T0408443

DIAGNOSTIC ASSESSMENT OF LEARNING DISABILITIES IN CHILDHOOD

DIAGNOSTIC ASSESSMENT OF LEARNING DISABILITIES IN CHILDHOOD

Jerry Concepcion Reyes

www.societypublishing.com

Diagnostic Assessment of Learning Disabilities in Childhood

Jerry Concepcion Reyes

Society Publishing
224 Shoreacres Road
Burlington, ON L7L 2H2
Canada
www.societypublishing.com
Email: orders@arclereducation.com

ISBN: 978-1-77469-877-8 (Hardcover)

ABOUT THE AUTHOR

Jerry Concepcion Reyes is an Instructor III, Extension Implementing Unit of the College of Teacher Education at the Laguna State Polytechnic University Siniloan Campus. Philippines. He graduated Bachelor of Secondary Education major in Biological Science, Master of Arts in Education major in Science and Technology, and Doctor of Philosophy in Education major in Science Education (CAR). He teaches Biological Science, Earth Science, Anatomy and Physiology, and Astronomy in the undergraduate teacher education programs. He presented research paper at National Conference in the Philippines.

TABLE OF CONTENTS

LIST OF FIGURES

LIST OF ABBREVIATIONS

AAIDD	American Association on Intellectual and Developmental Disabilities
AAP	American Academy of Pediatrics
ADHD	Attention Deficit Hyperactivity Disorder
ANS	Approximate Number System
APA	American Psychiatric Association
ASD	Autism Spectrum Disorder
BERS	Behavioral and Emotional Rating Scale
BOLD	Blood Oxygen Level Dependent
CAM	Center of Multiple Attention
CAPD	Central Auditory Processing Disorder
CBM	Curriculum-Based Measurement
CD	Conduct Disorder
CEC	Council for Exceptional Children
CNS	Central Nervous System
CNV	Copy Number Variant
CRPD	Convention on the Rights of Persons with Disabilities
CWSLD	Children with Specific Learning Difficulties
DALY	Disability-Adjusted Life Year
DBDs	Disruptive Behavior Disorders
DD	Developmental Dyscalculia
DLD	Developmental Language Disorder
DMDD	Disruptive Mood Dysregulation Disorder
DSM	Diagnostic and Statistical Manual
DSM-IV-TR	Diagnostic and Statistical Manual of Mental Disorders, Fourth Edition, Text Revision
EAHCA	Education for All Handicapped Children Act
EF	Executive Function
EFD	Executive Function Disorders

EFL	English as a Foreign Language
FAPE	Free and Appropriate Public Education
FAS	Fetal Alcohol Syndrome
FBA	Functional Behavior Assessments
FMRI	Functional Magnetic Resonance Imaging
GBD	Global Burden of Disease Study
HICs	High-Income Countries
HKD	Hyperkinetic Disorder
IAD	Intelligençe-Achievement Discrepancy
ICD	International Classification of Diseases
ID	Intellectual Disability
IDEA	Individuals with Disabilities Education Act
IDs	Intellectual Disabilities
IEP	Individualized Education Plan
IFJ	Inferior Frontal Junction
IPL	Inferior Parietal Lobule
IQ	Intelligence Quotient
LBLD	Language-Based Learning Disabilities
LD	Learning Disabilities
LDA	Learning Disabilities Association of America
LEA	Local Education Authority
LICs	Low-Income Countries
LMICs	Low and Middles Income Countries
MDD	Major Depressive Disorder
MIDAS	Multiple Intelligences Developmental Assessment Scales
MR	Mental Retardation
MRI	Magnetic Resonance Imaging
MTG	Middle Temporal Gyrus
NAEP	National Assessment of Educational Progress
NASP	National Association of School Psychologists
NCS-A	National Comorbidity Study-Adolescent Supplement
NHANES	National Health and Nutrition Examination Survey
NICHCY	National Dissemination Center for Children and Youth with Disabilities

NINDS	National Institute for Neurological Disorders and Stroke
NJCLD	National Joint Committee on Learning Difficulties
NSCH	National Survey of Children's Health
OCD	Obsessive-Compulsive Disorder
ODD	Oppositional Defiant Disorder
OTS	Object-Tracking System
PBD	Pediatric Bipolar Disorder
PDD	Persistent Depressive Disorder
PSW	Pattern of Strengths and Weaknesses
Q-EEG	Quantitative Electroencephalography
RCLD	Reading Comprehension Learning Disabilities
RD	Reading Disabilities/Reading Disorder
RESA	Regional Education Service Agencies
RTI	Response to Intervention/Right to Information
SD	Standard Deviations
SEA	State Educational Agencies
SES	Socioeconomic Status
SLD	Specific Learning Disabilities/Specific Learning Disability/ Specific Learning Disorders
SLI	Specific Language Impairment
SSA	Social Security Administration
TD	Typical Development
ToM	Theory of Mind
TTCT	Torrance Tests of Creative Thinking
UNICEF	United Nations Children's Fund
USAER	Units of Service and Support to Regular Education
USDOE	United States Department of Education
VIA-IS	VIA Inventory of Strengths
WHO	World Health Organization
WISC	Wechsler Intelligence Scale for Children
YLD	Years Lived with Disability
YLL	Years of Life Lost

LIST OF GLOSSARY

A

ADHD – One of the most prevalent neurodevelopmental diseases in children is ADHD.

Adolescents – Adolescence is a time of transitional physical and psychological growth that typically occurs between puberty and adulthood.

Alternative – something that is different from something else, especially from what is usual, and offering the possibility of choice

Aphasia – A communication condition called aphasia affects how you speak.

Autism Spectrum disorder – Autism spectrum disorder (ASD) is a developmental disability caused by differences in the brain.

C

Central Nervous System – The brain and spinal cord make up the central nervous system. The brain directs our thoughts, memories, movements, and emotions. The spinal cord relays information back and forth between the brain and the body's network of nerves.

Comorbidities – There is a medical term referred to as comorbidity. It depicts when the body has several diseases or conditions going on at once. Commonly, comorbidities are chronic or long-lasting.

D

Demographic – the statistical characteristics of human populations (such as age or income) used especially to identify markets.

Discrepancy – an illogical or surprising lack of compatibility or similarity between two or more facts.

Dyslexia – Due to issues recognizing spoken sounds and understanding how they relate to letters and words; dyslexia is a learning impairment that makes it difficult to read (decoding).

E

Endophenotype – Endophenotypes are heritable features that are identified through laboratory tests for abnormalities in the electroencephalogram, cognitive performance issues, and the ability to recognize facial emotions.

Epidemiology – the branch of medicine which deals with the incidence, distribution, and possible control of diseases and other factors relating to health.

Etiology – The cause or origin of a disease is known as its etiology. The term "etiology" also refers to the study of illness etiology.

Evaluation – An evaluation is a thorough assessment of a single student that can reveal details about the academic or behavioral needs of the student.

I

Idiopathic – Of unclear reason. Idiopathic disease refers to any illness whose cause is unclear or unidentified.

Individualized Education Plan (IEP) – A student with a disability must have an IEP, which is a plan or program created by a committee often composed of the student's teacher, resource staff, parent, and the student.

Intellectual – the intellectual is a person possessing superior powers of intellect

Intellectual Disabilities – An examination can be used to gauge intellectual capacity. Problems with thinking and comprehension are the main symptoms.

Intervention – the act of interfering with the outcome or course especially of a condition or process (as to prevent harm or improve functioning)

M

Manifest – to make evident or certain by showing or displaying

Mental Retardation – Mental retardation is a permanent condition that causes limitations in learning and adaptive functioning, which is a chronic illness marked by subaverage IQ.

Mental Retardation – Mental retardation is characterized by suboptimal intelligence is a lifelong condition that limits learning and adaptive functioning.

Motor Disorders – Motor disorders are nervous system abnormalities that result in atypical and uncontrollable movements.

N

Neurological – According to medical terminology, neurological disorders are conditions that affect the spinal cord, brain, and body's nerves.

Neurological Disorder – According to medical terminology, neurological disorders are conditions that affect the spinal cord, brain, and body's nerves.

P

Perceptual Development – The term "perceptual development" describes how young toddlers begin to assimilate, interpret, and comprehend sensory data.

Phonemes – A phoneme is a unit of sound used in phonology and linguistics that can differentiate one word from another in a specific language.

Phoneticization – Phoneticization is the process of representing speech in writing by employing a system in which individual symbols consistently represent speech sounds.

Pseudowords – A pseudoword is a piece of text or speech that looks to be a real word in a language but actually has no definition.

Psychology – The study of how the mind functions and how behavior is influenced by it, or how a person's character affects their behavior.

Pull-Out Model – A student with a disability is withdrawn from—or pulled out of—the general education classroom under a pull-out model of instruction so they can receive special education or supplementary supports in a different classroom or resource room.

S

Screening – The process of screening involves identifying students who may have difficulties utilizing tests and examinations.

Segregated Education – The education of students with disabilities in separate classrooms or schools is known as segregated education.

Short Attention Span: Short-attention-span individuals may find it challenging to concentrate on projects for any period of time without being sidetracked.

Speech Therapist – Children with speech-related issues are treated by skilled professionals called speech therapists or speech-language pathologists.

Speech Therapy – Speech therapy is a type of intervention that works to enhance a child's speech and their capacity to comprehend and use language, including nonverbal language.

Strauss Syndrome – An illness called Churg-Strauss syndrome is characterized by blood vessel inflammation.

Symptoms – A physical or psychological issue that a person has that could be a sign of an illness or condition.

T

Transition – A move from one condition or form to another is called a transition.

Treatment – the application of medicines, surgery, psychotherapy, etc, to a patient or to a disease or symptom.

V

Visuo-Spatial – Cognitive functions needed to "detect, integrate, and analyze space and visual shape, details, structure, and spatial relations" in more than one dimension are referred to as visuospatial functions.

Visuospatial Abilities – A person's ability to recognize spatial and visual links between items is referred to as their visuospatial ability.

PREFACE

Since the beginning of time, humans have been attracted to language and the capacity for communication. Without language, it would be impossible to communicate complicated concepts, discuss the meaning of events and potential results of various courses of action, or convey large amounts of complex information.

As we all know, a person's physical, mental, social, and spiritual states all interact to form who they are. Therefore, education should help a child grow in each of these areas. If a child is judged to be deficient in one or more conditions, they are classified as disabled or impaired.

Deficits in vision, hearing, limbs, and movements are simple to find, making physical and mental problems straightforward to identify. However, some emotional and neurological problems that affect how the brain processes information are difficult to diagnose because they are not readily apparent. These limitations are not visible.

For a variety of causes, including emotional, behavioral, and psychological ones, children with "learning disabilities" perform academically below average. Learning disabilities are not apparent until the child starts attending school. Many children don't show any symptoms until they perform activities that call for a specific kind of cognitive processing, at which point they become obvious.

Learning disability is when a child of average or above-average intelligence and who has good teaching is not learning and performing as they should. There are a variety of learning disabilities. They frequently have right hemispheres that are quite powerful, which can make reading more challenging but can also lead to more creativity and the capacity to solve nonverbal difficulties.

This book provides examples of assessment protocols, report writing, case studies illuminating diagnostic concerns, and discussions of the advantages and disadvantages of popular diagnostic approaches for learning disorders.

The prevalence of learning disorders, the improvement in recognizing kids with learning disabilities, warning signs of a learning disability, and methods to diagnose learning impairments are highlighted. The neurological causes and clinical characteristics of learning impairments have also been discussed in detail.

This book also covers the topics of screening versus evaluation and typical signs of a learning difficulty. It is critical to realize that assessing a student to see if they need additional learning requirements is different than screening to see if they have a learning issue.

The clinical characteristics of childhood mental disorders are discussed in the book along with their etiology, burden, risk factors, and consequences on childhood, and trends. This book highlights several techniques for identifying SLDs, including ability-achievement gap, response to intervention, and alternative research-based SLD identification procedures.

This book provides a summary of the evaluation of learning issues with speech and language components. Speech therapy is also extensively covered. How to handle the challenges faced by children with certain learning problems has also been covered at length.

This book emphasizes the need to change the notion that students with special needs should be accommodated in the current classrooms to the notion that all students, including those with special needs, should be accommodated in the classroom.

In the western world, there is a great deal of research and work being done on learning difficulties. However, there are many gray areas in this field that need more efforts, clarity, understanding, and discussion.

Due to their inability to read correctly, people with dyslexia frequently have to put in a lot of effort. Dyslexics have achieved success in a variety of professions. For example, Magic Johnson, Bill Gates, and Albert Einstein have all received a dyslexia diagnosis. The most crucial thing to keep in mind is that if your child is struggling, you should get assistance immediately. Speak with the teacher, the school, and the pediatrician to determine the best course of action for fixing the problem.

CHAPTER 1

Introduction of Learning Disability Assessment

Contents

This chapter will cover every aspect of learning disability assessment. At the beginning of this chapter, this chapter explains about the difference between myth and reality about learning disabilities. This chapter also provides highlights on types of learning disabilities. This chapter also helps to understand the prevalence of learning disabilities. At the end of this chapter, this chapter explains the warning signs of a learning disability.

1.1. INTRODUCTION

A generic term used to characterize particular categories of learning issues is "learning disability" (LD). A person with a learning disability may find it difficult to learn and apply particular abilities. Reading, writing, listening, speaking, reasoning, and mathematic skills are those that are most frequently impacted.

Individuals with learning difficulties are all different. A person with LD might not experience the same learning difficulties as another person with LD. An individual could struggle with both reading and writing.

Math comprehension issues may also be present in another LD person. According to the National Dissemination Center for Children and Youth with Disabilities (NICHCY), yet another person may struggle in each of these areas as well as with understanding what others are saying.

A collection of illnesses known as LD damage people's capacity to comprehend what they see and hear or to connect data from various brain regions. These limitations may manifest in a variety of ways, including particular issues with verbal and writing communication, coordination, self-control, or attention. These issues extend to academic work and can obstruct learning to read, write, or perform math.

A neurological condition known as a learning disability affects the brain's capacity to take in, absorb, store, and process information. The difficulty in learning fundamental academic abilities that a person of at least ordinary intellect experiences is referred to as a learning disability.

These abilities are crucial for academic and professional success as well as for surviving life in general. There is no specific disorder denoted by "LD." It is a term used to describe a collection of illnesses.

It's interesting to note that there isn't a precise, generally agreed definition of learning disabilities. Due to the multidisciplinary character of the field, there is continuing discussion about its definition, and there are currently at least twelve definitions that are published in the academic literature.

Figure 1.1. Image showing inclusive classroom, kindergarten learner Jericho (right); who has a learning disability; is assisted by his classmate, Nikki Paul (left), in understanding their mathematics lessons.

Source: Image by Flickr.

There are several technical definitions offered by various health and education sources. Overall, most experts agree on the following descriptions:

- Individuals with LD have difficulties with academic achievement and progress.
- Discrepancies exist between a person's potential for learning and what that person actually learns.
- Individuals with LD show an uneven pattern of development (language development, physical development, academic development, and/or perceptual development).
- Learning problems are not due to environmental disadvantage.
- Learning problems are not due to mental retardation or emotional disturbance.
- Learning disabilities can affect one's ability to read, write, speak, spell, compute math, and reason. They also can affect a person's attention, memory, coordination, social skills, and emotional maturity.
- Individuals with LD have normal intelligence, or are sometimes even intellectually gifted.
- Individuals with LD have differing capabilities, with difficulties in certain academic areas but not in others.
- Learning disabilities have an effect on either input (the brain's ability to process incoming information) or output (the person's

ability to use information in practical skills, such as reading, math, spelling, etc.).

1.2. MYTH VS. REALITY ABOUT LEARNING DISABILITIES

1.2.1. People With LD Are Not Very Smart

Reality. Children with learning impairments are equally intelligent as other children. LD has nothing to do with intelligence. In actuality, those who have LD are intelligent on par with or beyond average. There are many people who can be classified as talented because of their intellectual, creative, or other ability. According to studies, up to 33% of students with LD are gifted.

1.2.2. LD Is Just an Excuse for Irresponsible, Unmotivated, or Lazy People

Reality. Not moral defects, but neurological disorders are what cause LD. The effort needed to go through a day can be taxing in and of itself for some persons with LD. To perform what other people take for granted requires a tremendous amount of motivation.

Children with learning disabilities struggle to learn while being intelligent and capable. Learning difficulties are issues processing words or information. Language is a factor in the difficulties, including reading, writing, speaking, and/or listening.

1.2.3. LD Only Affects Children. Adults Grow Out of the Disorders

Reality. The effects of LD are now understood to last a person their entire life and "may even exacerbate in maturity as jobs and environmental demands alter." Sadly, a large number of persons, particularly older adults, have never received a formal LD diagnosis.

It is impossible to outgrow learning difficulties, although they can be consistently detected in kindergarten or first-graders, or even earlier. The earlier a youngster receives effective therapy for a learning issue, the better the outcome, according to research.

1.2.4. The Terms Dyslexia and Learning Disability Are the Same Thing

Reality. A sort of learning disability is dyslexia. It does not serve as a synonym for a learning disability. It is a particular language-based disorder that impairs a person's capacity for verbal and written expression. Unfortunately, due to irresponsible usage, the term dyslexia has come to be seen by some as a synonym for LD.

A reading disability is recognized in four out of every five children with a learning disability (or dyslexia). Learning how spoken language is translated into written text is difficult for them. Since reading and writing are necessary for many subjects, including arithmetic, a reading disability impairs a person's school-based learning in general.

1.2.5. Learning Disabilities Are Only Academic in Nature. They Do Not Affect Other Areas of a Person's Life

Reality. Individualized reading, writing, or math issues can occur in some people with learning disabilities. Nevertheless, most individuals with learning difficulties struggle in multiple domains. Learning difficulties, according to Dr. Larry Silver, are permanent impairments. "The same limitations that interfere with reading, writing, and arithmetic also will interfere with sports and other activities, family life, and getting along with friends," the author says.

While some kids have strong verbal (speaking) abilities, they may struggle with visual and spatial perception, motor skills, and, most importantly, social skills, which can make it difficult for them to grasp the primary idea, "see the big picture," or comprehend cause-and-effect relationships.

1.2.6. Adults With LD Cannot Succeed in Higher Education

Reality. More and more adults with LD are going to college or university and succeeding. With the proper accommodations and support, adults with learning disabilities can be successful at higher education.

1.2.7. Children With LD Are Identified in Kindergarten and First Grade

Reality. Learning disabilities often go unrecognized for years; most are not identified until third grade. Bright children can "mask" their difficulties, and some kinds of learning problems may not surface until middle school, high school, or even college.

1.2.8. More Boys Than Girls Have Learning Disabilities

Reality. Although three times more boys than girls are identified by schools as having learning disabilities, research studies show that, in fact, equal numbers of boys and girls have the most common form of learning problem—difficulty with reading. Many girl's learning difficulties are neither identified nor treated.

1.3. HISTORY OF THE FIELD

Learning disabilities are becoming more broadly defined. These descriptions are an attempt to describe a condition that has also been referred to as aphasia, neurologically impaired, Strauss Syndrome, and minor brain malfunction, among other labels.

Based on his papers from the early 1960s and remarks he made at the April 6, 1963 Conference on Exploration into Problems of the Perceptually Handicapped Child, history suggests that Dr. Samuel Kirk invented the phrase learning disabilities and popularized it.

His suggested term was "enthusiastically embraced and assisted in bringing the participants together into the Association for Children with Learning Disabilities, the predecessor of the Learning Disabilities Association of today."

A group of kids with problems in language, speech, reading, and related communication skills necessary for social interaction have been referred to as having "learning disabilities."

Children with sensory impairments like blindness or deafness are not included in this group because there are ways to manage and train the deaf and the blind. Additionally, children who have broad mental disability are not included in this group.

During the latter part of the 1960s, there became greater awareness about learning disabilities, both from the general public and Congress. In response, the U.S. Office of Education was charged with creating a federal definition for what constituted a learning disability. Samuel Kirk chaired this committee. In 1968, the first annual report of the National Advisory Committee on Handicapped Children, headed by Dr. Kirk, wrote: Children with special learning disabilities exhibit a disorder in one or more of the basic, psychological processes involved in understanding or in using spoken or written languages.

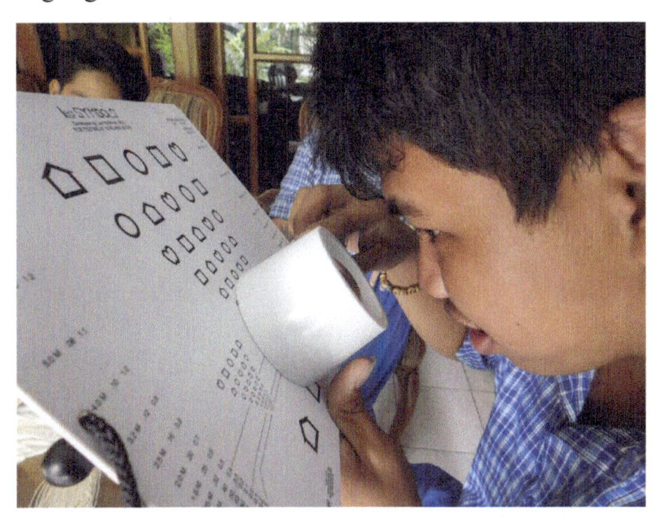

Figure 1.2. A child with a hearing impairment undergoes a low vision assessment at the school for children with disabilities which he attends, Cambodia.

Source: Image by Flickr.

These may show themselves as difficulties in reading, writing, spelling, math, thinking, talking, or listening. They include conditions that have been referred to as developmental aphasia, dyslexia, minor brain dysfunction, and perceptual handicaps.

They exclude learning issues that are predominantly brought on by mental retardation, emotional disturbance, environmental disadvantage, or physical, hearing, or vision impairments. (Special Education for Handicapped Children, 1968) The term "specific learning disability" (also known as SLD or LD) was officially recognized by the federal government as a special education category by the end of 1968 (U.S. Office of Education, 1968), and the Specific Learning Disabilities Act, also known as Public Law 91–230, was passed in 1969. P.L. 94–142, the Education for All Handicapped Children's Act, was passed by Congress in 1975. For kids in special education, the term "learning disability" was codified in this instance.

Under P.L. 94–142, a Specific Learning Disability Was Defined as Follows:

A disorder in one or more of the basic psychological processes involved in understanding or in using language, spoken or written, that may manifest itself in an imperfect ability to listen, think, speak, read, write, spell, or do mathematical calculations, including conditions such as perceptual disabilities, brain injury, minimal brain dysfunction, dyslexia, and developmental aphasia.

However, learning disabilities do not include, learning problems that are primarily the result of visual, hearing, or motor disabilities, of mental retardation, of emotional disturbance, or of environmental, cultural, or economic disadvantage.

Further investigation was warranted given the P.L. 94–142 definition's persistence in federal law. The National Joint Committee on Learning Difficulties (NJCLD), a coalition of parent and professional organizations, criticized the P.L. 94–142 criteria for incorporating terms that were ambiguous or challenging to apply to identify children with learning disabilities in the 1980s. The NJCLD put forth a different definition in response to the criticisms.

A wide range of diseases characterized by severe challenges in the development and use of listening, speaking, reading, writing, reasoning, or arithmetic skills are collectively referred to as learning impairments.

These illnesses can affect people of all ages, are innate to the individual, and are thought to be caused by central nervous system (CNS) dysfunction. Although they may coexist with learning difficulties, issues with self-regulation behaviors, social perception, and social interaction do not by themselves qualify as learning disabilities.

Learning difficulties are not a direct outcome of other handicapping conditions or external factors, despite the fact that they may develop concurrently with them (NJCLD, 1994).

The Individuals with Disabilities Education Improvement Act, Public Law 108–446, provides protection for kids in special education today (IDEA 2004). The standards and regulations under IDEA for what qualifies as a learning disability have not changed. Current federal legislation established the following phrase.

In General: A disorder in one or more of the fundamental psychological processes involved in comprehending or using language, whether spoken or written, is referred to as a "specific learning disability." This disorder may show up as a person's imperfect ability to listen, think, speak, read, write, spell, or perform mathematical calculations.

Figure 1.3. A girl holding a sign that says "LD = less equally intelligent/Strike out stigma" poses for a photo in Times Square with a man holding a sign that says "Take a picture with a proud Dyslexic."

Source: Image by Wikimedia commons

1.4. TYPES OF LEARNING DISABILITY

1.4.1. Dyslexia

Children that have a great deal of trouble learning to read are known as having dyslexia, which is frequently referred to as reading retardation. The young child may potentially be reading below grade level by two years. This child has not been able to learn to read using the conventional classroom teaching methods.

It's possible for a youngster with this condition to struggle with word formation, recalling auditory sequences, and further speech and language challenges. As a result, they struggle a lot with spelling. They are unable to appropriately comprehend what they observe. The child might view some letters upside down and backwards, as well as portions of words backwards.

A simple checklist that can help a teacher identify a child with dyslexia is provided below:

1. Does the child frequently reverse letters (b as d)
2. Does the child frequently reverse words (was as saw)

3. Does the child read a word inconsistently (girl as gril)
4. Does the child frequently reverse numbers (6 as 9)
5. Does the child repeat words while reading?
6. Does the child have trouble following written or oral directions?

Signs and Symptoms of Dyslexia are:

1. Reads slowly and painfully
2. Experiences decoding errors, especially with the order of letters
3. Has trouble with spelling
4. May have difficulty with handwriting
5. Exhibits difficulty recalling known words
6. Has difficulty with written language
7. May experience difficulty with math computations
8. Complains of dizziness, headaches or stomach aches while reading.
9. Confused by letters, numbers, words, sequences, or verbal explanations.
10. Reading or writing shows repetitions, additions, transpositions, omissions, substitutions, and reversals in letters, numbers and/or words.
11. Reads and rereads with little comprehension.
12. Spells inconsistently.

Strategies for Intervention:

1. Provide a quiet area for activities like reading, answering comprehension questions
2. Use books on tape
3. Use books with large print and big spaces between lines
4. Provide a copy of lecture notes
5. Don’t count spelling on history, science or other similar tests
6. Allow alternative forms for book reports
7. Allow the use of a laptop or other computer for in-class essays
8. Use multi-sensory teaching methods
9. Don’t teach using rote memory
10. Present material in small units.

11. Use lot of praise with these children
12. Don't give a punishment for forgetting books
13. Don't use the word lazy
14. Expect less written work
15. Prepare a printout of homework and stick it in their boo
16. Do not ask them to copy text from a board or boo
17. Accept homework created on a compute
18. Given the opportunity to answer questions orally.

1.4.2. Dysgraphia

It is a particular learning issue that has an impact on a child's fine motor and handwriting abilities. Despite receiving enough time and attention to write properly, some students nonetheless have dysgraphia. Although the exact cause of this disorder is yet unknown, it is suspected that a linguistic issue or motor system injury may be to blame.

The primary symptom of dysgraphia is illegible handwriting in students. Letters will be of varying sizes, with spaces between them, and the text may appear warped or inaccurate. Planning, arranging, and expressing thoughts are difficult for a youngster with learning disabilities who also has writing problems. He also has trouble explaining the order of events.

For instance, consider what is depicted in the tale or image. She or he has trouble describing things, persons, or situations (i.e., responding to inquiries like "How does it look?"). A child's writing is sloppy and lacks proper paragraph structure.

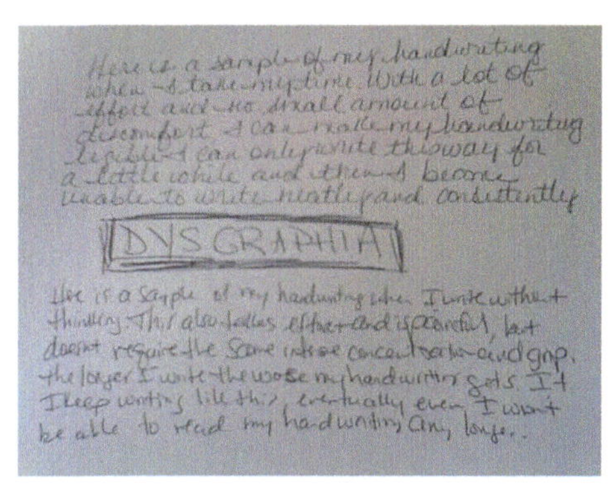

Figure 1.4. Example of motor dysgraphia.

Source: Image by Wikimedia commons.

A Checklist is to Help Teachers in Identifying Writing Errors in Children with Learning Disabilities is Given Below:

1. Does the child write too large or too small?
2. Does the child write the letter or word too close or too far apart?
3. Does the child very untidy in the written work?
4. Does the child make frequent grammatical, punctuation and spelling errors?
5. Does the child omit or adds parts of letters?
6. Does the child write numbers inconsistently or reverses them (31 as 13, 6 as 9)?
7. Does the child reverse forms or shapes of letters while writing (b as d)?

Signs and Symptoms of Dysgraphia

1. May have illegible printing and cursive writing (despite appropriate time and attention given the task)
2. Shows inconsistencies like mixtures of print and cursive, upper and lower case, or irregular sizes, shapes or slant of letters
3. Writes unfinished words or letters, omitted words
4. Inconsistent spacing between words and letters
5. Exhibits strange wrist, body or paper position
6. Has difficulty in letter formation
7. Copying or writing is slow or labored
8. Has cramped or unusual grip/may complain of sore hand
9. Has great difficulty thinking and writing at the same time (taking notes, creative writing).

Strategies for Intervention

1. Suggest use of word processor
2. Avoid penalizing student for sloppy, careless work
3. Use oral exams
4. Allow use of tape recorder for lectures
5. Allow the use of a note taker
6. Provide notes or outlines to reduce the amount of writing required

7. Reduce copying aspects of work (pre-printed math problems)
8. Allow use of wide rule paper and graph paper
9. Suggest use of pencil grips and or specially designed writing aids
10. Provide alternatives to written assignments (video-taped reports, audio-taped reports)

1.4.3. Dyscalculia

It is a particular learning disorder that impairs a person's capacity for both number comprehension and the acquisition of arithmetic facts. A special learning challenge in mathematics is called dyscalculia. Similar to dyslexia, dyscalculia can result from a problem with visual perception. The term "dyscalculia" relates specifically to the inability to carry out mathematical or arithmetic processes. It may be characterized as having a very hard time with numbers.

Although dyscalculia does not carry the same stigma, it is crucial to identify it as soon as possible, before it affects a child's self-esteem. There is no one etiology of dyscalculia, just as there is no set of characteristics that apply to all dyslexics. 'Dys' is a Greek term that means "difficulty with." Calcula is Latin for "calculation."

So, dyscalculia refers to a problem with math or calculations. A youngster with dyscalculia struggles with size relationships and spatial relationships (up, down, high, low, fat, near) (big, small, more, less). The kid also appears to be confused from left to right (disorientation with regard to number sequence).

Basic math skills are challenging for children with learning disabilities, even modest learning disabilities. Math difficulties include computational or conceptual issues.

The computational problems include:

- Poor addition, subtraction, multiplication, and division; and
- Failure in application of math rules.

The conceptual problems are developmental in nature and include:

- Poor understanding of questions,
- Difficulty in discriminating between the relevant and irrelevant aspects of math problems,
- Poor discrimination between different shapes, sizes, and quantities,

- Poor number sense,
- Poor spatial orientation (e.g., difference between `top' and `bottom,' `beginning' and `end'), and
- Poor problem solving.

Signs and Symptoms of Dyscalculia

- Shows difficulty understanding concepts of place value, and quantity, number lines, positive and negative value, carrying and borrowing
- Has difficulty understanding and doing word problems
- Has difficulty sequencing information or events
- Exhibits difficulty using steps involved in math operations
- Shows difficulty understanding fractions
- Is challenged handling money
- Displays difficulty recognizing patterns when adding, subtracting, multiplying, or dividing
- Has difficulty putting language to math processes
- Has difficulty understanding concepts related to time such as days, weeks, months, seasons, quarters, etc.
- Exhibits difficulty organizing problems on the page, keeping numbers lined up, following through on long division problems

Strategies for Interventions

- Allow use of fingers and scratch paper
- Use diagrams and draw math concepts
- Provide peer assistance
- Draw pictures of word problems
- Use mnemonic devices to learn steps of a math concept
- Schedule computer time for the student for drill and practice
- Use concrete material to teach children how to count such as buttons and beads;
- Teacher should use a lot of visual aids to teach simple mathematical operations and concepts
- Tactile materials such as embossed numerals, symbols should be used to teach simple concepts such as more or less, short or long.

Various lengths and sizes could be taught by tactile presentations

- Concepts such as time and money should be linked to day-to-day events. Use of meaningful vocabulary which includes phrases as tomorrow, in five minutes, as soon as possible will help the child in increasing his/her awareness about concepts related to time
- Worksheet activities are also useful in teaching math/math problems to children with learning disability having difficulty in math
- Give smaller number of problems to these children. These children can also be given some extra time to complete math assignments
- Playing cards can be used to teach computation skills to children. Some simple games could also be developed with the help of playing cards
- Blocks, puzzles and word games are always helpful in making the process of learning mathematical concepts more joyful for the child
- Use of colors again can give some useful hints. Highlighters can be used to specify directionality and signs (+, x)
- Display charts that explain the process, signs and tell what key words indicate in word problems are also of help these pupils
- Apply the basic concept in activities that could be practiced in and outside the classroom
- Have students estimate distance, weights, and sizes etc.
- Have students use an abacus to facilitate counting, calculations etc.
- Teach students to use rules (e.g., any number times 2 is double that number)
- Difficult problems should be taught with flash cards
- Play instructional math games
- Teach students the relationships between addition and subtraction or multiplication and division
- Use of colors (green means multiplication and red means addition) can prevent the children from being confused between number, symbols and signs
- Use the method of attack strategy training. In this method the child uses certain strategies for specific academic problems. Arithmetic computations can be taught with this method.

1.4.4. Dyspraxia

Dyspraxia is a condition that makes it difficult to plan, organize, and carry out sensory-motor tasks. The brain's immaturity is the cause of improper message transmission to the body. A child with dyspraxia may combine a number of issues to varied degrees.

1.4.4.1. Symptoms of Dyspraxia

- Poor fine and gross motor coordination
- Motor planning and perception problems
- Tactile dysfunction
- Poor awareness of body in space
- Difficulty with reading, writing and speech
- Poor social skills
- Poor sense of direction like finding rooms across the campus
- Poorly developed organizational skills
- Easy tiredness
- Problems with awareness of time
- Confusion over handedness
- Lack of awareness of potential danger

1.4.4.2. Identification of Dyspraxia

The following traits may be present in some or all dyspraxic children:

The Pre-school Child: Late rolling, crawling, and walking; difficulties with steps, climbing, and puzzles; trouble with eye motions that cause the head to move in place of the eyes; trouble learning new abilities automatically; and a delay in the development of speech.

The Older Child Exhibits the Following:

- Difficulty dressing
- Tying shoe laces
- Using cutlery
- Poor balance
- Difficulty with riding a bike
- Poor reading skills
- Poor handwriting

- Copying from blackboard
- Ability to express themselves.

Interventions to deal with Dyspraxia

The following can help dealing with dyspraxia:

- Break down tasks into smaller manageable slices
- Allow the child to finish a task before moving on
- Don't force the child to take part in team games
- Ensure they are aided to find their way round; they will forget where they should be
- Don't expect them to copy large chunks from the board or books, coordinating eyes, brain and hand are not easy for most of us, for these children it can be impossible
- Don't set them to fail. Do be aware of what you are asking them to achieve
- Ask them to repeat any series of instructions given, it helps to internalize it
- Never allow a child with Dyspraxia to be compared to an able child. Not by teachers or peers.
- Praise every effort and every small accomplishment. A Dyspraxic child has been used to failure repeatedly: every effort must be made to raise their self-esteem.
- Remember that they have difficulty in taking on board information during lessons. Allow them extra time: teach in small bursts, allowing opportunities to rest, if necessary.
- Ensure that the child has understood what is being taught, repeat if needed. Check that they are not falling behind because they cannot copy form the blackboard.
- Teach on a one-to-one level, with few distractions, when appropriate. If there is a learning support worker available, allow them to assist the child so they are taught at the same pace alongside their peers. Children with Dyspraxia so better in a relaxed environment with one-to-one support.
- Establish a parent- professional link.

1.4.5. Aphasia

Aphasia is a condition in which specific brain regions are damaged and the patient is unable to comprehend or make words. A person's speech or language must be considerably damaged in one (or more) of the four communication modes in order for them to be diagnosed with aphasia. Auditory comprehension, vocal expression, reading and writing, and functional communication are the four communication modalities.

Although level of intelligence remains unaffected, people with aphasia may experience challenges ranging from occasional difficulty finding words to losing their ability to talk, read, or write. Both receptive language and expressive language might be impacted. Visual languages like sign language are also impacted by aphasia.

Anomia, or a deficit in word finding abilities, is a common defect in aphasias. People with aphasia frequently use terms like thing to mask their inability to name items. So, when asked to name a pencil, they might respond that it is a writing instrument.

Dyslexia is a learning problem that makes it difficult for a person to read and write, whereas aphasia is a partial or complete loss of language abilities brought on by brain damage.

Signs & Symptoms

- Having difficulty finding words (anomia)
- Speaking haltingly or with effort
- Speaking in single words (e.g., names of objects)
- Speaking in short, fragmented phrases
- Putting words in the wrong order
- Inability to comprehend language
- Inability to pronounce, not due to muscle paralysis or weakness
- Inability to speak spontaneously
- Inability to form words
- Inability to name objects (anomia)
- Poor enunciation
- Excessive creation and use of personal neologisms
- Inability to repeat a phrase
- Persistent repetition of one syllable, word, or phrase (stereotypies).

Interventions

- Create a distraction-free learning environment for your aphasic students.
- When speaking with students who have aphasia, use straightforward language and basic sentences.
- If necessary, repeat words when conversing with aphasic students.
- When teaching vocabulary, give textual words, definitions, synonyms, antonyms, use examples, and pictorial representations (for example, orally, visually, and kinesthetically).
- Clearly explain syntax and semantics topics. To ensure the student understands the concepts, simplify them as much as possible, break them down into manageable chunks, and repeat them as needed.
- Allow students with aphasia as much uninterrupted time as needed to express themselves verbally.
- Make word choice boards.
- Use flashcards or index cards to build vocabulary.
- Encourage the students with aphasia to communicate in any way that feels comfortable to them, such as writing, drawing, pointing, gesturing, picture systems, sign language, or augmentative communication devices.
- Ask the students to repeat and explain ideas, instructions, and experiences.
- Work together with the speech therapist and special education case manager at the school to find potential assistive technology and augmentative communication devices for the aphasic students.

1.5. PREVALENCE OF LEARNING DISABILITIES

There is a very good probability that one knows someone who has a learning disability. In the United States, there are almost 2.9 million school-age children who are classified as having particular learning difficulties and who need some form of special education help. In actuality, learning disabilities are present in more than half of the students receiving special education (24th Annual Report to Congress, 2002).

They make up about 5% of all students in public schools that are of school age. Children who are homeschooled or attend private or religious schools are not included in these statistics. The most prevalent special education category by far is learning difficulties.

It should be emphasized that prevalence rates might differ significantly between states and even within one, depending on how rigorously eligibility is determined. For example:

Kentucky reports the lowest prevalence figure (2.9%) and Massachusetts the highest (7.35%). A study completed in Michigan compared the learning disabilities eligibility criteria and procedures for identification across the 57 regional education service agencies in the state (RESA).

The results indicated that 21% of the RESAs had no written eligibility criteria or policies, the length of the written policies varied from one sentence to 112 pages, and the severe discrepancy formula score varied from 15 to 30 standard score points! It is possible for a student to move a few miles to the next school district and no longer be considered to have a learning disability.

According to studies, learning problems do not affect all racial and ethnic groups equally. For instance, in 2001, 2.6% of non-Hispanic Black children and 1% of White children received special education assistance linked to learning disabilities. According to the same studies, economic standing, not ethnic heritage, is to blame for this.

Economic deprivation is not the cause of learning difficulties, but there is a higher chance of early exposure to toxic substances (such as lead, tobacco, alcohol, etc.) in low-income neighborhoods. In the LD group, boys outnumber girls by a ratio of around three to one. According to some academics, men are more likely than women to develop learning difficulties because of this.

However, others have suggested that "the higher prevalence of learning disabilities among males may be due to referral bias." They suggest that "academic difficulties are no more prevalent among boys than girls, but that boys are more likely to be referred for special education when they do have academic problems because of other behaviors, such as hyperactivity.

Additionally, LD prevalence varies by age. Unsurprisingly, between the ages of 6 and 9, an increasing number of students get special education services. However, the majority of children treated (42%) are between the ages of 10 and 13, while students between the ages of 16 and 21 experience a significant decline.

Because there is no accepted definition of learning disorders and no objective diagnostic standards, the actual prevalence of these conditions is a hotly debated topic. According to some academics, the 5% prevalence estimate that is now accepted is too high and is founded on ambiguous definitions, which causes incorrect identification.

However, research aimed at identifying objective early indications of LD in fundamental reading abilities has found that almost all kids who perform below the 25th percentile on standardized reading tests can be considered to have a reading impairment.

Although less is known about LD in written expression, experts believe that between 8% and 15% of students in schools actually have it. Additionally, according to research, 6% of students in schools experience math difficulties that cannot be explained by poor intelligence, sensory deficiencies, or financial hardship.

Finally, learning specialists have differing opinions about the sharp rise in the number of students who have been diagnosed with LD. Some people find the increase disconcerting and worry that too many students are being identified. However, other experts feel that given how nascent the area is, the rising occurrence is appropriate.

1.6. GROWTH IN THE IDENTIFICATION OF STUDENTS WITH LEARNING DISABILITIES

Since 1975, when the category of LD was first included in public law, the number of students identified as having a learning disability has grown by almost 250%, from approximately 800,000 students to almost 3,000,000 students (U.S. Department of Education, 2002).

There have been several theories put out as to why there has been such a huge increase in the identification of students with learning problems. These explanations, in accordance with Hunt and Marshall, include:

1. Children who are performing below grade level are mistakenly labeled as having learning difficulties. There are few, if any, alternative programs for these children since the evaluation and identification criteria are too arbitrary and unreliable.
2. Compared to many other special education diagnoses, such as moderate mental impairment and behavior issues, the diagnosis of LD is more socially acceptable. As a result, educators and parents "push" for this designation.
3. More accurate referrals and diagnoses have been made as a result of increased public awareness of learning difficulties. The

kinds of services that are offered are more known to teachers and parents.

4. The growth in social and cultural dangers over the past 20 years has been mirrored by an increase in the number of pupils with learning difficulties. More kids may be at risk of developing learning disabilities as a result of biological and psychological pressures, and as a result, more kids are found to have them.

1.7. WARNING SIGNS OF A LEARNING DISABILITY

There is no one symptom that identifies someone as having a learning problem. The gap between a child's performance in school and what would be expected of him or her given their intelligence or ability is what experts look for. There are more indicators that could point to a child's having a learning problem. A couple of them are listed below.

Since learning problems are frequently discovered in elementary school, the majority relate to assignments from that level. Most or perhaps all of these symptoms are unlikely to be displayed in children. However, if a child exhibit several of these issues, parents and the teacher should take the potential that the child has a learning disability into consideration.

Figure 1.5. Puzzle pieces and a notebook with learning disabilities text.

Source: Image by Flickr.

When a child has a learning disability, he or she may exhibit the following characteristics:

- Have trouble learning the alphabet, rhyming words, or matching letters to their sounds

- Make many mistakes when reading aloud, and repeat and pause often
- Not understand what he or she reads
- Have real trouble with spelling
- Have very messy handwriting or hold a pencil awkwardly
- Struggle to express ideas in writing
- Learn language late and have a limited vocabulary
- Have trouble remembering the sounds that letters make, or in hearing slight differences between words
- Have trouble understanding jokes, comic strips, and sarcasm
- Have trouble following directions
- Mispronounce words or use a wrong word that sounds similar
- Have trouble organizing what he or she wants to say or not be able to think of the word needed for writing or conversation
- Not follow the social rules of conversation, such as taking turns, and may stand too close to the listener
- Confuse math symbols and misread numbers
- Not be able to retell a story in order (what happened first, second, third)
- Not know where to begin a task or how to go on from there

1.8. WHY DIAGNOSE LEARNING DISABILITIES?

Half of the kids serviced by the Individuals with Disabilities Education Act (IDEA; U.S. Department of Education 2002) fall under the category of particular LD, and 6% of students in public schools are identified as having an LD, with state-specific identification varied (U.S. Department of Education, National Center for Education Statistics 2006).

Between the school years 1991–1992 and 2000–2001, there was a 28.5% increase in the number of LD diagnoses. Confusion over the proper criteria and methods for diagnosing the illness is thought to be a significant reason in the high percentage of students that receive the LD designation.

The categorization process used in the diagnosis of LD and other illnesses has five main functions: communication, information retrieval, description, prediction, and theory building. Classification serves the first goal by giving different people, including educators, clinicians, and doctors, a common vocabulary to communicate with one another. As opposed to needing exhaustive descriptions each time a symptom constellation is encountered, this enables experts to quickly develop at least a rough conceptualization of presenting problems. The recovery of information for treatment and the scientific investigation of particular illnesses is another function of diagnosis.

An educator can access intervention strategies that have been shown effective with other students with similar disabilities when they are informed that they would be dealing with a student who has an LD. In a similar vein, categorizing people according to shared traits and behaviors enables researchers to concentrate on particular groups of interest more readily.

Figure 1.6. Image showing classroom of Cornell university employment & disability institute.

Source: Image by Flickr.

Through classification, a shorthand description of co-occurring "symptoms" or problems is established, allowing professionals to quickly understand a given situation and formulate hypotheses. This leads to the fourth purpose, which is often the primary focus of attention, prediction of course and treatment.

The classification process's ultimate goal, concept generation, suggests that organizing the traits of disorders should provide theories of those conditions that direct study. In the instance of LD, the objectives of classification have not been achieved due to the lack of a consistent definition.

The term "LD" as it has been used in past and present practice refers to a large heterogeneous group that may include people who actually struggle with some learning tasks despite having average intellectual functioning, people who haven't had access to the right academic opportunities, and people who are gifted in some areas but perform within the average range in another, among others. The inability to organize the information that results hinders research efforts, which has a detrimental effect on advancements in detection, prevention, and correction. In addition to the need for a precise diagnosis to fulfill classification objectives, classification itself may have advantages.

For instance, the diagnosis of people with mental retardation and the greater focus on diagnostic precision were practices that helped to launch the deinstitutionalization movement. The need for classification is more recent evidenced by attention-deficit/hyperactivity disorder (ADHD).

Individuals with the constellation of symptoms defining ADHD (or ADD, as it was known at the time) were not recognized as having a disorder prior to the release of the Diagnostic and Statistical Manual of Mental Disorders Third Edition. Since these people were diagnosed as having ADHD, it is now known that ADHD has a biological foundation, and treatment research is making significant strides.

Advances in prevention and therapy are likely to not be made if children with LD are not recognized as such. Due to its predominance in educational settings, diagnosing children with an LD typically entails considerations that are different from those for other diseases.

Clinicians and educators frequently have to decide between diagnosing the concept of LD or labeling a child as having an LD so that the child can be placed in the chosen school. When determining a disorder's diagnosis, a theoretical construct must be inferred, whereas school placement solely considers a disorder's behavioral presentation.

While behavior may be enough for pre-referral intervention, the very nature of diagnosis requires that the construct be present, otherwise classification will not serve to enhance communication, prediction, or research. It is also necessary for educators and psychologists to weigh the benefits of special services with the stigma of a special education label and the cost of assessment.

Some individuals lean heavily toward a needs-based definition of LD that would allow any struggling child to receive services without a costly assessment. In addition, labeling a child as having an LD is often viewed as more desirable than classifying him/her as suffering from mental retardation (MR) due to the history of ethnic minority over identification in the latter diagnosis and resulting pressure to avoid disproportionate MR diagnoses. However, by incorrectly categorizing kids as having an LD, people undermine the validity of the LD construct and fail to benefit from categorization systems. The LD label loses all meaning and the associated special services' quality if students receive LD-related services when they should be receiving MR-related services or less strenuous treatments.

Shepard et al. (1983) investigated the special education records for a stratified sample of 800 students who had been diagnosed with LD in a ground-breaking study. Less than half of the sample met the diagnostic standards for LD at the time as stated by federal law or the professional literature, according to their findings.

The majority of the students in the category did have some form of learning difficulty, but these issues were brought on by other factors as MR, mental distress, and language obstruction. The researchers hypothesized that the excessive identification may have resulted from educators' attempts to justify their inability to educate pupils, a misunderstanding of definitions, and pressure from the bureaucracy and parents to identify and assist low-achieving students.

Figure 1.7. Learning disability week bus tour.

Source: Image by Flickr.

Research on LD will be complicated, and the construct might lose its significance in the public's eyes if the degree of LD misidentification in the Shepard et al. (1983) study is typical of practices across the USA.

Questions of bias akin to those surrounding moderate MR placements are likely to arise if the LD designation is applied to low achievers, such as non-native English speakers and members of ethnic minorities who may need services for different reasons than learning-disabled pupils.

In the best-case scenario, if misidentification becomes widespread, designating a child as having a learning disability will continue to be seen as more helpful than harmful, allowing it to function as a catch-all category that will eventually lose all significance and be eliminated from public policy. If this is the final result, students who actually have LD will not be able to get crucial therapies.

1.9. THE BEGINNING OF THE LD MOVEMENT

Samuel Kirk, a colleague of Monroe's, contributed significantly to the study of learning disabilities by laying the groundwork for a label that would establish a reputable field of study. The term "LD" was coined by Kirk, who defined it as a learning deficiency in a topic that results from a psychological impairment unrelated to mental retardation, sensory deprivation, cultural or educational variables.

Based on Kirk's theories, a group of parents established the Learning Disabilities Association of America in 1963, which sparked the creation of numerous organizations and the emergence of the LD movement (Hallahan & Mock 2003). In the 1960s and 1970s, parents started to actively lobby for their children who had learning challenges, and the government started to fund LD research in an effort to come to an agreement on its description.

Medical experts favored the term "minimum brain malfunction," whereas educators placed more emphasis on intraindividual differences and the gap between ability and accomplishment. Bateman (1965) revived this concept, which was missing from Kirk's influential formulation.

In contrast to Franzen's (1920) and Monroe's (1932) well-defined approaches to discrepancy, Bateman did not provide a model for quantifying discrepancy. Several researchers aligned with the medical model, focusing on visual and visual–motor disabilities with laterality training as remediation rather than academic intervention.

The US government, however, favored the educators' position. With the passage of the Education for All Handicapped Children Act (EAHCA) in 1975, all disabled students, including those with LD, were guaranteed a free and appropriate public education (FAPE).

A discrepancy model should be used to identify whether kids are qualified for services under the LD category, according to the US Office of Education's 1977 update of the EAHCA, which included a definition of LD that was identical to Kirk's from the decade before. The federal standards left it up to the individual states to determine how a major divergence should be calculated.

Unfortunately, identification issues were caused by the disparity rule. Different techniques were being used across states and school districts because there were no standards for defining how to establish whether a discrepancy existed.

Schools not only identified various numbers of kids as having learning disabilities, but also different kids, so a kid could have LD in one district and not have any issues in another. Some schools even used grade-level discrepancy models, considering ordinal scores as interval data, resulting in calculations that had no real value and overidentifying "slow learners" who had no real learning problems.

There has long been disagreement in the field of LD on the best diagnosis procedures. Concerns about the over- and incorrect identification of pupils as having LD in schools have sparked the discussion. Researchers have developed a variety of classification algorithms in response to these worries, each with unique strengths and weaknesses.

Some of these methods propose making a diagnosis of LD based on the assumed underlying cause of the disability, the simple demonstration of underachievement in comparison to some standard or expectation, or the existence of a specific profile that is presumed to indicate the most effective remediation method.

Certain supporters and critics of a particular diagnostic technique may disagree on what they believe to be the main tenets of that approach, and some diagnostic procedures may include more than one of these concepts. The debate about LD diagnosis has become more heated as a result of recent laws that provide states and school districts the option of using either the traditional discrepancy model or the response to intervention.

The focus of the pertinent research has been on the validity and reliability of the numerous models that have been put out, but beneath the discussion is a frequently unmentioned concern with the ability of the classification methods to capture the essence of what it means to have an LD. When the fundamentals of an LD are not entirely agreed upon, this makes things more difficult.

For instance, some people could think that a significant underachievement is what distinguishes LD, while others would think it is a "unexplained" failure in a particular academic endeavor. The idea of "unexplained" underachievement is false, according to Stanovich (1999), because individuals with learning disabilities have deficiencies like low phonological awareness that actually explain their academic performance.

According to this reasoning, the defining characteristic of LD must be academic underachievement. However, other academics and professionals may contend that the presence of a process deficit is the defining feature of LD because underachievement is caused by observable deficiencies, frequently referred to as cognitive processes.

Many respond to this assertion with the fact that most individuals' profiles consist of significant strengths and weaknesses across areas. Thus, the debate continues and the field of LD continues its search for a diagnostic panacea. The diagnostic confusion and resulting high identification rate are likely to continue and become more problematic given the recent changes to IDEA, or now IDEIA.

This latitude will undoubtedly result in differing diagnostic practices, pre-valences, and symptom constellations across geographic locations as has been noted for decades. More importantly, diagnostic confusion will threaten the viability of the very construct of LD, which would be a disservice to children and adults who genuinely have learning differences that require specialized instruction and services.

Children who have learning challenges are still directed to professionals for tests while researchers look for the gold standard of LD diagnosis. The ideal way to evaluate a child for an LD, taking into account LD definition and reliable assessment methods, is still up for debate.

Of course, the practitioner's type of setting and location will influence the suitable assessment approach to some extent. Although IDEA education legislation does not apply to clinicians in private practice, they should still take this law into consideration to ensure that their conclusions and recommendations are taken into account and carried out by schools.

The state's application of the federal legislation as well as the district's implementation of the state interpretation must be understood by school psychologists and other practitioners working in public schools.

1.10. CONCLUSION

The introduction of the assessment of learning disabilities is summarized in this chapter. This chapter also discusses the fiction versus reality of learning difficulties and illustrates the description of those conditions. Highlights on history, different learning disabilities like dyslexia and dysgraphia, dyscalculia, dyspraxia, and aphasia are also included in this chapter.

Provides highlights on the frequency of learning disorders, progress in identifying students with learning disabilities, warning indicators of a learning disability, and how to diagnose learning disabilities toward the end of the chapter.

REFERENCES

1. Amber E. Brueggemann Taylor, (2014). *Diagnostic Assessment of Learning Disabilities in Childhood: Bridging the Gap Between Research and Practice*. Springer Verlag. Available at: https://cloudflare-ipfs.com/ipfs/bafykbzacecobvadnmam2jb6ax6 rdecohc u34vlo2qnedlxgglaqfb3b6tf4qi?filename=%28Contemporar y%20 Issues%20in%20Psychological%20Assessment%29%20Amber%20E.%20Brueggemann%20Taylor%20%28auth.%29%20-%20Diagnostic%20Assessment%20of%20Learning%20Disabilities%20in%20Childhood_%20Bridging%20the%20Gap%20Between%20Research%20and%20Practice-Spri.pdf (accessed on 14 October 2023).
2. HopeQure, (2021). *Learning Disorders- its Types, Diagnosis and Assessment*. HopeQure. Available at: https://www.hopequre.com/blogs/learning-disorders (accessed on 14 October 2023).
3. Logsdon, A., (2020). *Learning Disability Assessment Process and Testing*. Verywell Family. Available at: https://www.verywellfamily.com/testing-for-learning-disabilities-2161888 (accessed on 14 October 2023).
4. Naset.org Home Page, (2011). NASET News Alert RSS. Available at: https://www.naset.org/publications/ld-report/introduction-to-learning-disabilities (accessed on 14 October 2023).
5. NICHD, (2018). *Eunice Kennedy Shriver National Institute of Child Health and Human Development*. U.S. Department of Health and Human Services. Available at: https://www.nichd.nih.gov/health/topics/factsheets/learningdisabilities (accessed on 14 October 2023).
6. Taylor, A. E., (2014). Introduction/history of learning disability assessment. *Diagnostic Assessment of Learning Disabilities in Childhood*, 1–18. Available at: https://doi.org/10.1007/978-1-4939-0335-1_1.

CHAPTER 2

Learning Disabilities: Neurological bases and Clinical Features

Contents

This chapter will talk about the concepts and ambiguities in the field of learning disabilities. At the beginning of this chapter, this chapter explains about the prevalence and gender differences in specific learning disorder. This chapter also helps to understand the concept of neural correlates in learning disabilities. At the end of this chapter, this chapter also explains the cognitive bases of learning disabilities. This chapter also explains about the neurobiological bases of learning disabilities.

2.1. CONCEPTS AND AMBIGUITIES IN THE FIELD OF LEARNING DISABILITIES

A diverse range of illnesses known as learning disabilities are characterized by an inability to acquire, retrieve, or utilize information correctly. They represent the most severe and persistent kind of learning difficulties in kids.

They may already exist at birth or develop as a result of disease, toxic exposure, inadequate nutrition, medical care, sociocultural deprivation, or trauma. Lack of proficiency in reading, writing, or math, which are often regarded as core domains, is the root cause of most learning issues.

Learning disabilities (LD) or specific learning disabilities (SLD) have been the most well-known and well-studied category of special education during the past several years, with the term becoming synonymous with special education itself because of how frequently kids are assigned to this group.

Nevertheless, given that LD have not been established as a distinct discipline, that is, until now no causal relationship has been determined between the phenomenology of LD and the factors which cause them, it is also the special education category which has brought the most disagreement between academics, researchers, and educators.

Despite formal definitions, there is a lack of comprehension of their nature and interpretation, which shows that the primary objective of a particular field is not achieved. Scientific opinions about learning impairments remain "in doubt" or "unfounded" without a knowledge of their nature and interpretation, and this is the fundamental source of the "identification difficulty," which is the lack of agreement on how to better define a classification category for LDs.

Over the course of more than a century of research, people have not been able to reach a consensus on a clear definition of learning disorders. People are thought to know a lot about their traits and the practices that have been used today, but they have not yet addressed the question of whether they represent a specific group of students with low academic achievement or if they are a category that all low-performing students can be grouped into.

These two aspects have been meticulously studied over time, albeit not cohesively; consequently, even today some claim that LD represent a specific difficulty, since these children have high intelligence, while others believe that this category includes every child who is unable to learn.

Since the beginning of the twenty-first century, scientists from various disciplines, but mostly educators, often come across parents' questions such as "My child, who goes to kindergarten, writes backwards, is these dyslexia?," "Will my child be a future Einstein?," "My child has trouble understanding meanings. Could this be dyslexia?," or My child is distrait and performs poorly at school.

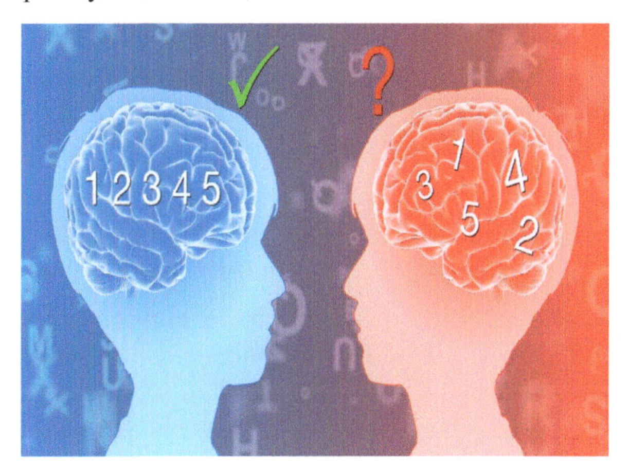

Figure 2.1. 3D medical animation still showing difference with normal brain and Dyslexia infected brain.

Source: Image by Wikimedia commons.

Could they be suffering from learning disabilities? Through international organizations like the Learning Disabilities Association (LDA), these researchers have tried to functionally operationalize the field in an effort to determine whether it is a scientific discipline with specific characteristics or a "pseudoscience," which encompasses everything. They have also looked for operational traits that would enable kids to achieve their full potential in the context of school and society.

2.1.1. Epistemological Ambiguities of the Field

Learning difficulties had not been given any attention in school before to the 1960s. However, the research of the school dropout issue, the development of school's knowledge-based character, and legally mandated compulsory education have resulted in the introduction of a new classification category, none other than LD.

The fact that academic performance was linked to later social and professional success and that LD related to those who had the potential for success because of their attributed superior cognitive ability also helped to create this specific group.

Over the course of time, this perception has consolidated, and learning disabilities have become the most important category of special education. An important indicator of this is the following: programs for children with LD congregate the highest number of students with special educational needs. 2.5 million Of American school students approximately 5% from the total public-school enrollment identified with learning disabilities in 2009.

These students represented 42% of the 5.9 million school-age children. This percentage varies across states. For example, in Kentucky, 3.18% of students belong in the specific learning disabilities category, while in Massachusetts and Port Island; the corresponding figures are 9% and 9.6%.

Both Canada and some European nations are currently observing similar differentiations. The wide range of prevalence reflects a number of factors, including the diversity of the population falling under this category, the pressure on students to perform better in school, which has raised standards, the various performance assessment criteria used, as well as the criteria used to define the field of learning disabilities.

The prevalence of these deciding factors has caused differences in LD student rates between US states. As a result, the main area of special education is LD.

Different definitions have been developed over time in an effort to highlight the essential elements of the field. But instead of being affirmative, positive, and tautological or overly broad or restrictive, each one of them has been ambiguous, metaphorical, and negative.

Every definition that came after that made an effort to improve the one before it. Therefore, their analysis is crucial, not in order to create a new definition but rather to expand the description and, particularly, the understanding of what learning disorders are.

Kirk came up with the original definition of learning difficulties and also developed the phrase itself. The idea of problems in the psychological processes involved in academic learning was first addressed in this definition. However, this definition still has some ambiguity regarding the field's delineation.

For instance, it notes that retardation, disorder, or delay are all examples of disabilities but doesn't go on to explain the differences between these categories. Along with introducing the concept of exclusion from other deficit-related illnesses, the definition also makes a case for differential diagnosis.

Figure 2.2. Learning disability week poster.

Source: Image by advocacy matter.

Exclusion, however, is not a criterion for specifying the characteristics that differentiate LD from other conditions. Despite its ambiguities, Kirk's definition marked the establishment of the new field of LD and became the basis for every formal definition in the USA.

Adoption of an operational definition was necessary to define LD's scope as a different type of special education in order for it to be recognized as a separate scientific discipline.

The US National Advisory Committee of Handicapped Children proposed such a classification in 1968; it served as the foundation for educational policy pertaining to children with LD and was incorporated into the Individuals with Disabilities Education Act (IDEA) in 1997.

Accordingly, research in Europe, and primarily in Britain, concentrated on specific reading difficulties—dyslexia—and, even as early as the 1960s, associations and treatment facilities for kids with this illness were developing.

Critchley, a key pioneer in the study of dyslexia in Britain, created a concept for developmental dyslexia, which he described as a learning disease that first manifests as reading difficulties and then as "strange" spelling and problems with the use of written language.

It has cognitive characteristics and is genetically based. It is not brought on by an intellectual handicap, a lack of social or cultural opportunities, ineffective teaching methods, or psychological problems. Furthermore, it is not brought on by any visible structural insufficiencies in the brain.

Finally, Critchley did not agree with the use of the term "learning difficulties," because he believed that the children's only difficulty had to do with language. Miles had another important scientific contribution in the study of dyslexia in Britain by conducting a large diachronic study during 1970–1980 on 14,000 children.

According to certain findings, 3% of students showed severe symptoms of dyslexia and 6% mild symptoms. Miles also accepted that it was a hereditary disorder. Rutter and his colleagues carried out epidemiological studies on children with reading difficulties and through them exhaustively highlighted specific reading difficulties.

He noted that the terminology and identification procedures for dyslexia were unorganized and unclear, which is brought on by the inability to comprehend the nature of learning difficulties and may be mistaken for general reading retardation.

The Warnock Report (1978), which was adopted and made into law in 1983, was the product of a study that was commissioned in 1978 by the British Department of Education and Science to establish a special education law in Great Britain, Wales, and Scotland in the interest of normalization and integration.

With more than 18% of the student population falling within this group, it appears that this statute takes a poor performance approach to the term "special educational requirements related LD." Although dyslexia is acknowledged as a special education need, in this instance it was not.

This is because, in order to meet any administrative and practical needs related to children's education, Britain established a purely pedagogical paradigm. The majority of European nations use the words dyslexia or learning impairments in place of Kirk's LD classification.

On the other hand, research on the nature of LD and the most effective methods for identifying them proceeded in the USA. Based on recent research and scientific discoveries, the National Joint Committee on Learning Disabilities created the following definition in 1989 in an effort to eliminate any remaining uncertainties in the field's identification:

A wide range of diseases characterized by severe challenges in the development and use of listening, speaking, reading, writing, reasoning, or arithmetic skills are collectively referred to as learning disabilities.

These conditions are innate to the person, thought to result from dysfunction of the central nervous system (CNS), and they can happen at any stage of life. Although they may coexist with learning difficulties, issues with self-regulation behaviors, social perception, and social interaction do not by themselves qualify as learning disabilities.

Learning disabilities may coexist with other disabilities (such as sensory impairment, intellectual disabilities, or emotional disturbance) or with extrinsic influences (such as linguistic or cultural differences, inadequate or inappropriate instruction), but these conditions or influences do not cause them.

> Kavale et al. point out that the term "in general" in this definition is ambiguous, just like the term "particular" in the IDEA's definition, allowing for many interpretations.

The SLD definition was preserved in the IDEA rule for 2004 in line with earlier iterations of the law and regulations. The use of alternative research-based techniques, such as the Patterns of Strengths and Weakness (PSW) model, as well as a process based on the child's reaction to scientific, research-based intervention, such as response to intervention (RTI), is notable as an attempt to broaden the identification process.

The IDEA definition, found in US Code (20 U.S.C. & 1401), reads as follows:

- "The term 'specific learning disability' means a disorder in one or more of the basic psychological processes involved in understanding or in using language, spoken or written, which disorder may manifest itself in the imperfect ability to listen, think, speak, read, write, spell, or do mathematical calculations.

- Such term includes such conditions as perceptual disabilities, brain injury, minimal brain dysfunction, dyslexia, and developmental aphasia.
- Such term does not include a learning problem that is primarily the result of visual, hearing, or motor disabilities, of mental retardation, of emotional disturbance, or of environmental, cultural, or economic disadvantage."

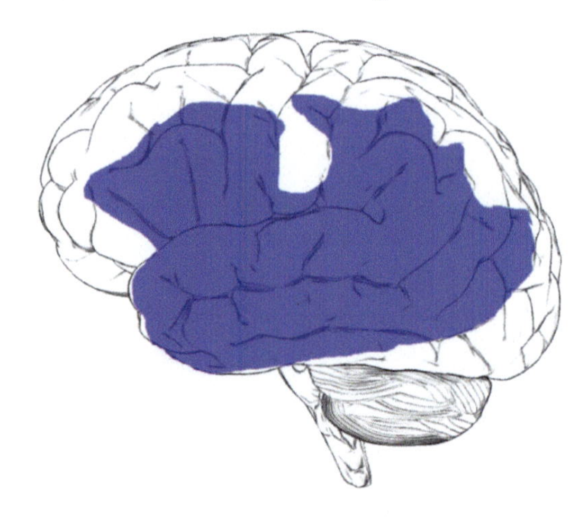

Figure 2.3. Global aphasia most commonly occurs due to a large lesion that encompasses much of the left hemisphere, specifically the left Perisylvian cortex.

Source: Image by Wikimedia commons.

Through the vague difference "in one or more," which is used in this official definition to introduce the "specific" part of the condition, it is not made clear how many difficulties must exist for the disorder to be termed specific.

Furthermore, it doesn't define what "specific" implies, making it unclear whether, for instance, it relates to distinctive characteristics of the relevant persons and their psychological makeup or whether the term suggests that the condition is idiopathic, or of unknown origin.

This definition also appears to establish a hierarchy of processes, with language—oral or written—being dominant. Additionally, the disease is linked to cognitive deficiencies (reasoning disorders), a characteristic that reflects what people today refer to as "metacognitive function," in addition to challenges with academic accomplishment.

Although there isn't yet any mention of CNS dysfunctions, there are allusions to cases that are comparable and arise from neurological illnesses.

According to this legislation, teachers are required to determine if a student who may have SLD is failing to make enough progress toward meeting age- and grade-level goals for achievement. This process presents crucial data and illuminates a model of accomplishments and aptitudes' strengths and shortcomings.

It is frequently claimed that intra-individual variances or variability is a sign of SLD. As part of the process, the gap between ability and achievement is also taken into consideration.

It is also argued that qualified staff should provide appropriate instruction. Students who have not received it cannot be considered as having SLD. Key instruction elements mainly regard reading, which, according to age, should be taught systematically:

1. Phonemic awareness;
2. Phonics;
3. Vocabulary development;
4. Reading fluency, including oral reading skills; and
5. Reading comprehension strategies.

Additionally, schools must regularly evaluate children' development and keep parents updated. The information acquired could demonstrate the efficacy of a teaching approach or program. With the parents' approval, an extension that cannot exceed 60 days may be given if the student shows no evidence of improvement.

Last but not least, the reauthorization regulations (NCLB) said that it is important to use reading instruction strategies that are backed by scientific reading research, mostly based on social construction. It has been suggested that issues with reading teaching may also be related to the overrepresentation of minorities in special education.

The updated definition gave US states the option to incorporate the RTI criterion in the diagnosis process rather than the IQ-achievement discrepancy or intelligence tests as part of the diagnostic process.

The phrase "specific learning disorder" is used in the DSM. The most recent edition, DSM-5, was updated in 2013 and broadens the prior definition to reflect the most recent advances in medical knowledge.

The diagnosis requires ongoing challenges with reading, writing, math, or mathematical thinking during the formal education years. Symptoms can include incorrect or laborious reading, unclear writing, trouble recalling number facts, and incorrect mathematical reasoning.

The range of scores on reading, writing, or math examinations that are culturally and linguistically acceptable must be substantially below the level of current academic proficiency. The person's challenges must considerably impede academic performance, occupational performance, or daily living activities and cannot be explained by developmental, neurological, sensory (vision or hearing), or motor disorders.

A clinical evaluation of the patient's developmental, medical, educational, and family histories, reports of test results and teacher observations, and the patient's reaction to academic therapies all go into the diagnosis of a specific learning problem.

Millions of dollars were spent on extensive study, especially in the USA but also on a global scale, in an effort to define the field. However, as of yet, no clear-cut description of the condition exists; instead, a broad picture of a group of students who are struggling to study exists.

Though many people are knowledgeable about the illness, many are unaware of its causes. Even the points of convergence among the definitions do not result in a common understanding of their nature.

Due to this, SLD are frequently studied and researched from various angles, and various labels are used to characterize them, such as dyslexia, specific language impairment (SLI), attention deficit hyperactivity disorder (ADHD), and learning disabilities. But the element of ability-achievement disparity consistently surfaces in all formal formulations.

The problem of discrepancy raises a reasonable question: "What is the meaning of concepts such as intelligence or general cognitive ability, learning or cognitive processes, and academic achievement—concepts that are included in every definition of SLD—and what is the causal relationship between them?." Unless this question is resolved, the identification of the field will remain vague and contentious.

An operational explanation of the condition was needed for actual implementation because conceptual and scientific definitions did not make it easier to identify the SLD field. The concept of intra-individual disparities was originally investigated, with a focus on the potential for some abilities to "malfunction" in contrast to the development of others.

Differences in intelligence functions, which are measured by intelligence tests like the Wechsler Intelligence Scale for Children (WISC), may reveal these developmental abnormalities. Children with SLD can be distinguished from other groups of students with average or low overall intelligence function scores using profiles of strengths and weaknesses identified using WISC composites.

This way of analyzing developmental disparities sparked debate over the characteristics of SLD. Are these pupils' profiles distinctive from the rest of the population? Does the profile of SLD subtests significantly differ from that of other individuals with normal IQs?

Kavale and Forness were unable to identify a specific WISC-based profile for students with LD in a meta-analysis of research because the imbalances between the subtests or between the verbal and practical portions of the criteria were deemed statistically unimportant.

They claimed that "particular" profiles could only be an indication of the children's competencies and in competences, which is a factor that is relevant in the design of pedagogical therapy. The same conclusion was reached by studies that produced comparable findings.

The inability to distinguish between intra-individual variations in cognitive capacities strengthened the idea that variations in intelligence and performance indicators might be distinguished—a quality that is first introduced in Bateman's characterization of the area.

This capacity and success criterion has gradually taken center stage in the classification of SLD. The fundamental issue with this strategy was that achievement was being evaluated using a variety of formal and informal criteria, but the WISC test remained the consistent criterion for intelligence quotient (IQ).

For this reason, the discrepancy criterion was disputed. A further reason of doubt was that meta-analyzes of studies determined a change in the rate of students with LD when different criteria were applied. For example, analyzes of findings in the state of Colorado showed that 26% of students did not meet the criterion, while 30% only did so in reading and math's.

By applying a different criterion for achievement among the same sample, 5% of students met the criterion in math's and 27% in reading. In another meta-analysis of findings, Cone, Wilson, and Bradley found that, in the state of Iowa, 75% met the discrepancy criterion. In a similar study, Kavale and Reese noted discrepancy rates between 33% and 75% depending on the tests being used. As a result, Lyon et al. came to the conclusion that discrepancy as a primary criterion for determining LD is more detrimental than helpful for children because achievement criteria include various external factors, including the educator, the infrastructure, the curriculum, etc.; these factors can neither be isolated nor interpret the complex interactions between "deficit" and pedagogical/social factors, which need to be taken into account during the diagnostic procedure.

Cruickshank described students with LD as students who are classified differently in each state in his description of them around 50 years ago.

Due to the lack of a clear definition of what LD is and the ambiguity surrounding the causal links between learning abilities and academic achievement as well as the question of whether they constitute a specific disorder and what that means, the term has been overgeneralized or, on the other hand, sub-generalized based on one symptom that is present in the majority of cases.

90% of students with LD do, in fact, struggle with reading. But is this issue a major or minor issue? What types of reading problems could be considered LD cases? Studies have shown that it is impossible to distinguish between children with reading difficulties brought on by a variety of factors and children who meet the criteria for SLD (dyslexia), as specified in the IDEA classification.

However, it has been suggested that even in cases of specific reading challenges, such as dyslexia, pupils with this disorder are at the bottom of the normal distribution of reading ability.

Ysseldyke et al. in their study of students who were diagnosed as having LD and students who were not diagnosed but were at the lowest level of the reading ability distribution, found no psychometric differences in the performance of the two groups. Based on these results as well as other studies, Algozzine concluded that in general, LD as a category is "non-existent and useless."

Also, the fact that the majority of these children exhibit reading difficulties has led—mainly in Europe—to the equation of LD with dyslexia, which, while representing one of their symptoms, according to IDEA's definition, has ended up becoming an autonomous scientific field.

Due to the ambiguous low reading performance criterion and the exclusionary characteristics included in all LD definitions, LD has primarily been equated with dyslexia in Europe.

On a global professional and administrative level, two patterns have emerged as a result of the lack of agreement. Those who view SLD as a separate category and those who associate them with all students who perform poorly in academics can be found on either side of the debate.

However, in the majority of nations, educators only use the standard of removing kids with low IQs; in other words, they try to distinguish between pupils with SLD and those who have intellectual ability deficiencies and corresponding adaptive skill deficits.

In conclusion, it is clear that the lack of agreement among academics, researchers, and practitioners regarding the crucial characteristics that set the LD category apart from other categories of low achievement, as well as the lack of a shared understanding of their nature and causes, has caused the field to stagnate. There are two opposing viewpoints in the general discussion.

While one views these pupils as belonging to a "umbrella" category that includes a wide variety of students with low accomplishment without developmental specificities, the other views them as having disabilities that are associated with their innately particular learning deficiencies.

According to those who agree with the "umbrella" description, LD is a creation of the contemporary educational system, which, in Senf's words, has attempted to purify general education like a sociological sponge, which is most "absorbing" when academic requirements are rigid or parental pressure for achievement is greater.

This sponge also takes in a multitude of pedagogical, behavioral, and psychosocial issues that can obstruct students' ability to learn in school, in addition to the individual variances among children. But LD cannot represent a scientific entity if the field has not been defined scientifically.

2.1.2. Contemporary Frameworks to Identify LD

Due to this, researchers are attempting to redefine the field of SLD in order to determine whether or not SLD represent a group with poorer achievement who do not require special care or teaching that has been specifically tailored for them.

According to a recent argument, the field delineation should include a summary of all the prior knowledge that is reflected in the various definitions and applied pedagogical practices. This will help determine the extent to which the deficiency is responsible as well as the extent to which various exogenous factors are responsible for their influences. The improvement of reading instruction, which has been the subject of research both domestically and internationally for more than 30 years, has been the focus of educational reform efforts in the USA. This has been accomplished by emphasizing the application of evidence-based instructional approaches.

The failure of educational systems to reduce the gap between children, especially those with disabilities and those belonging to minorities, became a major source of worry as a result of the research.

Despite the redefinitions and educational regulations, there are still ambiguities and contradictions regarding the conceptualization and identification of LD. Although there have been attempts to determine why they exist, and many neurobiological researchers have tried to attribute them to disorders of the CNS, so far, their causes have not been established.

The identification framework of intelligence-achievement discrepancy (IAD) is still used internationally by those who view LD as a distinct disorder, while the low-achievement model is applied by those who talk of a non-distinct group of low achieving students.

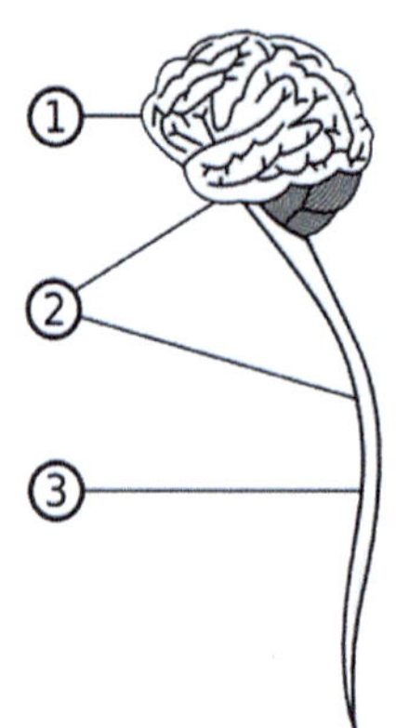

A diagram showing the CNS
1. Brain
2. Central nervous system
(brain and spinal cord)
3. Spinal cord

Figure 2.4. Central nervous system; diagram with labels.

Source: Image by Wikimedia commons.

In the USA, school districts in a number of states have begun using RTI as a supplement to the conventional testing methodology (such as IAD). As previously indicated, RTI is seen to be a useful tool for identifying students with LD.

In a national survey, 72% of teachers and 54% of parents were in favor of this decision, mainly because RTI's approach facilitates early intervention and pre-referral services. This way, inappropriate referrals to special education are reduced, and at the same time preventative intervention model is created for students who otherwise been referred for special education services after they demonstrated school failure.

In recent years, another framework—the pattern of strengths and weaknesses (PSW)—has emerged with the tendency to prevail; although not covered by federal law regulations, it is widely accepted and used in the USA because it supports research-based practices.

There are now four framework models that can be employed for the conceptualization and identification of SLD, notably in the USA, depending on the theoretical approaches to LD. Supporters of the disorder's non-distinctive nature have embraced the low-achievement framework, which ignores the component of unanticipated underperformance.

One or more of the remaining three frameworks—intelligence-achievement disparity, reaction to instruction-intervention, and intra-individual differences—is used by proponents of the disorder's specific nature (PSW).

The idea of unanticipated underachievement, which is portrayed by kids who should be able to learn but can't show academic success, without the presence of other learning barriers and despite receiving adequate instruction, is a significant component of the disorder's particular character.

Determining which of the frameworks produces a particular group of low achievers is therefore crucial to evaluating the validity of the identification. A categorization should accurately reflect the metrics that provide the concept of unexpected underachievement functionality.

Despite the debate it has sparked, the conventional framework of IAD continues to be prevalent in identification in the USA and abroad. When a student exhibits a considerable gap between academic accomplishment as determined by standardized reading, writing, and math exams and cognitive aptitude as commonly tested by IQ, that student is likely to have SLD.

Due to the multidimensionality of LD and the flaws in psychometric assessments, this framework has come under fire for being unreliable in both aptitude and achievement exams.

Another framework that, as was already indicated, makes it easier to teach both general education lessons and targeted interventions to kids who fall below the core curriculum level is response to intervention (RTI). A student's assessments are compiled, and his or her progress is tracked following particular treatments, in order to determine whether the student is at risk for academic issues.

When there is still a gap in achievement and progress after interventions have been put in place, the student is classified as having LD. This model is utilized in the USA; however, a different pedagogical dynamic evaluation paradigm is utilized in Britain.

The use of several evaluations in class to identify pupils who perform less well in each topic has also drawn criticism because it is an unstable strategy that is always dependent on the class as a whole. It is challenging to identify a student's latent skills and establish the cut-point that would put him or her in the LD group using either a single exam or the results of numerous tests.

As has already been mentioned, the IDEA's alternative research-based practice provision allows for the use of the framework of the PSW. There are other PSW models, including the discrepancy/consistency model, dual discrepancy/consistency model, and the concordance-dis-concordance model (also known as cross-battery evaluation).

These three theories have different methodologies, but they all agree that students can be diagnosed with SLD if they show unexpected academic underperformance and a corresponding impairment in one or more particular cognitive capacities connected to the academic deficit.

However, in reality, SDL is frequently detected in students by showing a PSW that is limited to academic success areas. Additionally, there may be several individual variances, which add to measurement mistakes and make them inaccurate.

Cottrell and Barrett recently conducted a survey on the frameworks used by school psychologists in the USA, and they discovered that 63.1% of them nearly always employed the IAD paradigm.

49.3% were using the RTI framework in most cases, and 29.4% were using the PSW framework in almost every case. However, they could not determine which framework was being primarily employed. For instance, 31.5% reported that they had been using the RTI framework most of the times, while only 17.8% reported that they were using this framework exclusively. In order to find out which one is being primarily employed, Maki and Adams surveyed 461 school psychologists in 2017. They discovered that only 30.4% reported primarily using the IAD framework, while they were primarily using almost equally the RTI (34.5%) and the PSW (35.1%) framework, respectively.

Benson et al. discovered that 37% of school psychologists used IAD, even in jurisdictions where it is not a part of the diagnostic process, in a national study of 1317 school psychologists conducted in the US. 51 % of respondents used RTI.

Finally, 53% of respondents said they were utilizing PSW. According to the age of the respondents, 49.2% of those who responded to the survey said they were involved in academic screening procedures that included monitoring early literacy, oral reading fluency, early numeracy, math computation, reading comprehension, math concepts and applications, spelling, and written expression prompts.

RTI and PSW, RTI and IAD, and PSW and IAD were frequently used in combination, according to many of the participants. This most recent poll indicates the lack of agreement among professionals about identification methods for SLD.

2.2. THE PREVALENCE AND GENDER DIFFERENCES IN SPECIFIC LEARNING DISORDER

Children's learning processes, which include learning to read, write, and do math, require a typical time of cognitive growth. When there are indications of these skills being disabled, a specific learning disability (SLD), a neurodevelopmental disease, needs to be clinically assessed.

Different prevalence rates for the three types of specific learning disorders included in the DSM-V vary by age, sex, stage of development, contextual factors, and the type of evaluation used in the study.

When it coexists with other mental illnesses, its symptoms are more severe. Additionally, behavioral and emotional problems may go along with this diagnosis if educational and clinical treatments are not made.

A neurodevelopmental illness known as SLD is characterized by challenges with comprehension and learning, issues with writing and written expression, and challenges with number perception and computation. Due to these issues, the child's academic performance is below par. This condition is biologically based and affects how well the brain can acquire or perceive information for both verbal and nonverbal information processing. The behavioral observations in its etiology are related with a cognitive impairment. As a result, it is described as the inability to achieve grade-level requirements in math computation and/or math problem-solving despite receiving age-appropriate learning opportunities and instruction in listening comprehension, reading comprehension, fundamental reading abilities, and reading fluency.

These deficiencies are ongoing and greatly impede one's ability to perform well at work or in daily activities.

SLD is a complex condition whose etiology includes genetic susceptibility, familial stress, cognitive and developmental variables, language spoken, and environmental factors such as socioeconomic status and educational attainment.

In many studies, gender, level of intelligence, higher family history of learning disabilities, low parental education, the exposure during pregnancy to the use of medicines, exposure to radiation, smoking, infections, hypoxia, complicated deliveries, hypoxia during labor, premature labor, low birth weight, low Apgar score, neonatal jaundice, convulsions, developmental delay, low-income families, and low socioeconomic status, leading to the occurrence of the SLD, are defined as predeterminants. In the clinical examination of SLD, children's developmental, medical, educational, and family history are assessed.

Test results, teacher comments, and student reactions to academic interventions are all reviewed as well. For a person to be diagnosed with SLD, their current academic abilities must be significantly below the range of expected scores given their chronological age (e.g., at least 1.5 SD i.e., standard deviations below the population mean for age and age-appropriate education on tests of reading, writing, and/or mathematics with normal levels of intelligence functioning, taking an IQ score of greater than 70 into account).

Mental retardation, sensory loss (vision or hearing), other psychiatric or neurological disorders, psychosocial difficulties, an insufficient language for use in an academic setting, or educational issues cannot explain these issues.

Dyslexia, dysgraphia, and dyscalculia are three different types of learning disorders that can be viewed collectively or separately.

Figure 2.5. Dysgraphia.

Source: Image by Wikipedia commons.

2.2.1. The Prevalence Rates Evaluated in Studies of Specific Learning Disorder

There are not many prevalence studies that include SLD diagnostic criteria or measures. On the other hand, SLD is regarded as being relatively common but is not well understood. From the past to the present, there have been several research on SLD, and various prevalence ratios have been announced.

Depending on the size of the sample and the inclusion criteria, different sources state the frequency and prevalence of the SLD at varying rates.

For example, Al-Yagon et al. reported different prevalence rates that included 1.2% from Greek epidemiologic study in 2004 and 20.0% from a study in Australia in 2000. A lifelong prevalence estimative of learning disability was found to be 9.7% in children from 3 to 17 years of age by the 2003 National Survey of Children's Health (NSCH) in the USA. The study in Finland in 2001 reported a prevalence of 21.2% in school-aged children referred to special education.

Del'Homme et al. reported this prevalence of 28.0% in 2004. In an epidemiological study with 2174 primary school children in Turkey by using checklists, the probable prevalence rates were found to be 13.6%.

The absence of commonly accepted definitions or diagnostic criteria for SLD and evaluations based exclusively on a scale or other assessments that reflect the degree of academic attainment are significant issues that are complicating the performance of epidemiological investigations. SLD was classified as a neurodevelopmental disorder in the DSM-V, and the severity of the disorder was rated.

This indicates that SLD is thought of as a dimensional developmental condition that resulted from the interaction of several risk factors. Even though intellectual disability is an exclusion criterion in DSM-V, one of the significant changes is the abolition of the IQ-achievement disparity criterion. Studies have shown varied prevalence rates because the DSM-IV criteria took into account the IQ-discrepancy criterion.

One recent study, for instance, examined the SLD frequency using DSM-V criteria and derived three distinct conclusions using the 1, 1.25, and 1.5 standard deviations for 1633 German students in the third and fourth grades.

Accordingly, the reading disorder for children having 1 as the standard deviation was estimated at 6.49%, written expression disorder was 6.67%, and mathematics disorder was 4.84%; the reading disorder for children having 1.25 as the standard deviation was estimated to be 5.14%, written expression disorder was 6.86%, and mathematics disorder was 3.31%; the reading disorder for children having 1.5 as the standard deviation had an estimated value of 3.8%, written expression disorder was 5.02%, and mathematics disorder was 2.39%.

Using DSM-IV and DSM-V criteria, distinct prevalence rates of SLD were discovered in a different study involving 1618 Brazilian children and adolescents in the second through sixth grades.

The SLD (global) impairment rate was 7.6%, followed by writing (5.4%), arithmetic (6.0%), and reading (7.5%). Using DSM-V criteria revealed higher prevalence rates than they had anticipated.

According to the American Psychiatric Association's (APAs) DSM-V, children from various linguistic and cultural backgrounds are 5–15% more likely to have SLD, 4–9% more likely to have a reading disorder, and 3–7 more likely to have a math disorder.

In research carried out in many nations, it was discovered that the difficulty rates varied depending on whether the reading, writing, and math problems were divided or combined.

Researchers have hypothesized in earlier studies that reading and math skills may be influenced by the same cognitive factors. It was discovered that the same phonological processing skills that are thought to influence reading development also seem to influence the development of general computation skills.

According to Geary's research, there is a connection between difficulties digesting words and having access to math information stored in long-term memory. Mathematical ability is a skill that is based on counting and uses phonological abilities and number words.

The relationship between a problem and a solution in long-term memory may be reflected, at least in part, in the same phonetic and semantic memory systems that facilitate word recognition since counting requires the activation of number words.

It was therefore proposed that the co-occurrence of reading and math difficulties might signify a more widespread impairment in the representation or retrieval of data from semantic memory.

It is suggested that phonologic issues mentioned in the etiology of the reading difficulties can produce different rates of reading difficulties interculturally, depending on the spoken language, and that the roles of family history and genetic load are taken into consideration in reading difficulties and mathematical difficulties.

It is hypothesized that reading challenges are less common in nations with good phoneme-grapheme harmony and more common in nations with poor phoneme-grapheme harmony because the difficulties in phonemic compliance led to phonologic issues, which led to reading difficulties. The majority of research indicated that 5–17% of people had a reading issue.

In the study conducted with 1476 children in 1983, the mathematics disorder rate was 3.6%, and the reading disorder was 2.2%; in the study conducted by Lewis et al. in 1994 with 1056 children who were 9–10 years old, the mathematics disorder was found to be 1.3%, and the reading disorder was 3.9%.

In the study conducted by Miles et al. in 1998, the reading disorder prevalence was suggested to be 4.19%, and also in the study of Badian in 1999 with 1075 children, the reading disorder was suggested to be 6%, and the mathematics disorder was suggested to be 3.9%.

The studies of Badian and Lewis et al. were designed to obtain an estimation of the prevalence of combined reading and arithmetic, reading only, and arithmetic-only disabilities. Badian found that the prevalence rate in arithmetic and reading was 3.4%, for reading only 6.6%, and for arithmetic only 2.3%.

And Lewis reported prevalence proportions as follows: 2.3% for combined reading and arithmetic, 3.9% for reading only, and 1.3% for arithmetic only. When different methods and materials are used in the prevalence studies, different results are obtained as in the studies of Badian and Lewis.

Lewis assessed word weakness while Badian assessed reading comprehension. Despite the fact that they are both reading processes, they call on various cognitive abilities. As a result, it helps to identify a distinct group of poor readers.

The use of various cut-off scores for the diagnosis of reading and math difficulties in these researches is another factor that causes inconsistent outcomes among studies. In a manner similar to the findings of Badian and Lewis et al., Dirks et al. discovered a larger percentage of combined reading and arithmetic difficulties than the handicap in either reading or arithmetic alone.

They also emphasized the cognitive and neuropsychological differences between children with combined reading and math disabilities and those who only had reading or math disabilities.

2.2.2. Comorbidity of Specific Learning Disorder

ADHD, which has the highest rate of comorbidity and is the subject of the most research, should be taken into account in studies on the incidence of particular learning problems. The same researchers identified a 4% prevalence of comorbidity in two American national investigations.

According to DuPaul et al. this comorbidity rate ranged from 18 to 60%, and they discovered that ADHD patients had a 7-fold greater incidence of SLD than the general population. In comorbid instances, some clinical research found that the prevalence of SLD was 70% and that of ADHD was 82.5%.

These two illnesses may be related to comparable hereditary causes, according to genetic studies. When determining the prevalence of SLD, varied study techniques, poor SLD criteria, and the significant comorbidity between SLD and ADHD may produce varying results.

Additionally, compared to SLDs without ADHD or any other comorbidity, symptoms of children with SLD are more enduring when they exhibit behavioral issues during the early years of school. As a result, SLD incidence and prevalence rates can be greatly altered by early diagnosis and treatment approaches.

2.2.3. Gender Differences of Specific Learning Disorder

DSM-5 is stated that SLD is two to three times more prevalent in boys than in girls. In 4 different epidemiologic studies including 9799 children from England, Wales, and New Zealand, boy/girl rates of reading difficulties were 21.6%/7.9%, 20.6%/9.8%, 17.6%/13.0%, and 18.0%/13.0%.

In various studies, reading and spelling deficits were not analyzed separately, so that it remained unresolved. Landerl and Moll reported balanced gender ratios for reading (fluency) deficits but a disproportionate number of boys for spelling deficits in German population.

In research by Moll et al. combined reading and spelling issues were shown to affect boys more frequently than girls, but when separate spelling disorders were assessed, gender ratios were found to be equal. These investigations revealed that boys were more likely than girls to have dyslexia. The most typical example of a mathematical disability reported in the literature is one where there is no gender difference.

The results of the other research indicated that math difficulties were more common in boys or girls. Additionally, other research revealed contradictory results. For instance, Devine et al. found that girls had math challenges far more frequently than boys did, despite their being no gender difference in the prevalence of math learning issues.

2.3. NEURAL CORRELATES IN LEARNING DISABILITIES

In terms of understanding cognitive and physical pathways, researchers have made great strides in the study of learning disorders in recent years. Understanding the neurological basis of learning problems is important for managing them and providing cognitive therapy.

With the development of functional neuroimaging techniques, it is now possible to identify anatomical networks and neuronal learning systems, furthering our understanding of the neurobiology of learning disabilities. On the other hand, neuropsychological testing, using extensive tests or specific cognitive tasks, has proven to be effective in analyzing certain cognitive deficiencies in order to identify prospective targets of intervention for cognitive compensation.

2.4. COGNITIVE BASES OF LEARNING DISABILITIES

Over the past 50 years, learning disorders have been investigated by neuropsychological researchers, leading to the publication of numerous scholarly articles on the subject.

Assessment and cognitive therapies can benefit from a better understanding of learning difficulties. An ophthalmologist who researched children with reading difficulties without brain injuries first identified cases of learning abnormalities in children and labeled these kids as having "word blindness."

Subsequently medical researchers used the term "dyslexia" to describe children with troubles in reading and spelling isolated words; they attributed dyslexia to a disorder of cerebral dominance for language. Other authors used the term "learning disabilities" to refer to children with unexpected difficulties secondary to language disorders, differentiating learning disabilities from behavioral disorders and intellectual disabilities.

Neuropsychologists began their investigation into the cognitive underpinnings of learning disorders in the 1970s. The significance of profile interpretations for implying brain damage in learning impairments was highlighted in particular.

Other researchers have discovered cognitive correlates of reading problems, such as finger agnosia, right-left confusion, auditory-visual integration, trouble naming colors, or other linguistic issues.

Some researchers proposed that developmental Gerstmann syndrome or parietal lobe disorders may be linked to learning impairments. Some scholars linked reading problems to a delay in brain development or to issues with language.

In favor of multivariate techniques, other scholars rejected theories based on group comparisons of single variables. This prompted studies that helped to better understand the cognitive deficiencies of learning disabilities by identifying the profile of neuropsychological testing.

The "theory of speech processing" as a segmented signal of phonological representation was one of the major influences on the scientific understanding of learning impairments. This hypothesis holds that phonological awareness is a metacognitive comprehension of the spoken sound structure.

To access the growing lexical system, young readers must connect the orthographic patterns of written language to the underlying structure of speech. This notion has been supported in a number of languages with different levels of phonological and orthographic transparency.

Since a certain phonological awareness and cognitive capacity was thought to be linked to decoding a particular academic talent, explaining success or failure in reading, these discoveries were crucial in the understanding of learning disabilities.

The division of learning impairments into academic domains led to a growth in the body of basic research on cognitive correlates and neurobiological aspects of learning disabilities' cognitive domains.

Thus, learning disorders were separated into three principal domains and six subdomains:

1. Oral reading domains that occur at the level of word (dyslexia) and the level of text (reading comprehension disorders)
2. Math domains that could be computational (dyscalculia) or involve executive mathematical functions (math problem-solving disorders)
3. Written language domains that could involve basic skills needed for transcription (handwriting and spelling dysgraphia) and generating text in essays or stories (text generation disorders)

Higher-order language, attentional, and executive impairments that influence both oral and writing language are thought to be the result of issues in these cognitive domains, according to Pennington and Peterson. In other instances, attention-deficit/hyperactivity disorders (ADHD) or developmental language problems are frequently co-occurring with these cognitive disorders.

In order to lay the groundwork for effective interventions, international researchers have mapped the framework of various sources of variability that affect learning difficulties across time.

According to this concept, cognitive processes (such as phonemic awareness), psychosocial factors (such as attention, anxiety, and motivation), and environmental context are all associated to learning impairments (socioeconomic conditions, schooling, instruction, home environment).

Intellectual quotient (IQ) is not a reliable indicator of learning impairments, but processing speed and working memory issues are. These issues are also often co-occurring with ADHD. Phonological awareness is a powerful predictor of success or failure in learning to read. In more transparent languages, spelling and time reading assessments may be used to detect dyslexia, whereas tests that tested vocabulary, listening comprehension, and attention/executive function could be used to examine diseases that affect text-level reading.

Serial response time measurements were used to test the learning capacities of people with dyslexia, and the results showed a mild effect that suggests that automatization of learning is hampered in people with this disorder.

According to neuropsychological studies, the declarative learning system is thought to be relatively intact, while the procedural learning system, which is involved in implicit learning and impaired in people with SLIs, has a neurological and functional distinction between different types of learning.

Implicit learning mechanisms are active in dyslexic patients, which is supported by the fact that children with dyslexia appear to have problems deriving structure from novel sequences in artificial grammar learning paradigms and issues in making judgments about grammaticality.

People with learning disabilities may experience greater challenges in language tasks requiring them to extract and produce sequential information due to prominent difficulties in procedural learning in sequence-based tasks and relative preservation on declarative and nonsequential procedural learning.

Math disabilities without reading difficulties are very common as comorbidity in children with learning disabilities. Attention, working memory, and phonological processing are also overlapped with math problem-solving disorders, even if less studied than computational skills.

These findings support the view that mathematical abilities involve multiple cognitive processes and that math disorders reflect more generalized cognitive difficulties. Executive functions that affect self-regulation are relevant for text generation disorders.

2.5. NEUROBIOLOGICAL BASES OF LEARNING DISABILITIES

New non-invasive structural and functional technologies have been utilized in recent years for study on the cerebral anatomy and function of children with learning impairments. The majority of research on dyslexia has used neuroimaging techniques like magnetic resonance imaging (MRI) or functional investigations (electroencephalography, Functional Magnetic

Resonance Imaging (FMRI), event-related potentials, positron emission tomography).

Studies based on functional neuroimaging have identified a network of three regions localized in the left hemisphere mediating word reading:

1. A sub lexical dorsal stream localized in temporoparietal areas
2. A lexical ventral stream localized in occipitotemporal region
3. A cerebral area in the left inferior frontal lobe under activated or overactivated by temporoparietal or occipitotemporal regions.

The dorsal and ventral components of this network, which is common to all languages and orthographies, function simultaneously and connect to the inferior frontal gyrus. The ventral stream is dedicated to the visual processing of orthographic patterns, whereas the dorsal stream is related with the sub lexical pathway to word meaning, corresponding with word reading.

The fusiform gyrus is thought to be a region that mediates word recognition with easy access to inferior temporal semantic regions.

Researches based on functional MRI have demonstrated that the development of ventral system is dependent on exposure to print and that in children this system shows reorganization with explicit instructions in reading.

Quantitative analyzes of MRI have shown reduced volume of the network of pre-scholars before the onset of formal reading instructions.

The dorsal and ventral pathways have resulted similar pattern of activation in children with word-level learning disabilities when compared with children developing reading comprehension learning disabilities (RCLD).

The left angular, left inferior frontal, and left hippocampus and Para hippocampal gyri all displayed lower deactivation in the group of children with RCLD, in contrast. Reduced gray matter in the right frontal areas was discovered in other structural studies on adolescents with RCLD, explaining their executive function issues.

Adult functional MRI investigations have discovered that the corticostriatal and hippocampal systems are also involved in language learning. The cortex and other subcortical structures are related to these structures as well as to one another and to the cortex. During learning processes, functional interactions between these regions have been described. Therefore, modifications in functional brain activity in one of these areas throughout language learning may be an indication of a local alteration in a complex learning network.

Learning the phonology and grammar of a language seems to involve the frontal cortex and basal ganglia. In fact, fMRI studies show that the hippocampus is engaged during the process of learning new vocabularies and during encoding processes connected to words, demonstrating the importance of the hippocampus in word learning.

When learning new words, the ventral striatum (nucleus accumbens) is active, but the dorsal striatum reacts to feedback in verbal paired-associated activities. Children with language difficulties have also been found to have abnormalities in the striatum.

Some studies suggest a reduction of volume of the caudate nucleus in children with specific language and learning impairment, while others have reported increases in caudate nucleus volume. Functional studies conducted on adults with dyslexia show hyperactivation of the striatum, not seen in children with dyslexia, suggesting to be a compensatory mechanism in adulthood.

Structural network analysis in children with a higher risk for dyslexia and other reading difficulties have showed that the hippocampus, temporal lobe, and putamen are less strongly connected in these individuals.

Studies conducted on children with math disabilities have found disorders of connectivity in temporoparietal and inferior parietal white matter.

Researchers have not found consistent structural differences across all studies in dyslexic patients, probably since this disorder is the result of a combination of multiple risk factors including motor, oral language, phonological disorders, and executive deficits.

A brain network connecting frontotemporal regions with the superior parietal, intraparietal, and inferior parietal circuits has also been shown by functional neuroimaging studies on numerical processing and mental arithmetic. Children with learning impairments in math are more active in this network, which is what it is known for.

Other studies have shown that some cerebellar regions are involved in cognitive, emotional, and behavioral activities in children with learning problems, particularly those with linguistic short-term memory deficiencies and reading development.

Specific areas of the cerebellum are functionally linked to the cerebral reading network, according to the cerebellar deficiency theory.

The inferior frontal junction (IFJ), the middle temporal gyrus, and the inferior parietal lobule (IPL) are thought to be the three reading-related brain areas that end up having functional connection with the cerebellum (MTG).

2.6. CONCLUSION

The neurological causes and clinical characteristics of learning impairments are all summarized in this chapter. This chapter's introduction gives highlights on the ideas related to learning impairments. The incidence of particular learning disorders and gender disparities are also explained in this chapter.

It addresses the neural correlates of learning disorders, the cognitive causes of learning difficulties, and the neurobiological causes of learning disabilities toward the end of the chapter.

REFERENCES

1. Görker, I., (2020). The prevalence and gender differences in specific learning disorder. *Learning Disabilities – Neurological Bases, Clinical Features and Strategies of Intervention* [Preprint]. Available at: https://doi.org/10.5772/intechopen.90214.
2. Krishnan, S., Watkins, K. E., & Bishop, D. V. M., (2016). Neurobiological basis of language learning difficulties. *Trends in Cognitive Sciences*, *20*(9), 701–714. Available at: https://doi.org/10.1016/j.tics.2016.06.012.
3. Liang, F., & Li, P., (2019). Characteristics of cognitive in children with learning difficulties. *Translational Neuroscience*, *10*(1), 141–146. Available at: https://doi.org/10.1515/tnsci-2019-0024.
4. Moll, K., et al., (2014). Specific learning disorder: Prevalence and gender differences. *PLoS One*, *9*(7). Available at: https://doi.org/10.1371/journal.pone.0103537.
5. Sahu, A., et al., (2019). Psychiatric comorbidities in children with specific learning disorder-mixed type: A cross-sectional study. *Journal of Neurosciences in Rural Practice*, *10*(4), 617–622. Available at: https://doi.org/10.1055/s-0039-1697879.
6. Sandro, M., (2020). Neural correlates in learning disabilities. *Learning Disabilities – Neurological Bases, Clinical Features and Strategies of Intervention* [Preprint]. Available at: https://doi.org/10.5772/intechopen.92294.
7. Tzouriadou, M., (2020). Concepts and ambiguities in the field of learning disabilities. *Learning Disabilities – Neurological Bases, Clinical Features and Strategies of Intervention* [Preprint]. Available at: https://doi.org/10.5772/intechopen.90777.

CHAPTER 3

Screening and Evaluating Learning Disabilities

Contents

This chapter will provide highlights on the screening and evaluation of learning disabilities. This chapter will also explain the concept of engaging families in the screening and evaluation process. This chapter also helps to understand various elements of disability screening. This chapter also explains different types of elements of evaluation. This chapter also provides highlights on the challenges related to screenings and evaluations. At the end of this chapter, this chapter will explain the phased approach to screening and evaluating students at school level.

3.1. INTRODUCTION

According to the World Health Organization [WHO], 2011] more than a billion people, or roughly 15% of the world's population, are affected by some form of disability, including sensory impairments (such as blindness and deafness), intellectual impairments, developmental impairments, physical impairments, and psychosocial impairments.

Although some people may have a disability as adults, many people are born with it or develop it as children. 150 million children under the age of 18 are thought to be disabled, according to the United Nations Children's Fund (UNICEF). These kids frequently need special education assistance in schools (UNICEF, 2005).

Children with disabilities must have access to inclusive education, according to the United Nations Convention on the Rights of Persons with Disabilities (CRPD), which was ratified in 2006. Children who receive an inclusive education attend their local schools with their peers and receive the necessary supports, rather than being educated in segregated facilities depending on their disabilities.

Many of the 177 nations (as of April 2018) that have signed the CRPD are therefore creating new systems and supports to encourage and guarantee inclusive educational opportunities for all children with disabilities (United Nations, 2006). But for many nations, creating an inclusive education system is frequently difficult and challenging.

Complicating this educational reform process are the challenges of identifying students with disabilities. Some disabilities may be apparent (e.g., mobility impairment), but others—such as learning disabilities—cannot be determined based on appearances alone.

Identifying a student with a learning disability requires

- A multistep process,

- The use of tools and resources that are translated and adapted to the local cultural context, and
- The participation of a multidisciplinary team of experts.

Many nations are exploring for solutions to support students with learning difficulties since they see the need for it. Unfortunately, many people have done this without having the procedures, techniques, or resources necessary to successfully diagnose learning problems.

This form of identification is not in accordance with global best standards. Large rates of misdiagnosis may result from an inadequate or poor screening and evaluation procedure, and students may not get the help and supports they require to succeed academically.

RTI takes seriously the responsibility to meet the needs of young children who are at risk and to provide every child with the best education possible. RTI encourages inclusive, egalitarian education in all of its projects and works with governments to implement the necessary laws and programs to achieve this long-term objective.

This manual is one of several manuals created to assist school districts, institutions of higher learning, and educators in meeting the educational requirements of all students, including those with disabilities.

The process of determining if a pupil has a learning disability is intricate and multidimensional. Unfortunately, some educational institutions and ministries have made attempts to streamline the procedure at the expense of pupils. Screening and evaluation procedures, when carried out properly, can aid in locating students who might require additional educational supports in order to realize their full academic potential.

On the other hand, harmful outcomes can occur when screening and evaluation of learning disabilities are carried out in a hasty, haphazard manner or without adhering to international best practices, such as incorrectly identifying students who may have learning disabilities as having disabilities or improperly identifying students who may have disabilities.

This section of the manual explains typical indicators of learning disorders, the method for identifying children who require special education, and the procedures for conducting an efficient evaluation of a student for a particular disability. In contrast to early identification procedures or other identification procedures unrelated to the classroom, this manual concentrates on screening and evaluating pupils in the classroom (usually in primary and secondary schools).

3.1.1. Typical Signs of a Learning Disability

The identification process usually begins when either a family member or a teacher becomes concerned that a student is not making adequate progress in school. Common characteristics of learning disabilities include the following, as described by the Learning Disabilities Association of America (2017):

1. Short attention span
2. Poor memory
3. Difficulty following directions
4. Inability to discriminate between/among letters, numerals, or sounds
5. Poor reading, writing, and/or math ability
6. Eye-hand coordination problems, poor coordination
7. Difficulty with sequencing
8. Disorganization and other sensory difficulties

Regardless of impairment, all people exhibit these traits at some point during their development.

However, a person with a learning disability could exhibit more than one of these traits (Learning Disabilities Association of America, 2017). Depending on a student's age and developmental stage, a learning disability may also fluctuate in its characteristics.

Depending on the cultural setting, these qualities could differ slightly. Because many students may struggle to study and communicate in their non-native language, it is important to take into account a student's native language.

Such difficulties are not indicative of a learning disability and should not be taken as such. For instance, 1989 research in Morocco indicated that Berber-speaking pupils performed worse in their first year of school than their Arabic-speaking peers in terms of Arabic reading.

However, after five years of public schooling in Arabic, both groups scored similarly in reading (Wagner, Spratt, & Ezzaki,1989). As a result, it is crucial to take language and culture into account when assessing a student's learning challenges.

Usually, additional tests or a thorough evaluation are required when a student exhibits the signs of a learning disability in order to help identify that student's learning challenges and capabilities.

3.1.2. Screening versus Evaluation

A learning deficiency can be difficult to diagnose and can occasionally seem onerous. A two-step procedure is ideal for determining whether a person has learning disabilities: (1) an initial assessment to see if a child needs more support in the classroom, and (2) a more thorough evaluation to see if a child has a learning disability and, if so, where areas of learning may be affected.

It is crucial to understand the difference between screening to see whether a kid has additional learning requirements and evaluating to determine a diagnosis of a learning disorder. Additionally, admission to a school shouldn't be based on a screening or assessment. Only necessary services and supports should be offered to pupils after being screened and identified, not a student's admission to a school.

Children and their families may experience issues if they need to receive an official diagnosis in order to access education. In many nations, screenings and evaluations are carried out in assessment or evaluation institutions that are either public or private, which can be quite expensive for many families.

Even though many nations demand a diagnosis before allowing a kid suspected of having a disability to enroll in school, this diagnosis is occasionally used to force enroelment in segregated schools or classes.

As a result, many families of disabled children decide against having their child evaluated for fear that their child will be turned away from a school because they have a learning problem (Ahmad, 2015). Some nations, including Costa Rica, are actively working to transition away from diagnosis-based systems and toward more customized and needs-based ones (Stough, 2003).

The origins of a student's learning challenges may be explained by a diagnosis, but it may not give enough information about the kind of services a student might need because learning disabilities can impact people differently, even those who share the same diagnosis.

As an alternative, every student should be evaluated for their unique learning strengths and weaknesses in order to determine the best supports and services. Even with a diagnosis, thorough evaluations are still necessary in the US to fully comprehend a student's strengths and flaws (Turnbull, Stowe, & Huerta, 2007).

By gathering this data, teachers may better understand the student's needs and develop an Individualized Education Plan (IEP) that will help the kid succeed in the classroom (Parent Center Hub).

Screening potential challenges in learning and development are very different from a comprehensive evaluation, which is used to identify specific learning disabilities, other disabilities, and other related challenges. Unfortunately, many countries do not recognize the difference between these two methods and often apply screening procedures to attempt to determine a learning disability.

For instance, teachers in Jordan frequently use self-made achievement tests to determine eligibility for learning disabilities support services (Al-Natour, Al-Khamra, & Al-Smadi, 2008) rather than using several tools and engaging a multidisciplinary team.

3.2. ENGAGING FAMILIES IN THE SCREENING AND EVALUATION PROCESS

During the process of screening, evaluating, and providing services, family involvement is crucial. In order to determine the appropriate assessment methods and tactics for their children, families can be of great assistance (Rutland & Hall, 2013). However, families must be informed about and participated in all parts of screening and evaluation in order for them to contribute to the process in a meaningful way (Boone & Crais, 1999).

Tools and guidance materials should be used in conjunction with standards on when and how to engage families most effectively when nations start to establish systems to support screenings and evaluations inside schools. Supporting children with disabilities and ensuring that the education and supports provided in the classroom are supported and reinforced at home require close collaboration with families.

Assistive device referral procedures, family history information for screenings and evaluations, parental agreement for evaluations, and family involvement in the IEP process are a few examples of standards that might be included.

Expanding parental participation to include other family members and carers (engaged in the child's upbringing) might be useful in nations where biological parents may not always be the primary carers.

Additionally, many parents and families may be unfamiliar with the notions of learning difficulties, screens, and evaluations, so schools should be sure to fully explain the procedure and go over the potential role of parents in all phases (Aro & Ahonen, 2011). Given the significance of family and parental involvement, this subject is weaved throughout the entire work.

3.3. ELEMENTS OF DISABILITY SCREENING

An identification screening, also known as a screening assessment, offers both broad information about a student who could require further services and a more thorough assessment (Bergeson et al., 2008). The screening process is frequently fast-paced and brief. When a student is suspected of having learning difficulties, screenings can also be carried out on an individual basis.

Screenings can give more detailed and preliminary information about a particular student's potential learning difficulties and strengths. Another advantage is that screenings can be conducted by those without extensive specialized training.

Parental approval may not be required for all screenings, particularly those that are school-wide (National Center for Learning Disabilities, 2006); nonetheless, screeners should abide by local regulations as parental consent policies might vary by nation.

A best practice, parental consent should be promoted whenever possible. The following are screening recommendations:

3.3.1. Screening Should Take Place as Early as Possible

As early as age three, learning issues can start to manifest. So that the child might prevent years of scholastic trouble, screening should be done as early as feasible, and the child should be regularly rescreened.

Once a child enrolls in school and then every 2–3 years after that, instructors should screen as necessary; they should observe the child both inside and outside the classroom (for example, during recess), and they should share their concerns with the child's parents or guardian(s) (Aro & Ahonen, 2011).

Children with suspected vision or hearing loss should be referred for further assessment and services. Screenings should include vision and hearing tests to track any changes over time.

Families can discuss their expectations for their kid's education with their child's teachers as well as pertinent facts about their child, such as strengths and hobbies (Aro & Ahonen, 2011). After then, screening might be conducted on a family member or teacher's advice.

3.3.2. Screening Should Rule Out Other Potential Causes of Learning Difficulties

Before a student is suspected of having a learning disability, it is important to rule out any other possible explanations of their learning difficulties. Before doing a more thorough evaluation, it is especially crucial to rule out hearing and vision issues.

Students with vision or hearing challenges may:

1. Require frequent breaks due to fatigue;
2. Have difficulty sustaining attention;
3. Be unable to finish timed tests;
4. Be unable to sit for long periods of time;
5. Have difficulty with sitting or balance, maintaining posture, and/or arm-hand use;
6. Have trouble answering questions;
7. Have difficulty pointing at something or looking someone in the eye; and
8. Have challenges communicating effectively (Farrall, Wright, & Wright, 2015).

These symptoms are often mistaken for indicators of learning disabilities. A teacher or other trained professional should conduct the vision and hearing exam because many nations have not adopted standard screening programs. This will help to guarantee that a student's learning difficulties are not caused by low vision or hearing impairment.

Additionally, screening should rule out any other elements that can affect a student's capacity to succeed academically, such as the environment or language. These elements could give the impression that a student has a learning problem.

Ruling out external factors is especially important in situations where the language spoken in a student's home may not be the same as the language of instruction at school. In fact, some experts do not recommend evaluating students for learning disabilities if their first language differs from the language of instruction.

They suggest that evaluations for learning disabilities can only take place once students clearly have a strong written and oral understanding of the primary language of instruction (Dunn & Walker, 2008).

3.3.3. Be Culturally and Linguistically Relevant

Misidentification can occur when screening technologies are used that have not been customized to the regional language or culture. Every screening method should be conducted in the student's original language and tailored to the cultural setting.

It is not the same thing to simply translate a tool into the native tongue as to adapt it. To represent a country's cultural setting, the tool should be modified instead. Early developmental stages, for instance, change considerably depending on the culture and reality of the country (e.g., catching a ball may be an inappropriate milestone in countries where children do not play with balls or typically have access to playing with balls).

3.3.4. Have Clear Procedures and Standards for Initiating an Evaluation

Screenings do not exist for their own sake. Instead, there must be clear policies in place regarding what to do if a student is found to have additional learning needs and what resources are available to help that student and their family. In most instances, doing a thorough examination should be the following step.

3.3.5. Use Multiple Tools and Sources of Information

The screening procedure must make use of a variety of informational tools and resources (described in more detail later in the guide). Utilizing a variety of tools and information sources improves the accuracy of the evaluation results and helps to eliminate any potential bias on the part of the assessors.

3.3.6. Don't Use Screening Methods to Diagnose a Learning Disability

The purpose of screening should be to determine the additional need for a thorough evaluation and not to try to pinpoint a specific learning problem. Finding a specific learning problem is far more difficult, and only specialists should do it.

3.4. ELEMENTS OF EVALUATION

An evaluation is a thorough process carried out by qualified specialists (using a wealth of detailed information) in order to discover or diagnose the root of the student's learning issues, ascertain the severity of the handicap, and identify specific remedies. These evaluations' results should also be utilized to create an IEP and establish goals for a student's academic advancement. Examinations ought to:

3.4.1. Take Place Upon Completing an Initial Screening

As stated before, a general screening must be conducted before a comprehensive evaluation is done because screenings can rule out other factors that may be confused with characteristics of learning disabilities. Evaluations can be time-consuming for all members of the evaluation team, so it is important that there be a suspected need before moving forward.

3.4.2. Use Multiple Evaluation Tools and Sources of Information

In order to evaluate whether a student has a learning disability, no one test or score is adequate (NJCLD, 2011). Therefore, it is necessary to perform an evaluation using a variety of tools and information sources. Although there is no set standard for the minimum number of tools that should be employed, an evaluation should include at least two tools.

According to each student's particular requirements, the precise quantity will be decided on an individual basis. IDEA, a US education statute for children with disabilities, states that several examinations and procedures must be carried out in order to determine eligibility, and that doing so is wrong and unacceptable (Turnbull, Stowe, & Huerta, 2007).

A student's health, vision and hearing, general intelligence, social and emotional status, communication abilities, academic performance, and motor skills should all be evaluated as part of an effective examination (Farrall, Wright, & Wright, 2015).

Additionally, "background and family history, formal and informal testing, observations in the classroom and other settings, as appropriate; interviews with family, teacher(s), and the child; additional testing, depending on the presenting problem and the test findings" are some examples of the types of information that can be used to evaluate a student (Farrall, Wright, & Wright, 2015).

3.4.3. Be Culturally and Linguistically Relevant

Every tool needs to be customized and standardized to take into account the regional standards for the culture and language in which it will be used.

Sadly, diagnostic tools for learning problems are frequently imported using Western criteria.

This practice "raises ethical issues as a lack of sensitivity to cultural differences can result in misdiagnosis or mislabeling" (Aro & Ahonen, 2011). If tools may not have been culturally adapted or are not available, evaluators should develop, adapt, and pilot tools before conducting evaluations. During this time, students can receive additional supports in the classroom without having received a diagnosis.

3.4.4. Be Conducted by A Trained Multidisciplinary Team

To get a range of viewpoints, it is crucial that a multidisciplinary team take part in all reviews. A student's care givers, the general education teacher, and a special education teacher at the school should be the core components of this team. Where possible, a social worker or school psychologist's equivalent should also take part.

Speech therapists, physical therapists, occupational therapists, reading specialists, and others may also be requested to join the evaluation team. The team should have at least one member who is capable of leading the process and has received training in conducting an extensive review.

An educational specialist who is conversant with the student's ethnic and language culture, if necessary, is another desirable team member. A school administrator or a representative of the district or regional offices of the ministry of education will frequently also take part in the review.

However, only a qualified clinical psychologist, educational psychologist, school psychologist, or neuropsychologist should make the diagnosis if the team has reason to believe that a kid has a particular learning problem (Ross Kidder, 2002).

A student with suspected learning difficulties should receive additional support rather than an actual diagnosis if these skilled professionals are not present in their nation. By doing this, the student will, at the very least, get the necessary learning supports, and the likelihood of a mistaken diagnosis or incorrect labeling is decreased.

Countries should simultaneously endeavor to increase their domestic workforce's capabilities to promptly fill professional gaps.

3.4.5. Be Conducted Over an Extended Period

It's crucial to acquire information about a student from many sources and throughout a period of time that is reasonable—possibly one to two weeks—as well as at various times. The precision of the results will be improved by gathering data over a number of days and hours. For instance, if testing always takes place before lunch, when a student could be hungry, or if a student isn't feeling well on a particular day, these factors could affect the data results.

On the other hand, an evaluation shouldn't go too long because doing so could produce unduly significant delays in the student's services and results. For instance, all evaluations must be finished within 60 days of families giving their written agreement, according to US statute IDEA.

3.4.5.1. Engage Families

An increasing amount of research demonstrates that a student's academic success depends heavily on family engagement in general, but particularly in relation to special education services (Family Empowerment and Disability Council, 2012). To make sure that the evaluation is pertinent and can serve as a basis to support a student, involving families in the evaluation process is crucial.

Families should:

1. Be informed about why the evaluation is being suggested;
2. Provide their consent to have their child evaluated;
3. Be involved in the evaluation process to provide important family and historical background; and
4. Be fully informed of the evaluation results with a copy of the final report.

The consent phase of the evaluation process is crucial because it guarantees that families are fully informed of the purposes of an evaluation and enables them to participate in the process going forward. Throughout the review process, families should be requested to participate and should be encouraged to do so.

Engaging families can include

1. Allowing them to receive important information about their children's strengths and needs;
2. Providing important and relevant historical information;
3. Assisting in the selection of the appropriate evaluation tools; and

4. Allowing them to advocate for school services for their children (Hall, Rutland & Grisham-Brown, 2011).

3.4.6. Include a System for Consent

The permission to obtain special education services is distinct from the consent to have a student evaluated. A different consent procedure should be developed if the evaluation leads to the conclusion that special education services are required. The family's native tongue must be used for all forms of communication, including verbal and written permission procedures, to guarantee that they comprehend the proposals being made.

3.4.7. Have Clear Procedures and Standards Related to Referrals

In order to create support systems that address the obstacles and capitalize on the strengths, evaluation seeks to identify a student's academic weaknesses and strengths. Therefore, prior to conducting the evaluation, a system supporting a student's educational needs should be in place. As soon as a kid is given the go-ahead to access services, it is important to operationalize clear rules and processes for referrals and supports.

The interdisciplinary team that conducted the evaluation should give specifics regarding suggested services if it is found that a student has a learning disability and would benefit from special education services.

These services must to be tailored to each student and take into account both their academic talents and weaknesses. When feasible, students themselves should take part in all talks pertaining to service as well as parents or guardians.

3.4.8. Record Results of Evaluation in a Comprehensive Report

A thorough report should include the information gleaned from the evaluation. The student's family is the report's primary audience, but a copy should also be kept in the student's file for use by any present or future teachers.

The person in charge of the evaluation usually writes the report primarily, with assistance and feedback from the other members of the multidisciplinary team. Both the student's academic achievements and weaknesses should be highlighted in this report. Additionally, recommendations for additional services and supports for future IEPs should be included in this report.

Technical language or anything that can be confusing should be avoided because this report should be accessible to families. Reports should offer the facts in an ordered manner and be thorough and succinct.

The report should be delivered in person to the families so that they can be guided through the conclusions and suggestions and have a face-to-face discussion. Frequently, the report is distributed to the families ahead of time so that there can be a more thorough and educated conversation.

3.4.9. Re-Evaluate on a Recurring and Consistent Basis

Because the needs of students with learning disabilities may change over time, periodic reevaluations must be conducted to ensure that the supports and services are still appropriate and meet the respective student's needs.

Although reevaluations typically occur every 3 years, some educational systems allow for reevaluations as needed within this 3-year period. Just as in the evaluation process, the Ministry of Education should develop the standards related to periodic reevaluations.

3.5. CHALLENGES RELATED TO SCREENINGS AND EVALUATIONS

Finding kids with learning difficulties has obvious advantages, including facilitating access to assistance, obtaining reasonable accommodations, and creating an IEP. However, a few related obstacles must be taken into account, including the following:

- **Lack of Qualified Professionals:** In many nations, special education and related services are still in their infancy. Although qualified specialists in special education might offer assistance in inclusive schools in low- and middle-income nations, qualified specialists in psychology, occupational therapy, and speech-language pathology are uncommon at the school level. Additionally, even if these specialists are present and accessible to a school system, it's possible that they lack the necessary training for screening or evaluation procedures. For instance, it is not required in Namibia to screen or assess students for learning difficulties using multidisciplinary teams. No official procedure is in place to determine a student's learning needs or method to inform eligibility for special education services; instead, the administration and school counselor call the parents to review their child's academic achievement and behavior (Aro & Ahonen, 2011).

- **Lack of Tools and Guides Adapted to Local Language and Culture:** One study that polled testing experts in education from 44 nations found that 85% said they needed access to tests that identify and diagnose pupils with disabilities. The experts determined that the most urgent requirement was testing for learning difficulties. The countries with the highest likelihood of producing tools include Australia, Canada, Western Europe, or the United States, while those with the lowest likelihood are those in Africa or the Arab world. Despite the ease with which tools can be obtained, "their availability and use varied greatly among more than 220 countries" (Oakland, 2009). In the same survey, 68% of participants claimed to have evaluated disability using tests created in other nations. It is unethical to employ Western diagnostic tests to identify or treat learning problems in low- and middle-income nations (Oakland, 2009).

  Such examinations are frequently not translated into local languages nor tailored to a sample of the local community (Aro & Ahonen, 2011). (Oakland, 2009). Additionally, some instrument features might not be suited for use in various cultures. For example, non-Western cultures may have different expectations than Western societies regarding when children should attain particular developmental milestones (Fernald et al., 2009). The danger of misidentification and misdiagnosis can increase if Western-made tools are not adapted to the student's nation, language, and culture (Oakland, 2009). Before promoting their usage, nations without adaptable tools should seek to make the tools culturally appropriate for their own nations.

- **Lack of Evaluation Standards:** Along with the lack of suitable tools and manuals, the general screening and evaluation process also frequently lacks standards and rules. Standards or guidelines for the use of multidisciplinary teams, testing adaptation, family participation, and service referral have not yet been developed in many nations. Without these agreed-upon procedures to support legitimacy, accountability, or uniformity, the screening or evaluation process can differ greatly by region or even by school.

  For instance, there are no established standardized procedures or instruments in Jordan for recognizing learners in the classroom. The majority of special education eligibility assessments therefore rely on achievement tests created by teachers (Al-Natour, Al-Khamra, & Al-Smadi, 2008). The validity and accuracy of such assessments are unknown because they are frequently created by people who lack knowledge or experience in learning impairments.

- **Possible Misclassification or Misdiagnosis:** The National Joint Committee on Learning Disabilities in the United States "believes that insufficient diagnostic processes and procedures have contributed to misclassification of individuals and questionable incidence rates of learning disabilities" (NJCLD, 1994). Misclassification and misdiagnosis can manifest in two ways:
  - Overrepresentation of individuals who do not have learning disabilities but may have other related challenges in areas such as speech processing or behavior. Evaluation tools that do not take language or cultural diversity into account can also cause overrepresentation.
  - Underrepresentation of individuals who may have challenges from a learning disability, but are not recognized as having a disability (NJCLD, 1994).

Macedonia is one place where overrepresentation is evident. Romani pupils make up 46% of the population in special education although making up only 2.66 % of the total. Roma students are disproportionately overrepresented in learning disability programs and schools.

Evaluation procedures that do not take into consideration linguistic variety and contain social bias can result in this mistake (European Roma Rights Center, 2012). The identification of those studying English as a second language as having a learning disability has also been problematic in the United States.

Evaluators and other professionals must make sure that the student being evaluated has a solid grasp of the language used in the classroom (both written and oral) before conducting a learning disability exam (Dunn & Walker, 2008).

On the other hand, inadequate evaluation procedures may result in pupils going unidentified and not receiving help. For instance, in Kenya, it is less common for teachers to identify a handicap among pupils who are poor. Since screening and evaluations are only conducted at assessment or evaluation facilities and many low-income families cannot afford to travel to these locations, the number of students with impairments is frequently underreported (Mukria & Korir, 2006).

3.5.1. Labeling

Although knowing a student's specific learning disability is helpful to provide the appropriate services and support, students can also be harmfully labeled. As UNICEF stated, "there are dangers in 'labeling' children according to their diagnosis as it can lead to lower expectations and denial of needed services, and overshadow the child's individuality and evolving capacities" (World Health Organization (WHO) and United Nations Children's Fund (UNICEF), 2012).

Figure 3.1. World health organization headquarters.

Source: Image by Wikimedia commons.

Being classified as having a disability can also result in increased stigma, rejection from peers, lowered self-esteem, and fewer possibilities for the student (Florian et al., 2006). Due to these possible risks, evaluations should have a purpose and result in services and supports that will enhance the educational experience for each student.

"To mitigate potential prejudicial labeling, all identification systems should be coupled with disability awareness programs to help administrators, teachers, students, and parents better understand and fully accept diversity and disability," according to the RTI Disability Inclusive Education Systems and Policies in Low- and Middle-Income Countries (Hayes & Bulat, 2017).

Figure 3.2. UNICEF.

Source: Image by Needpix.

3.5.2. Segregated Settings

3.5.2.1. Pull-Out Model

It is crucial to understand that special education is a service rather than a location. Specialized schools and segregated classrooms are only a few examples of places where special education services are offered around the world. This paradigm is predicated on the idea that kids with disabilities need a setting aside from the general education classroom where they can receive specialized teaching.

A special education teacher "pulls out" a pupil from a general education class to get training in this "pull-out model." The method may promote stigma and have a detrimental effect on a student's self-esteem, even if this approach can provide pupils with specialized teaching and support (Barton, 2016).

Most crucially, the pull-out approach lessens a student's exposure to teacher teaching in the general education context, which frequently results in the already-struggling student missing important curricular components.

The pull-out model can result in increased academic gaps between students with disabilities and students without disabilities (Bouck, 2006). If a full evaluation team decides that individualized instruction outside the classroom is necessary, it is important that the student is not pulled out during instructional time or during the student's preferred activities (such as recess or art time).

3.5.2.2. Push-In Model

The "push-in" concept of special education has gained popularity recently in many nations. In this model, kids with disabilities attend general education classes with their peers without impairments and receive special education services there.

The special education teacher and general education teacher work together to ensure that students are "receiving full access to the general education curriculum while limiting any disruption to their daily schedule (such as pulling students out of a classroom).

This model also includes the implementation of specially designed modifications within the classroom setting" (Professional Learning Board, 2017). Researchers found that students with disabilities make more progress in the push-in model than in the pull-out model.

The amount of time a kid with a disability spends in a general education class is actually positively connected with better math and reading test scores, less disruptive conduct, and more job chances in the future.

Regardless of the type or severity of the disability, this outcome was observed in all kids with disabilities (Wagner et al., 2006). In the push-in model, resource room or special education teachers can assist general education teachers, function as advisers and mentors, and mentor general education teachers while co-teaching students with disabilities using differentiated learning strategies.

The instructor in the resource room is still able to give the kid individualized instruction, although it is usually done in a small group in the general education classroom.

Many nations use the pull-out model while trying to increase the number of resource rooms. For instance, Chinese legislation mandates that primary schools create resource rooms if they have sufficient resources or a particular percentage of children with disabilities. Over the past 20 years, the government has significantly increased the number of such settings (Xiaoli & Olli-Pekka, 2015).

This model's drawback is that it might be pricey due to the increased equipment and classroom space requirements. When specialized and rigorous training outside of the general education classroom has proven helpful for particular pupils, countries may want to take into consideration the push-in strategy rather than using the pull-out method all the time.

3.6. SCREENING AND EVALUATION METHODS AND TOOLS

There is no one technique or technology that can reveal all of a student's abilities, deficiencies, and educational requirements. Teachers should use a variety of screening and evaluation instruments, and data for both should be gathered using various techniques or ways to gather information.

This section offers more details on the many methods a teacher can use to gather data for screening as well as clarification on the various data collection methods.

3.6.1. Screening and Evaluation Information Sources

For both screening and evaluation, professionals must collect as much information as needed and appropriate to assess (1) a student's possible educational needs, and (2) which instructional strategies can be immediately implemented. They should collect information about the following.

- **Family Background:** Knowing a student's family background and history can assist identify whether they have experienced difficulties since birth and whether other elements at home may have an impact on their current academic performance. Meetings with families should be productive and cooperative to reduce the chance of assigning blame for a student's potential academic difficulties to their parents.
- These conversations and exchanges should be held in the family's native tongue to allow for full communication between the family and school staff as well as to guarantee that the information is useful.
- **Observation:** Teachers can have a better understanding of a student's behavior through observations of them in various situations. Observations need to be made over time and at various periods during the day in order to be useful.
- Additionally, observations ought to be made in a variety of contexts and settings, such as during various forms of instruction and in informal settings at school, as these contexts might reveal

how a student's behavior may vary depending on the situation. When gathering information, the observer must be as unobtrusive as possible.

- Furthermore, other students in the classroom should never be told that a specific student is being observed; such a statement could increase stigmatization. Whenever possible, observers should use a standardized checklist and include a way to record the information in a report shared with parents or other members of the multidisciplinary team.
- **Review of Past Exams and Assignments:** Analyzing previous assignments and tests might be helpful in determining a student's potential educational demands and difficulties. This procedure can demonstrate whether any academic trends or problems were noticeable during a specific period of time.
- For example, if a student only began having challenges in reading, writing, or mathematics at a certain time but did well previously, this timing might indicate that other factors besides a learning disability should be considered. Reviewing past work can help measure a student's academic progress and compare growth to an expected rate of progress (Overton, 2012).
- **Formal Testing and Tools:** To identify a barrier in a particular subject, such as reading, writing, or mathematics, standardized screening and evaluation tools may be useful in addition to the methods mentioned above. However, relying too much on these technologies without utilizing other information-gathering techniques can result in inaccurate information.

Additionally, it's crucial to create guidelines for tool usage, the localization of tools into other languages, and the suggested method for modifying tools to fit the specific cultural context of a location.

3.6.2. Screenings and Evaluation Tools

The evaluation and screening of learning difficulties can be done using a variety of formal procedures and resources; the recommended tools are mentioned below.

3.6.2.1. Vision and Hearing Screening Tools

In cooperation with the Ministry of Health, regular screenings for vision and hearing should be conducted. These tests should reveal any issues with how well a student can see objects up close and, in the distance, as well as how well they can hear various tones at various frequencies.

A functional vision evaluation should be part of vision testing as it may detect issues (such problems with eye movement and night vision) that aren't addressed by screening alone.

The expense of conducting hearing and vision screenings is inexpensive, and teachers can undertake them. With the help of good headphones and an app on a tablet or smartphone, hearing tests can be conducted. Because a student may not yet be literate or may have difficulty naming letters, the equipment used for vision testing should be culturally appropriate and use symbols rather than letters.

In a perfect world, screenings would be accompanied by recommendations for additional testing and services, such spectacles or hearing aids.

3.6.2.2. Speech and Language Assessment Tools for Evaluation

The capacity of a learner to appropriately create sounds or pronounce words may be hampered by speech problems (American Speech-Language-Hearing Association). Language disorders can impact either receptive language or expressive language, which is the capacity to verbally communicate ideas, thoughts, and feelings (the ability to understand oral communication).

Before doing a learning disability test, any communication issues must be checked out even though students with speech and language impairments may also have learning disabilities. Furthermore, autism may be indicated—though not always—by speech and language issues as well as issues with social skills.

Similar to learning disabilities, speech and language disabilities are also considered to be high-incidence disabilities. In the United States, approximately 5% of all elementary students have some form of speech or language disorder (National Institute on Deafness and Other Communication Disorders, 2016).

Trained speech therapists typically administer assessments for potential speech and language disorders. However, because many countries lack trained speech therapists, implementing these tools and evaluations may not be feasible.

3.6.2.3. Intelligence Assessment Tools for Evaluation

Intelligence tests have historically been a crucial aspect of diagnosing learning disabilities, especially when used to assess the gap between a student's intelligence and academic performance. However, during the past few decades, the use of IQ tests in the evaluation of learning disabilities has become more and more contentious in the United States and other high-income nations.

For instance, such assessments might be unfair to students from low-income households and those from varied cultural and linguistic backgrounds (Connecticut State Department of Education, 2010). As a result, intelligence tests shouldn't be used as the main indicator of whether a learning problem is present.

3.6.2.4. Reading Assessment Tools for Evaluation

There are various techniques to evaluate a student's ability to read at the same level as their peers. Additionally, reading tests can offer crucial baseline data that can be used to analyze a student's development and performance. They can also tell teachers about how to create effective lessons and enhance education (Rhodes & Shanklin, 1993).

3.6.2.5. Writing and Spelling Assessment Tools for Evaluation

As with reading, it's crucial to assess a student's prospective writing and spelling challenges. Each student's writing issues may seem differently. For instance, some students could find it difficult to communicate their ideas in writing, while other students may find that their handwriting is difficult to read and understand. Additionally, difficulties with spelling frequently point to a more pervasive learning problem because spelling is a "essential component of written language" (Farrall, Wright, & Wright, 2015).

3.6.2.6. Mathematics Assessment Tools for Evaluation

In the past within the United States, most evaluations for learning disabilities relied primarily on reading tests. However, assessing a student for difficulties in mathematics is just as critical as assessing reading or writing difficulties.

Mathematics assessments can reveal information about a student's skills in understanding numbers and quantities, writing numbers, producing basic calculations from memory, and mastering basic calculation operations (Aro & Ahonen, 2011).

3.6.2.7. Motor Skills Assessments Tools for Evaluation

Evaluation is required to identify if a student's learning issues are mostly caused by their motor skills challenges rather than a learning disability because these obstacles might negatively impact a student's performance in school (for example, difficulty with handwriting) (Connecticut State Department of Education, 2010). Such difficulties could be a sign of a disability like cerebral palsy.

These tests can determine whether a student has a motor handicap as well as whether the disability happens while preparing for or engaging in a particular activity (Aro & Ahonen, 2011).

3.6.2.8. Functional Behavior Assessments (FBA)

An FBA is used to identify the causes, or triggers, of a student's behavior that is interfering with learning. An FBA analysis includes:

- The setting in which the behavior took place (the time of day, the location, etc.)
- The antecedent (what happened directly before the behavior)
- The aspects of the behavior itself (what does the student do that is interfering with their education)
- The consequence (what happens after the behavior, and how do the people around the student respond to the behavior)

FBAs are often administered by behavior analysts who have been trained to study behavior. Analysts should speak with the student's instructors, family, and anybody else who may be able to offer insightful commentary on why the behavior is occurring in addition to conducting this assessment. FBA may be difficult to undertake in many nations right now, but it may be a goal in the future.

3.7. PHASED APPROACH TO SCREENING AND EVALUATING STUDENTS AT THE SCHOOL LEVEL

Low- and middle-income nations are increasingly looking for strategies to detect and assist pupils with learning difficulties in the classroom. However, because screening and evaluation are difficult processes, nations frequently are unsure of where to begin or where to concentrate their limited resources.

Some nations may already have some procedures in place, but they might not have all the resources available to carry out effective screenings and evaluations that are in line with global best practices. This patchy accessibility of services could unintentionally result in a misdiagnosis of learning difficulties and prevent pupils from getting the help they require to succeed academically.

For instance, some nations might utilize screening methods to evaluate a learning disability or might use just one kind of diagnostic tool that isn't customized or standard for the region. Similar to this, a single person rather than a diverse team may frequently be in charge of conducting an evaluation at the school.

These procedures could produce data that inaccurately portrays a student's academic demands and limitations. This chapter offers a staged method for countries to help them assess existing levels of service availability, as well as any potential gaps in services, and provides advice on how to prioritize and expand services. It recognizes the problem of incomplete screening and evaluation systems.

The core elements of this phased approach can be defined as follows:

Phase 1: Nascent Screening and Differentiated Instruction. In this phase, countries or educational systems may have some, but not all, systems in place to identify students with learning disabilities effectively. Countries in this phase should focus on conducting effective vision and hearing screening techniques in the classroom while simultaneously developing the systems needed to screen for other challenges in academic instruction. During this phase, teachers should focus on diversifying instruction to differentiate learning, if they have not done so already.

Phase 2: Emerging Screening and Individualized Instruction. In this phase, all students routinely receive vision and hearing screenings and a system is also in place to assess and rule out other challenges (such as medical or environmental factors) to academic instruction. Systems required to conduct evaluations can be developed. As these supports are put in place, teachers can provide more fully differentiated instruction, support intensive instructional strategies, begin to develop IEPs, and provide reasonable accommodations.

Phase 3: Established Systems and Support. In this phase, the systems, standards, and tools are in place to provide comprehensive screening and evaluation services that can be implemented in the school setting. In this phase, teachers should provide individualized learning supports in the classroom. Systems established for screening and evaluations should be monitored and updated as needed.

3.8. CONCLUSION

The evaluation and screening of learning disorders are summarized in this chapter. This chapter also discusses screening versus evaluation and common indicators of a learning problem. It is crucial to understand that evaluating a student to determine whether they have additional learning requirements differs from screening to determine whether they have a learning problem. Additionally, screening or evaluation should not be a requirement for admission to a school.

Additionally, this chapter highlights the components of evaluation and discusses issues with screening and evaluations such as a lack of qualified professionals, a lack of resources and instructions in the local language and culture, a lack of evaluation standards, and the potential for misclassification or misdiagnosis. Additionally, the tools for screenings and evaluations were discussed.

REFERENCES

1. Hayes, A. M., et al., (2018). *Learning Disabilities Screening and Evaluation Guide for Low – and Middle-Income Countries*. www.ncbi.nlm.nih.gov. Research Triangle Park. Available at: https://doi.org/10.3768/rtipress.2018.op.0052.1804; https://www.ncbi.nlm.nih.gov/books/NBK545498/#_ch6_ (accessed on 14 October 2023).
2. Hayes, A. M., et al., (2022). *Learning Disabilities Screening and Evaluation Guide for Low – and Middle-Income Countries. RTI*. RTI International. P.O. Box 12194, Research Triangle Park, NC 27709-2194. Tel: 919-541-6000; e-mail: publications@rit.org; Web site: http://www.rti.org. Available at: https://www.rti.org/rti-press-publication/learning-disabilities-screening (accessed on 14 October 2023).
3. *Screening for Indicators of a Specific Learning Disability*, (n.d.). ADCET. www.adcet.edu.au. Available at: https://www.adcet.edu.au/oao/for-disability-practitioners/screening-for-indicators-of-a-specific-learning-disability (accessed on 14 October 2023).

CHAPTER 4

Clinical Characteristics of Mental Disorders in Children

Contents

This chapter will provide highlights on the clinical characteristics of mental disorders in children. At the beginning of this chapter, this chapter explains about the nature of childhood mental and developmental disorders. This chapter explains the diagnosis and classification of mental disorders in children. This chapter helps to understand the comorbidity and co-occurring mental disorders in children. This chapter also explains about the clinical characteristics of attention deficit hyperactivity disorder (ADHD). This chapter also provides highlights on the clinical characteristics of oppositional defiant disorder (ODD) and conduct disorder. At the end of this chapter, this chapter will explain the clinical characteristics of intellectual disabilities and mood disorders.

4.1. INTRODUCTION

Neurodevelopmental, emotional, and behavioral abnormalities that affect the brain's ability to develop in children can have substantial negative effects on their psychological and social well-being. Families and school systems must provide a lot more care for these illnesses in children because they commonly last into adulthood (Nevo & Manassis, 2009, Polanczyk & Rohde, 2007, Shaw et al., 2012).

These children are more likely to have damaged developmental trajectories, require more medical and disability services, and run a higher risk of coming into touch with law enforcement (Fergusson et al., 1993).

4.1.1. Childhood Mental and Behavioral Disorders

The following five conditions are the only ones covered in this chapter: autism, conduct disorder, childhood anxiety disorders, and ADHD (intellectual developmental disorder).

- **Anxiety disorders:** Excessive or inappropriate fear, along with behavioral problems that go along with it, characterize anxiety disorders and hinder functioning (American Psychiatric Association, 2013). Clinical symptoms of an anxiety disorder in children include extreme physiological symptoms, behavioral problems, such as avoiding frightened objects, and related suffering or impairment (Beesdo et al., 2009).
- **ADHD:** Inattention and disorganization, either with or without hyperactivity-impulsivity, are symptoms of ADHD, a neurodevelopmental disease that impairs functioning (American Psychiatric Association, 2013). About 20% of people with ADHD

continue to struggle with it as adults (Polanczyk & Rohde, 2007).

- **Conduct Disorder:** A pattern of antisocial acts that violate others' fundamental rights or important age-appropriate societal norms characterizes the disorder, which is diagnosed in children under the age of 18.
- **Autism:** A neurodevelopmental disorder marked by substantial impairment in social interaction and communication abilities as well as the existence of constrained and stereotypical behaviors.
- **Intellectual disability:** A generalized disease known as intellectual disability is defined by two or more adaptive behavioral deficiencies and markedly reduced cognitive performance (American Psychiatric Association, 2013).

4.2. NATURE OF CHILDHOOD MENTAL AND DEVELOPMENTAL DISORDERS

Mental and developmental issues in children are a growing problem for the world's health care systems. Due to the decline in infant mortality, there are now more children and adolescents in the populations of LMICs (Murray et al., 2012), and many adult mental and developmental illnesses begin in childhood and adolescence (Kessler et al., 2007), which are two variables that contribute to this.

4.2.1. Global Epidemiology and the Burden of Childhood Mental and Developmental Disorders

Given the severe lack of data for many geographical regions and the cultural variances in presentation and measurement, determining the worldwide epidemiology of mental diseases is a challenging undertaking.

These issues are exacerbated when investigating mental disorders in children, particularly in LMICs where other health concerns, such as infectious diseases, are priorities. The issue of data paucity was highlighted in the Global Burden of Disease Study 2010 (GBD 2010), which quantified the burden in terms of years lived with disability (YLD), years of life lost (YLL) due to premature mortality, and disability-adjusted life years (DALYs = YLDs + YLLs) (Murray et al., 2012).

Burden calculation first required systematically reviewing and modeling the available epidemiological data for mental disorders to provide the necessary prevalence outputs (Baxter et al., 2014, Erskine et al., 2013,

Whiteford et al., 2013). The 2010 global and regional prevalence of anxiety disorders, ADHD, conduct disorder, and autism in males and females ages 5–9, 10–14, and 15–19 years are shown in tables 8.1, 8.2, and 8.3 (Baxter et al., 2014, Erskine et al., 2013).

Since the burden of this disorder was handled as a residual category after all other intellectual disabilities had been reattributed to particular causes, such as newborn encephalopathy, the prevalence of idiopathic intellectual disability (Whiteford and colleagues, 2013) was not determined (Vos et al., 2012).

The 21 world areas identified by GBD 2010 showed a very consistent pattern in the epidemiology of pediatric mental illnesses. These prevalence estimates, meanwhile, were based on scant data; in some areas, like Sub-Saharan Africa, there are either no statistics at all for various illnesses or none at all for specific children's disorders. Regional differences might exist, but they are difficult to determine due to a paucity of data and the ensuing large uncertainty gaps.

From an epidemiological standpoint, the 21 geographical areas identified by GBD 2010 showed rather constant rates of childhood mental disorders.

Patterns of burden followed those of prevalence in terms of gender, age, period, and region. Due to its high population and decreased baby and young child mortality, South Asia has the highest prevalence of children and adolescents with mental and developmental disorders (Murray et al., 2012).

The populations of LMICs tend to have higher proportions of children and adolescents than high-income countries (HICs). For example, 40% of the population in "least developed countries" is younger than age 15 years, compared to 17% in "more developed regions" (United Nations, 2011).

Furthermore, population aging is occurring more slowly in low and middles income countries (LMICs), with some low-income countries (LICs) predicted to have the youngest populations by 2050, given their high fertility rates (UN 2011).

These patterns indicate that childhood mental illnesses will become more significant in LMICs. Additionally, if infectious disease-related infant mortality continues to decline, more children may reach the ages at which mental problems manifest, putting additional strain on these nations already underdeveloped mental health systems.

4.2.2. Risk Factors for Childhood Mental and Developmental Disorders

There are lifelong risk factors and age-specific risk factors among the table 8.5 mental and developmental disorders of children risk factors (Kieling et al., 2011). Children's health is strongly influenced by their carers' health and wellbeing, their living conditions at home and at school, and the peer pressure they experience as they enter adolescence.

Consideration should be given to a risk factor's prevalence, degree of correlation with a negative result, and ability to limit exposure to that risk factor when determining its relative importance (Scott et al., 2014). Using these standards, attempts to deal with maternal mental health issues or enhance parenting abilities may enhance many children's mental health and development.

4.2.3. Consequences of Childhood Mental and Developmental Disorders

Both the effects on children and the continuation of mental illness into adulthood are repercussions of these disorders. Children's suffering on an individual level, as well as the detrimental impacts on their families and peers, are all part of the impact in childhood.

Aggression against other students and peer distraction from learning are two examples of this impact. Children with mental and developmental difficulties are more likely to experience physical and mental health issues as adults, as well as more likely to be unemployed, interact with law enforcement, and require assistance with daily living.

4.2.4. Trends in Childhood Mental and Developmental Disorders

The prevalence and burden of childhood mental disorders remained consistent between 1990 and 2010 (GBD 2010). Although the rates themselves may not have changed, population and aging do have impacts on the number of YLDs and DALYs attributable to mental disorders in childhood. As the population of children increases globally, the number of DALYs attributable to mental disorders in children will increase.

4.3. DIAGNOSIS AND CLASSIFICATION OF MENTAL DISORDERS IN CHILDREN

Various health providers can make a diagnosis of a mental condition. A child psychologist, psychiatrist, pediatrician, family doctor, or counselor may conduct an examination that identifies a kid as needing mental health treatment.

Pediatricians and family doctors are typically the ones who first notice serious behavioral abnormalities and are increasingly making diagnoses like ADHD.

The severity of mental problems cannot be determined using any precise metrics or benchmarks. The context has a role in severity, since certain settings and circumstances can exacerbate symptoms and make it difficult to cope. Children with particular disorders may exhibit less severity and dysfunction when placed in other, more supportive environments.

Diagnoses might be challenging since developmental problems can alter presenting manifestations. In actuality, diagnoses can alter with age because each disorder's manifestation changes as a child gets older. Symptoms could wax and fade.

A student's response to treatment also differs from one individual to another and from one point in their development to another. As the following chapters of this report will show, it's not uncommon for a child to have numerous contemporaneous or sequential mental diagnoses or for a mental condition to co-occur with a physical disorder. A primary mental disorder is typically used to describe a diagnosis that appears to be the primary contributor to disability, while secondary disorders are used to describe diagnoses that co-occur.

A complex collection of criteria, such as those in the Diagnostic and Statistical Manual of Mental Disorders (DSM), published by the American Psychiatric Association (APA), are typically used to make diagnoses.

There have been multiple versions of the DSM, the most recent being the DSM-5, which was published in 2013 and which was preceded by the DSM-IV-TR (2000), the DSM-IV (1994), the DSM-III-R (1987), and the DSM-III (1980).

The sets of criteria vary in substantial ways, and with a new diagnostic standard, changes in diagnostic categories will be encountered. Almost all of the criteria involve both a set of symptoms and some evidence of impairment, although not necessarily the level of impairment that would qualify for designation as severely or moderately impaired according to the SSI definitions.

The DSM-III serves as a general framework for the SSI mental health listings for kids. Unknown is how SSI determinations were impacted by the subsequent development of diagnostic standards.

Understanding the applications and constraints of a "primary diagnosis" is crucial when analyzing the data available about kids with mental health issues. Different diagnostic labels are used depending on the purpose (e.g., clinical, research, or public health).

A child either has or does not have a specific diagnosis according to official classification systems like the DSM or the International Classification of Diseases (APA, 2013; WHO, 1992).

Clinical professionals treat patients rather than the "diagnostic" since that is more practical. Diagnoses are given to make billing easier, however in the absence of a conclusive laboratory or blood test, the label's accuracy might vary greatly.

However, some diagnoses can be made more consistently (such as ASD and ID) and others require the input of numerous respondents (such as ADHD) to increase accuracy. Due to these problems, the idea of a "diagnostic" needs to be viewed as a dynamic process (Jensen & Hoagwood, 1997).

4.4. COMORBIDITY AND CO-OCCURRING MENTAL DISORDERS IN CHILDREN

Children with mental illnesses co-occur quite frequently. One disorder may make a youngster more susceptible to developing another. For instance, a youngster with ADHD may also display behavioral issues. The likelihood of intellectual disability is also higher in autistic children.

Furthermore, in young children, it may be difficult to determine the difference between autism or an intellectual disability and the impairments brought on by speech, language, and communication issues. Treatment choices could become more difficult if there are several co-occurring disorders.

Co-occurring physical and mental illnesses are possible. It is well known that co-occurring mental and physical health issues frequently occur, especially in adults, and often have complex causal relationships (Druss & Walker, 2011).

A mental health illness raises the likelihood of developing mental health issues, which in turn increases the likelihood that any mental health issues would result in disabilities (Honey et al., 2010). There are a ton of studies on children who have co-occurring physical and mental health issues.

Children with various forms of chronic health issues have higher rates of emotional and behavioral issues, and the likelihood that they will receive a mental diagnosis is higher, according to data from Canada's Bergen Child Study (Hysing et al., 2009).

Merikangas and colleagues discovered, using information from the Neurodevelopmental Genomics Cohort Study, that children with moderate to severe physical conditions have a greater prevalence of mental health disorders than children with no physical conditions or mild physical conditions (Merikangas et al., 2015).

Children enrolled in Medicaid who had serious mental health issues were far more likely than other kids to have ongoing physical health issues (Combs-Orme et al., 2002). It was discovered that having both physical and mental health issues had a negative impact on general health status and functioning (Combes-Orme et al., 2002).

In a study of Florida Medicaid-enrolled children, 35% of children with physical disabilities had mental health problems and 42% of children with mental health disabilities had other health problems (Boothroyd & Armstrong, 2005).

The risk factors for having comorbid physical and mental health problems include poverty and social disadvantage (Honey et al., 2010). These children are at high risk for unmet needs which can further worsen their health and functioning (Boothroyd & Armstrong, 2005).

Comorbidity SSI statistics are not available. A single diagnosis is selected as the principal cause of disability for the purposes of SSI determinations—and consequently for the purposes of this report. The ailment that is most easily assessed as fitting the standards of disability in the SSI system is frequently the one that is selected with the diagnosis when there are numerous diagnoses that contribute to a noticeable impairment, either physical or mental.

Patterns of comorbidity within the SSI program cannot be evaluated and contrasted with patterns of comorbidity seen in the broader population due to the limitations of the SSI data.

4.5. CLINICAL CHARACTERISTICS OF ATTENTION DEFICIT HYPERACTIVITY DISORDER

The diagnosis of ADHD has increased during the past few decades. The majority of diagnoses among school-aged children are made as a result of teacher and parent worries about a child's conduct and performance at home and at school.

A variety of medical specialists, such as family doctors, psychologists, and child psychiatrists, make diagnoses. Several organizations, like the American Academy of Pediatrics (AAP, 2011) and the American Psychiatric Association (APA, 2011), have created diagnostic and treatment guidelines; nonetheless, adherence to standards varies, especially for straightforward cases (Garner et al., 2013).

The current diagnostic criteria outlined in the Diagnostic and Statistical Manual of Mental Disorders, 5th Edition (DSM-5) require that a child's behavior be developmentally inappropriate (i.e., the child's behavior is substantially different from other children of the same age and developmental level) and that the symptoms must begin before age 12 and be present for at least 6 months; must be present in two or more settings; must cause significant impairments in home, school, occupational, or peer settings; and must not be secondary to another disorder (APA, 2013).

The DSM-5 distinguishes between three basic manifestations of ADHD. Inattentive ADHD is the first type; hyperactive-impulsive ADHD is the second; and mixed ADHD is the third.

Preschool-aged toddlers frequently exhibit motor restlessness and aggressive, disruptive conduct, while later adolescents and adults are more likely to exhibit disorganized, distractible, and inattentive symptoms. As distractibility and inattention are within the range of developmental norms during this time, it can be challenging to diagnose ADHD in preschoolers (APA, 2013).

The majority of the time, a diagnosis of ADHD is made in a clinical setting following a thorough evaluation that includes taking a careful history, conducting a clinical interview to rule out or identify other causes and contributing factors, using behavior rating scales, performing a physical exam, and performing any necessary or appropriate laboratory tests.

A variety of sources, including the kid, parents, teachers, doctors, and, if necessary, other carers, should be thoroughly gathered and evaluated (APA, 2013).

There are objective measures of impairments that are being used more frequently in ADHD, such as measures of adaptive functioning in general and specific ADHD impairment measures, despite the fact that the evaluation of impairment in ADHD is thought to be more subjective than that of intellectual disability (Gordon et al., 2006). (Biederman et al., 1993; Fabiano et al., 2006).

Clinical interviews enable a thorough examination of whether the symptoms correspond to the ADHD diagnosis criteria. During an interview, details on the child's past experiences with the challenges they are currently experiencing, their general health and development, as well as their social and familial history, should be acquired.

Additionally, a child's functioning may be impacted by circumstances that could disrupt the development or integrity of the central nervous system (CNS) or that could be revealed during an interview, such as the presence of a chronic disease, sensory impairments, or medication use.

Hyperactive or nervous behaviors may be brought on by disruptive social factors such family strife, situational stress, abuse, or neglect. Last but not least, a family history of alcohol or drug misuse, mood or anxiety problems, learning disabilities, antisocial disorder, or ADHD may point to an elevated risk for ADHD and associated diseases (Larsson et al., 2013).

In addition to conducting a clinical interview, healthcare professionals should use parent and teacher behavior checklists to determine the number and severity of ADHD symptoms present at home and at school. Behavior rating measures are helpful in determining the scope and severity of the symptoms, but they are insufficient in and of themselves to diagnose ADHD.

However, a number of validated behavior rating scales are available that may accurately distinguish between children with ADHD and controls as well as between ADHD and other pediatric psychiatric problems (APA, 2013).

Currently, there are no laboratory tests available to identify ADHD in children. Although genetic and neuroimaging studies are able to discriminate between subjects with ADHD and normal subjects, these findings apply to differences among groups and are not sufficiently precise to identify single individuals with ADHD.

Competing medical and biological explanations for ADHD must first be ruled out. Thus, the presence of hypertension, ataxia, or thyroid disorder should prompt further diagnostic evaluations. Fine motor coordination delays and other "soft signs" are common but are not sufficiently specific to contribute to a diagnosis of ADHD. Vision or hearing problems should also be evaluated.

Children with ADHD may also have medical histories that are associated with exposure to meningitis, diseases like lead poisoning, or prenatal alcohol consumption. It is significant to remember that a child's behavior in a medical office or a controlled laboratory setting might not correspond to how they typically behave at home or in the classroom.

Therefore, basing a diagnosis solely on observed behavior in a doctor's office has the risk of being wrong. Analyzes of electroencephalograms and computerized attention tests also cannot be used to make the diagnosis. To rule out any contributing problems, standard office exams for vision and hearing are an integral element of the total assessment. (APA, 2013).

4.5.1. Demographic Factors and Duration of the Disorder

Most ADHD diagnoses are made when children are in elementary school. Children who struggle to control their impulsivity and hyperactivity as well as their inability to stay focused on the educational lesson become more apparent because of their behaviors' potential to disrupt the classroom environment. In an educational setting, the demands for attentiveness and orderly behavior are increased.

Until early adolescence, when the hyperactive symptoms may be less visible, the inattentive and unmindful features, as well as the issues with restlessness and impulsivity, tend to linger. In general, ADHD symptoms do not wax and wane but rather tend to be consistent.

- **Age:** Clinical manifestations of ADHD may change with age (APA, 2013). A childhood diagnosis of ADHD often leads to persistent ADHD throughout the lifespan. Sixty to 80 % of children diagnosed with ADHD will continue to experience symptoms in adolescence, and up to 40 to 60 % of adolescents exhibit ADHD symptoms into adulthood (APA, 2013).
- Young adult functioning suffers greatly as a result of symptoms like inattention, impulsivity, and disorganization. In addition, children with ADHD who are not treated may experience a number of risk factors as adults. These include participating in risky behaviors (sexual, delinquent, drug usage), underachieving in school, having trouble finding work, and having relationship problems.

- **Sex:** Compared to girls, boys are more likely to have an ADHD diagnosis. According to estimates of prevalence, there are about twice as many male children with reported ADHD diagnosis as female children.

  According to the 2011 National Health Interview Survey, the estimated prevalence of ADHD in men was 12 %, compared to only 4.7 % in women (Perou et al., 2013). Similar to this, a recent meta-analysis of 86 pediatric ADHD studies found that the ratio of diagnosis for all subtypes of ADHD for men and women varied from 1.9 to 1 to 3.2 to 1. (Wilcutt, 2012).
- **Race/Ethnicity:** There is currently no convincing evidence that the incidence of ADHD diagnoses in children vary by race or ethnicity, according to recent population-based studies. According to some prevalence estimates, more white people than African Americans or Hispanic Americans are given an ADHD diagnosis; however, this could be because non-white children with ADHD take longer to be diagnosed clinically (Miller et al., 2009; Morgan et al., 2013).

Cultural differences in the acceptance of a child's ADHD diagnosis are another obstacle to persuading some parents to seek treatment for their children and to adhere to that therapy. These differences may also affect attitudes toward or interpretations of children's behavior (Bailey et al., 2010).

4.6. CLINICAL CHARACTERISTICS OF OPPOSITIONAL DEFIANT DISORDER AND CONDUCT DISORDER

ADHD, conduct disorder (CD), ODD, intermittent explosive disorder, and disruptive behavior not otherwise specified are among the disruptive behavior disorders (DBDs) of childhood. Disruptive mood dysregulation disorder (DMDD) has also been added to several nomenclatures, albeit there aren't much official epidemiological statistics on this most recent inclusion.

Children or teenagers are officially diagnosed with DBD if their actions and related repercussions "abuse the rights of others and/or that bring the individual into substantial conflict with society norms or authoritative structures" (APA, 2013).

ODD and CD are the two DBDs that are most frequently studied among those other than ADHD, and they will be the only DBD categories covered in the rest of this section since they are the only ones that have any bearing on the Social Security program.

The World Health Organization and the APA both define ODD as a persistent pattern of angry, rebellious, or disobedient behavior. Among addition to the impairment brought on by these antisocial behaviors, such as lying and stealing, CD is also regarded as "disruptive" due to the prevalence of these behaviors in young people with CD.

ODD and CD are sometimes combined into one group in prevalence and epidemiologic research because they have similar antecedent risk factors and are both characterized by difficult interactions with parents and other authority figures.

Several scientists contend that there are important differences between the two, pointing out that while there are conflicting results on gender differences in ODD, CD has a very clear male-to-female risk ratio. Therefore, these writers advise documenting and researching these disorders individually (Burke et al., 2002; Maughan et al., 2004). ODD and CD show a lot of overlap in item analysis on risk scales, but they still seem to be different constructs (Cavanagh et al., 2014).

The latest guidelines for assessing ODD/CD in children were issued in 2007 and 1997, for ODD and CD, respectively, by the American Academy of Child and Adolescent Psychiatry (Steiner et al., 1997, 2007). The diagnosis of ODD/CD requires a comprehensive diagnostic evaluation, which includes interviews with the child or youth, the primary caregiver, and collateral informants, such as teachers.

Standardized reporting tools are recommended for gathering complete data from diverse informants, but no tool is thought to be specific, nor are there any biological markers for these disorders. It is not clear if the distinction between ODD and CD is important for the care of individual patients.

The suggestions emphasize the significance of the doctors' ties with both the family and the patient in assessment and therapy because the ODD/CD diagnoses and symptoms are intertwined with families and social interactions.

When children or teenagers engage in aggressive or similar behaviors that generate ongoing issues, including negative legal and social repercussions, and when other factors are absent, an ODD/CD diagnosis is made. Since these disorders frequently show along a continuum and typically do not resolve rapidly, continued therapy and follow-up are required. Although the causes of ODD and CD are not completely understood, it seems that genetic, environmental, and familial variables all have a role. As a result, a review of a kid's past should include exposures during pregnancy, exposure to traumatic situations as a child, and cognitive or other developmental issues.

Additionally, it's important to compile a history of the current illness, which should include the age of onset, the environmental circumstances in which the symptoms appear, the length of the symptoms, and any situations or events that may have contributed to the current illness. It should also include people, locations, or occasions that either lessen or exacerbate the behavior problems.

It is also important to perform a mental health assessment for conditions like substance misuse, trauma-related symptoms, and ADHD.

Since ODD and CD are known to cluster in families, it's crucial to learn about any medical and psychological illnesses that have run in the family. In addition, it's important to evaluate the family's coping mechanisms, communication, and interactional patterns.

Once a release of information has been approved, information about a child's performance in a school environment should be acquired from the appropriate staff, including the principal, teacher, school psychologist or counselor, and nurse.

Teacher evaluations on structured types of behavior are frequently highly beneficial. It is important to be examined for any potential intellectual, communicative, or motor ability impairments. By definition, ODD and CD are conditions that frequently include social service providers including foster care and the juvenile court system. Agency reports of symptoms and outcomes are crucial for accurate diagnosis and care.

To exclude medical causes, a comprehensive physical examination is required. It's important to take into account any medical issues that lead to agitation, violence, or impulsive rage. Routine laboratory tests, such as blood counts, kidney and liver functions, thyroid functions, toxicology screens, pregnancy tests, and urinalysis, are typically not necessary until a particular history or examination finding indicates it. However, when age-appropriate, screening for depression, substance misuse, and HIV is recommended.

4.7. CLINICAL CHARACTERISTICS OF AUTISM SPECTRUM DISORDER

The neurodevelopmental disorder known as autism, also known as autism spectrum disorder (ASD), was first identified in 1943 (Kanner, 1943) and is characterized by impairments in social interaction and communication as well as repetitive or stereotyped behavioral patterns and frequently constrained interests.

The diagnosis of ASD is typically made during childhood, based on comprehensive behavioral evaluations by specialists in child psychiatry or psychology or by those in behavioral and developmental pediatrics. ASD was not officially recognized until DSM-III, the third edition of the Diagnostic and Statistical Manual of Mental Disorders, in 1980 (APA, 1980; Kanner, 1943).

The current version of the DSM introduced in 2013, DSM-5, is the first edition of the DSM to use the term "ASD." This version does not distinguish subtypes such as "autistic disorder" or "Asperger syndrome," and the diagnostic criteria specified in the DSM-5 for ASD are somewhat narrower than used previously.

According to the DSM-5 criteria, a child must exhibit restricted or repetitive patterns of behavior, interests, or activities across a variety of contexts, have symptoms that first appear in early childhood and cause significant functional impairments, and the impairments must not be better explained by an intellectual disability (APA, 2013).

DSM-5 made significant changes by removing subcategories and offering a comprehensive method for diagnosing ASD (Volkmar et al., 2014a). A "grandfather clause" allowing continuous diagnostic assignment to cases previously diagnosed under DSM-IV was included to the DSM-5 in response to worries that people may lose their services.

Although many affected children can have an ASD diagnosis made by the age of two by skilled clinicians, and most cases can have an ASD diagnosis made very clearly by the age of three, population-based studies in the United States have shown that the median age at first diagnosis of ASD is older than five years (Maenner et al., 2013; Shattuck et al., 2009).

A pediatrician or other primary care practitioner may frequently send a patient to a clinical center or care provider who has experience diagnosing ASD as part of the process of getting an ASD diagnosis. Families may have to wait 6 to 12 months or longer for the first appointment after making a referral. Financial and cultural obstacles might cause diagnostic delays at every stage, especially for socioeconomically deprived children (Magaa et al., 2013).

Several sets of practice guidelines are now available to provide guidance on screening and diagnosis (McClure, 2014). Current practice guidelines suggest that there should be a comprehensive assessment involving structured observations of the child's behavior; extensive parental interviews; testing of cognition, speech and language, hearing, vision, and motor function; a physical examination; and a collection of medical and family history information (Millward et al., 2008; Nye & Brice, 2005; Reichow et al., 2010, 2013). The assessment may also involve genetic testing, neuroimaging, or other studies.

It is advised to start early screening at 18 months and continue through preschool. ASD is typically a disorder with early beginnings, however early screening may miss a small percentage of cases when parents report regression following a period of normal development. In other situations, symptoms may go undetected on early screening in children with greater cognitive ability.

Early diagnosis and evaluation are crucial to maximize the likelihood of a successful outcome (McClure & Melville, 2007; Volkmar et al., 2014a). A family history of ASD (such as in a sibling) should raise clinical worry levels.

It is advised to get a clinical evaluation to seek for symptoms and indications of related illnesses (notably seizure disorder or epilepsy). Although occasionally linked to single-gene diseases (most notably fragile X and tuberous sclerosis), the genetics of ASD appears to be quite complex, with probable associations with numerous different genetic pathways (Geschwind, 2011).

Aside from a few well-known single-gene disorders, genetic testing is still scarce, despite the growing recognition of the involvement of genetic variables in etiology. Based on the clinical presentation or family history, more extensive genetic testing may be required. There are now guidelines for genetic testing (Schaefer et al., 2013).

To evaluate developmental stages and the need for occupational and physical therapy, a variety of tests are performed. There are numerous screening and diagnostic tools available (see Volkmar et al., 2014a). Multiple areas of difficulties are frequently found when cognition and communication are assessed. Unusual learning methods in ASD result in difficulties with generalization, which can make it difficult to master adaptive abilities. Thus, it is important to evaluate a student's capacity for applying knowledge in real-world situations.

4.8. CLINICAL CHARACTERISTICS OF INTELLECTUAL DISABILITIES

The general mental ability of reasoning, planning, problem-solving, abstract thought, understanding difficult concepts, effective learning, and experience-based learning is known as intelligence (AAIDD, 2010).

Historically, intellectual disability (previously known as "mental retardation") has been characterized by both significant deficits in functional and adaptive skills as well as significant cognitive deficits, as demonstrated by an IQ score of less than 70 (two standard deviations below the population mean of 100).

The capacity to perform age-appropriate everyday tasks is a component of adaptive skills. The Diagnostic and Statistical Manual of Mental Disorders, Fifth Edition (DSM-5) published by the American Psychiatric Association and the American Association on Intellectual and Developmental Disabilities (AAIDD) are the two different classification systems for intellectual disability (ID) used in the United States. Both of these methods categorize ID severity in accordance with the kind of assistance required to enable an individual to operate at their best.

DSM-5 defines intellectual disabilities as neurodevelopmental disorders that begin in childhood and are characterized by intellectual difficulties as well as difficulties in conceptual, social, and practical areas of living. The DSM-5 diagnosis of ID requires the satisfaction of three criteria:

1. Deficits in intellectual functioning—"reasoning, problem solving, planning, abstract thinking, judgment, academic learning, and learning from experience"—confirmed by clinical evaluation and individualized standard IQ testing (APA, 2013, p. 33);
2. Deficits in adaptive functioning that significantly hamper conforming to developmental and sociocultural standards for the individual's independence and ability to meet their social responsibility; and
3. The onset of these deficits during childhood.

In contrast to the fourth edition, DSM-IV, the DSM-5 definition of ID promotes a more thorough understanding of the person. The DSM-IV classification included general mental ability impairments that influence how a person behaves in social, cognitive, and everyday life contexts.

Specific IQ scores were no longer used as a diagnostic criterion in the DSM-5, although the overall idea of functioning two or more standard deviations below the general population was kept. The DSM-5 has given adaptive functioning and the use of common life skills more importance.

The DSM-5 criteria indicate impairment in one or more superordinate skill domains, such as conceptual, social, or practical, as opposed to the DSM-IV criteria, which required impairments in two or more skill areas (Papazoglou et al., 2014).

4.9. CLASSIFICATIONS OF SEVERITY

The terms "mild," "moderate," "severe," and "profound" have been used to describe the severity of the condition. This approach has been helpful in that aspects of mild to moderate ID differ from severe to profound ID. The DSM-5 retains this grouping with more focus on daily skills than on specific IQ range.

4.9.1. Mild to Moderate Intellectual Disability

Most ID sufferers are categorized as having modest intellectual impairments. In all facets of conceptual development as well as social and everyday living abilities, those with mild ID lag behind. These people can pick up useful life skills that enable them to function in daily life with the very minimum of assistance.

People with mild ID can take care of themselves, visit locations they are familiar with in their neighborhood, and learn the fundamentals of health and safety. Their moderate self-care needs some assistance.

4.9.2. Severe Intellectual Disability

People with severe ID frequently have the ability to understand speech but have limited communication skills as a result of significant developmental delays (Sattler, 2002). Even though they can learn basic daily routines and self-care skills, people with severe ID require supervision in social situations and frequently require family care to live in a supervised environment like a group home.

4.9.3. Profound Intellectual Disability

Congenital syndromes are common in people with severe intellectual disabilities (Sattler, 2002). These people need constant monitoring, assistance with self-care, and are unable to live freely.

They frequently have physical restrictions and a very restricted capacity for communication. People with mild to moderate disabilities are less likely than people with severe or profound ID to have concomitant medical issues.

4.10. CLINICAL CHARACTERISTICS OF LEARNING DISABILITIES

Learning disabilities (LDs) are identified by both academic and medical methods (Cortiella & Horowitz, 2014). The federal special education statute known as the IDEA has the definition that is most frequently used from the standpoint of education (IDEA).

The medical perspective on LDs is reflected in the Diagnostic and Statistical Manual for Mental Disorders (currently the DSM-5 and previously the DSM-IV) published by the American Psychiatric Association (APA, 2013). There is considerable overlap in the definition of LD used by professionals in educational and medical settings (Cortiella & Horowitz, 2014).

4.10.1. Individuals with Disabilities Education Act

A specific learning disability, according to the IDEA, is a disorder in one or more of the fundamental psychological processes involved in comprehending or using language, whether it is spoken or written. This disorder may show up as a person's inability to listen, think, speak, read, write, spell, or perform mathematical calculations.

This phrase covers a variety of ailments, including dyslexia, brain damage, mild brain dysfunction, and perceptual difficulties. Specific learning difficulties are not primarily brought on by physical, mental, or hearing impairments, emotional disturbance, mental retardation, or economic, social, or cultural disadvantage. (DOE, 1995)

Prior to obtaining educational interventions and adjustments, children are often diagnosed in educational settings following the IDEA criteria (Cortiella & Horowitz, 2014). The usage of diagnostic terms like "perceptual impairments" and "minimal brain dysfunction" that are no longer accepted presents an issue with the IDEA definition. Some evidence suggests that dyslexia, or trouble with reading, may be the most prevalent type of learning disability among the major categories (Ferrer et al., 2010). Other significant categories of specific disabilities include dysgraphia (difficulties with writing), dyscalculia (difficulties with mathematical calculations), and others. Studies that analyze every student have revealed as many as 21.5% to be dyslexic; nevertheless, schools only report 4–5% of students to be dyslexic (Ferrer et al., 2010).

4.10.2. Diagnostic and Statistical Manual for Mental Disorders

According to DSM-5, the diagnosis of a specific learning disorder includes the following symptoms:

1. Persistent difficulties in reading, writing, arithmetic, or mathematical reasoning skills during formal years of schooling. Symptoms may include inaccurate or slow and effortful reading, poor written expression that lacks clarity, difficulties remembering number facts, or inaccurate mathematical reasoning.
2. Current academic skills must be well below the average range of scores in culturally and linguistically appropriate tests of reading, writing, or mathematics. Accordingly, a person who is dyslexic must read with great effort and not in the same manner as those who are typical readers.
3. Learning difficulties begin during the school-age years.
4. The individual's difficulties must not be better explained by developmental, neurological, sensory (vision or hearing), or motor disorders and must significantly interfere with academic achievement, occupational performance, or activities of daily living (APA, 2013).

It should be noted that the fourth version of the DSM (i.e., DSM-IV-TR) did not include a general category of LD but rather many diagnoses specific to deficiencies in reading, arithmetic, and written language (APA, 2000).

When a person does much worse on individually offered standardized tests than would be expected given their age, education, and level of IQ, the DSM-IV-TR classifies them as having learning disabilities (LD) (APA, 2000).

Three well defined diagnostic categories are recognized under the DSM-IV-TR approach: reading disorders, math disorders, and disorders of written expression. There is also a residual category for learning deficits that are not further described. In federal regulations, these words are frequently used interchangeably with the phrase "learning disability" generally.

The now more than 20-year-old DSM-IV approach was founded on techniques that relied on discrepancy scores; that is, a learning difficulty was said to exist in a specific area, such as reading, when the scores in that area were noticeably below what would be expected based on the person's overall cognitive ability.

Although these disorders are defined somewhat similarly in the International Classification of Diseases (ICD), Ninth Revision, it makes clear that the school setting must be conducive to the child's potential to learn the skill. However, the additional learning problem is only identified when the accomplishment delays are far more severe than would be predicted. Sensory abnormalities can be present.

By including LDs into a single, comprehensive diagnosis, the DSM-5 has adopted a novel approach to the diagnosis of LDs. The diagnostic is more generic and highlights issues with acquired academic skills with the opportunity to specify the more conventional areas rather than restricting it to reading, math, or written language (APA, 2013).

A clinical evaluation of a person's history, academic records, and responses to therapies are used to make a diagnosis. The problems must not be better explained by other illnesses, the scores on the applicable measures must be significantly below the range, and the difficulties must be persistent. There must be a considerable obstruction to success, employment, or daily life activities.

The term "dyslexia," which predates the term "LD," refers to problems with accurate or fluent word recognition, bad spelling, and deficiencies in coding skills (International Dyslexia Association, 2015). It is still used in clinical and research contexts and is covered by the single LD diagnosis in the DSM-5.

4.10.3. Standardized Instruments for Assessment

There are many well-standardized tools available for evaluating LDs. Commonly utilized is a cognitive ability test, such as the most recent Weschler Intelligence Scale for Children (Prifitera et al., 2005). The Woodcock-Johnson IV, the Wechsler Individual Achievement Test II, and the Wide Range Achievement Test III are other regularly used measurements.

Additionally, there are specialized exams like the thorough phonological processing test and measures of fluency like the Test of Word Reading Efficiency. The results of the assessment help with diagnosis, intervention planning, and locating any other comorbid disorders or issues that can obstruct therapy. Different tools should be used to evaluate children who are growing up in various cultures, with the instruments being tailored to the culture.

4.10.4. Response to Treatment Intervention

An awareness of the potential problems with diagnosis led to the introduction of a new concept, response to treatment intervention (RTI), in the 2004 amendment of IDEA. The RTI approach has emerged as a possible alternative to the discrepancy-based diagnostic approach (Vaughn & Fuchs, 2003). This model combines aspects of assessment with intervention, and its approach includes an emphasis on early screening and closer follow-up to clarify the need for additional intervention.

Interventions of varying intensities, from less to more, are used. Only when all other attempts to adjust the child's usual classroom and program have failed or when issues still exist with the child's overall performance or rate of skill development is a diagnosis of LD made. This diagnostic procedure may take a while.

Annual testing is used by alternatives to the RTI system to identify pupils whose abilities have not advanced as anticipated and who may require more rigorous and targeted intervention. To determine which child's score falls below a predetermined level, another method makes use of normalized references. These topics are still being hotly contested in the industry. The strategies used by different school systems to address these issues vary greatly.

4.11. CLINICAL CHARACTERISTICS OF MOOD DISORDERS

The criteria for the following diagnoses are included in the same diagnostic category in the Social Security Administration's (SSA) Listing of Impairments for mood disorders: Manic depression, severe depression, and bipolar disorder, sometimes known as cyclothymic syndrome.

Figure 4.1. Social security administration.

Source: Image by Flickr.

However, according to the Diagnostic and Statistical Manual of Mental Disorders, Fifth Edition (DSM-5) (APA, 2013), the mood disorders that may have a childhood onset are (1) major depression, (2) persistent depressive disorder (PDD), and (3) DMDD. In a departure from DSM-IV, DSM-5 treats bipolar disorders as a separate category. Pediatric bipolar disorder (PBD) will be addressed separately following a discussion of depression.

4.11.1. Depression

According to the DSM-5, major depression is characterized by the occurrence of all five symptoms, which include being sad, empty, or hopeless for the majority of the day (depressed mood); having a markedly decreased interest in most activities (anhedonia); and experiencing severe, recurrent verbal or behavioral outbursts three or more times per week.

Figure 4.2. Depression.

Source: Image by Flickr.

Irritability may serve as a stand-in for children's chronic depressive symptoms, but it is not a sufficient indicator of serious depression in children (Stringaris et al., 2013). The most noticeable aspect of PDD is its chronic nature, which can encompass both chronic major depression and sub threshold depression in children (formerly known as dysthymia).

Major depressive disorder (MDD) and PDD can both be diagnosed at any age; however, the latter is labeled as "early onset" if the first episode occurs before age 21. Only children between the ages of 6 and 18 are affected by DMDD.

A new diagnosis called DMDD was created to lessen the possibility of misdiagnosing children with chronic and non-episodic irritable mood as having bipolar disorder (Roy et al., 2014). Estimates of prevalence, clinical traits, and course may alter when these criteria are used in further study because PDD and DMDD are new diagnostic categories.

The distinction between "depressive disorders" and "bipolar and associated disorders" is the most significant between DSM-IV and DSM-5 in the diagnosis of mood disorders. Depressive disorders are classified differently in DSM-IV and DSM-5; however, these modifications are often quite minor and are not expected to significantly affect estimates of prevalence or incidence.

A thorough mental diagnostic evaluation, involving interviews with the child, the child's primary carers, and collateral informants like teachers, is necessary for the diagnosis of a childhood-onset depression disorder (Birmaher et al., 2007). Although there are screening techniques that identify depressed symptoms, their results do not replace a clinical diagnosis (Birmaher et al., 2007).

For these diagnoses, there are no reliable biologic indicators. Studies looking at the contributing aspects such genetics, sleep, neuroendocrine, inflammatory, metabolic, and neurotrophic factors are among those being done on the biological correlates of child depression.

These factors as well as neural networks are in the exploratory phase of research development (Li et al., 2013a, b; Miller and O'Callaghan, 2013; Mills et al., 2013; Nivard et al., 2015; Palagini et al., 2013; Penninx et al., 2013; Rao, 2013; Schmidt et al., 2011; Schneider et al., 2011). Early findings using brain neuroimaging, for example, have suggested that alterations in the developmental trajectories of limbic and striatal regions may increase the risk of adolescent-onset depression (Whittle et al., 2014).

According to the theory of impaired regulation of emotional processing in early childhood-onset severe depression, Luking and colleagues found a weaker link between the amygdala and cognitive control areas (Luking et al., 2011). Additionally, preliminary neuroimaging research concerns whether alterations in brain white and gray matter distinguish between unipolar and bipolar depressive illnesses with early start (Serafina et al., 2014). None of these scientific breakthroughs are now used for diagnostic purposes.

4.11.2. Demographic Factors and Duration of the Disorder

4.11.2.1. Age

Because the manifestation of depressive symptoms can vary by developmental stage, the age of onset for depression in children and adolescents is diverse. For instance, irritability may be more pronounced in younger depressed youngsters (Birmaher et al., 2009). Preschoolers with the depressive syndrome may display symptoms that fall below the threshold for a shorter-term depression (Luby et al., 2014).

These early depressed symptoms are important because, even after adjusting for a mother's history of depression and other risk factors, they are predictive of severe depressive disorder in later childhood in clinical samples (Luby et al., 2014).

Sub threshold depressive symptoms have also been reported to predict the start of major depressive disorder (MDD) in young adults, suggesting that this association may endure (Klein et al., 2013). Two of the most well-established risk factors for MDD are parental depression and anxiety in children (Thapar et al., 2012).

4.11.2.2. Sex

Although there is no gender-specific difference in the risk of developing early-onset depression in children (i.e., those 12 years or below), the risk for girls significantly rises during adolescence. The majority of child studies have found that boys and girls experience depression at similar rates, or at somewhat higher rates in males than in girls (Brooks-Gunn & Petersen, 1991; Costello et al., 1996; Garrison et al., 1989; Lewinsohn et al., 1998b; Nolen-Hoeksema et al., 1991; Petersen et al., 1991; Rutter et al., 1986; Wesselhoeft et al., 2014).

In contrast, during adolescence the rate of depression among girls almost always exceeds that of boys (Avenevoli et al., 2015; Costello et al., 2003; Ferrari et al., 2013; Lewinsohn et al., 1998b; Offord et al., 1989), and this trend persists into early adulthood (Costello et al., 2003; Ferrari et al., 2013; Rao et al., 1999; Rohde et al., 2013).

There is evidence that hormonal, rather than psychological or sociological, reasons account for the appearance of this adolescent gender difference, which persists until menopause (Angold et al., 1998).

4.11.2.3. Race/Ethnicity

The results on differences in rates of depression among young people by race or ethnicity are conflicting, and the variation is probably caused by variations in study designs, target groups, and methods used to diagnose depression. Based on symptoms reported by teens, major depression among a nationally representative sample of teenagers did not differ by race or ethnicity (Avenevoli et al., 2015).

No differences in the prevalence of mental disorders by race or ethnicity were detected in a study using data from the National Health and Nutrition Examination Survey (NHANES) for kids aged 8 to 15 years, presumably due to the small sample size (Merikangas et al., 2010).

However, an examination of data from the National Comorbidity Study-Adolescent Supplement (NCS-A) revealed that Hispanic adolescents had greater incidence of mood disorders than non-Hispanic White adolescents (Merikangas et al., 2010).

Additionally, results from the National Longitudinal Study of Adolescent Health showed that minority youth reported depressed symptoms more frequently than non-minority youth (Rushton et al., 2002). This result is in line with a study that looked at the prevalence rates of depression among Medicaid-eligible children and adolescents (Richardson et al., 2003).

4.11.2.4. Socioeconomic Status

Although research on adults suggests a link between depression and lower social class (Kessler et al., 2003), findings from research on kids and teenagers are contradictory (Merikangas et al., 2009). According to some studies, there is no correlation between socioeconomic class and depression or anxiety disorders (Costello et al., 2003), while others find a strong correlation, at least for the most disadvantaged populations (Costello et al., 1996; Gilman et al., 2003; Reinherz et al., 2003).

A poor socioeconomic level (SES) in childhood is linked to a higher risk of depression later in life, according to data on the lifetime risk of depression

(Gilman et al., 2002). As a result, it is unclear exactly how poverty and childhood or adolescent mood disorders are related.

4.11.2.5. Duration

Depression that starts in childhood is a chronic condition that lasts, on average, six months. The mean age of beginning of depression was 15 years among a longitudinal cohort of 816 high school students (aged 14 to 18), and the average length of a severe depressive episode was 26 weeks, but the range was extremely large, ranging from 2 to 520 weeks (Rohde et al., 2013).

Early start (15 years and younger), suicidal ideation, and seeking mental health therapy were risk variables associated with prolonged depressive episodes (Rohde et al., 2013). These results are in line with the NCS-A, which discovered that among a nationally representative sample of American youth, the mean length of a major depressive episode was 27 weeks (Avenevoli et al., 2015).

The median length of severe depressive episodes was found to be much longer in samples from patients who had been referred by doctors, which most likely reflects the higher clinical severity among kids who have access to and get ongoing mental health care.

These samples had median depression durations of 7 to 9 months, which was more than three times higher than the median depression duration observed in a community-based sample (Kovacs, 1996).

Adolescent depression also tends to recur. A recent review of outcomes of childhood depression reached the following conclusions (Costello & Maughan, 2015):

1. One in two children with a diagnosis of depression had one or more further episodes as an adult;
2. Depression alone has a much better prognosis than depression accompanied by any of the following: anxiety disorders, ODD, or substance use disorder; and
3. Family conflict predicts continuity of depression into adulthood.

In the community, among teenagers who had previously recovered from a depressive episode, 5% did so again within six months, 11% within a year, and about 33% within four years (Rohde et al., 2013).

An estimated 70% of young patients with depression who were clinically referred samples have at least one recurrence within five or more years

(Kovacs, 1996). These results are in line with research from other countries that indicates depressed children and adolescents are more likely to develop serious depression and suicidal thoughts as adults (Fergusson et al., 2005; Harrington et al., 1990).

4.12. CONCLUSION

The clinical features of mental disorders in children are outlined in this chapter. This chapter also describes the causes, burden, risk factors, effects on childhood, and trends in childhood mental and developmental disorders. It also discusses the nature of childhood mental and developmental disorders. Additionally covered were the identification and categorization of childhood mental illnesses.

Additionally, this chapter discusses the clinical characteristics of ODD, conduct disorder, learning impairments, mental disorders, intellectual disabilities, autistic spectrum disorder, and ADHD.

REFERENCES

1. Boat, T. F., & Wu, J. T., (2015). Clinical characteristics of attention deficit hyperactivity disorder. In: *Mental Disorders and Disabilities Among Low-Income Children*. Washington, D.C.: National Academies Press. Available at: https://www.ncbi.nlm.nih.gov/books/NBK332879/ (accessed on 14 October 2023).
2. Boat, T. F., & Wu, J. T., (2015). Clinical characteristics of autism spectrum disorder. In: *Mental Disorders and Disabilities Among Low-Income Children*. Washington, D.C.: National Academies Press. Available at: https://www.ncbi.nlm.nih.gov/books/NBK332891/ (accessed on 14 October 2023).
3. Boat, T. F., & Wu, J. T., (2015). Clinical characteristics of intellectual disabilities. In: *Mental Disorders and Disabilities Among Low-Income Children*. Washington, D.C.: National Academies Press. Available at: https://www.ncbi.nlm.nih.gov/books/NBK332877/ (accessed on 14 October 2023).
4. Boat, T. F., & Wu, J. T., (2015). Clinical characteristics of learning disabilities. In: *Mental Disorders and Disabilities Among Low-Income Children*. Washington, D.C.: National Academies Press. Available at: https://www.ncbi.nlm.nih.gov/books/NBK332886/ (accessed on 14 October 2023).
5. Boat, T. F., & Wu, J. T., (2015). Clinical characteristics of mood disorders. In: *Mental Disorders and Disabilities Among Low-Income Children*. Washington, D.C.: National Academies Press. Available at: https://www.ncbi.nlm.nih.gov/books/NBK332873/ (accessed on 14 October 2023).
6. Boat, T. F., & Wu, J. T., (2015). Clinical characteristics of oppositional defiant disorder and conduct disorder. In: *Mental Disorders and Disabilities Among Low-Income Children*. Washington, D.C.: National Academies Press. Available at: https://www.ncbi.nlm.nih.gov/books/NBK332890/ (accessed on 14 October 2023).
7. Scott, J., et al., (n.d.). *Chapter 8; Childhood Mental and Developmental Disorders*. dcp-3.org. dcp. Available at: https://www.dcp-3.org/sites/default/files/chapters/Ch%208%20Childhood%20mental%20and%20developmental%20disorders.pdf (accessed on 14 October 2023).

CHAPTER 5

Essentials of Specific Learning Disability Identification

Contents

This chapter talks about essentials of specific learning disability identification. At the beginning of this chapter, this chapter provides a brief introduction to the classification systems of learning disability. This chapter explains different methods of SLD identification and the 2006 federal regulations. This chapter also provides highlights on how SLD manifests in reading, mathematics, writing. This chapter also explains how SLD manifests in oral expression and listening comprehension. This chapter also helps to understand the response to intervention (RTI) approach to SLD identification.

5.1. OVERVIEW OF SPECIFIC LEARNING DISABILITIES

This chapter's goal is to give a quick review of the definitions, categorization schemes, and procedures for identifying particular learning problems (SLD). In the past, evaluations of children who did not perform academically as expected frequently resulted in the diagnosis of a learning impairment (LD) (Kavale & Forness, 2006).

The number of children in the United States identified as having LD has tripled since the enactment of the Education for All Handicapped Children Act of 1975 (P.L. 94–142; Cortiella, 2009). This landmark legislation included criteria for the identification of exceptional learners, including children with LD, and mandated that they receive a free and appropriate public education (FAPE).

Each reauthorization of P.L. 94–142 maintained its original intent, including the most recent reauthorization, the Individuals with Disabilities Education Improvement Act of 2004 (P.L. 108–446; hereafter referred to as "IDEA 2004").

Data on students who are eligible for special education services have been gathered by the United States Department of Education (USDOE) since 1975. According to the most recent data, 2.6 million school-aged children are labeled as SLD. In addition, SLD accounts for 43% of all students who have been diagnosed with an educationally restrictive condition.

5.1.1. A Brief History of the Definition of Learning Disability

The first descriptions of LD appeared in the domains of neurology, psychiatry, and education in the middle to late 1800s (Mather & Goldstein, 2008). The earliest definitions of learning disabilities (LD) were created by clinicians based on their observations of people who had significant problems learning fundamental academic skills despite having average or above-average general intelligence or people who lost their ability to perform certain tasks after suffering a brain injury as a result of a head injury or stroke (Kaufman, 2008).

The medically focused study of LD stalled because clinicians at the time lacked the technology or psychometrically sound instrumentation to test their theories about brain-based LD, which resulted in the development of socially constructed, educationally focused definitions that assumed an underlying neurological etiology (Hale & Fiorello, 2004; Kaufman, 2008; Lyon et al., 2001).

In 1963, Samuel Kirk addressed a group of educators and parents at the Exploration into the Problems of the Perceptually Handicapped Child conference in Chicago, Illinois.

The purposes of the conference were to

- Gather information from leading professionals from diverse fields about the problems of children who had perceptually based learning difficulties; and
- Develop a national organization that would lobby to secure services for these children.

At this conference, Kirk presented a paper entitled "Learning Disabilities" that was based on his recently published book, Educating Exceptional Children (Kirk, 1962).

Kirk defined LD as a psychological disability brought on by a potential cerebral dysfunction and/or emotional or behavioral disturbances, and resulting in retardation, disorder, or delayed development in one or more of the processes of speech, reading, language, writing, arithmetic, or other school subjects. Mental retardation, sensory deprivation, cultural, or educational factors are not to blame.

The conference attendees not only agreed with Kirk's use of the name "LD" and its description, but they also established the Learning Disabilities Association of America (LDA). As it relates to diagnosing and educating people with LD, the LDA still has an impact on "frameworks for legislation, theories, diagnostic processes, educational practices, research and training models."

Kirk's definition of LD affected federal law as well as definitions of LD by other organizations, such as the Council for Exceptional Children (CEC) (e.g., P.L. 94–142). In addition, Kirk's 1962 definition was incorporated into 11 other definitions of LD that were in use between 1982 and 1989.

It is therefore not unexpected that a thorough analysis of these definitions indicated greater consensus than disagreement about the LD construct (Hammill, 1990). It's interesting that none of the definitions had a significant impact on changes in LD identification. This is mostly because they tended to emphasize conceptual rather than operational features and exclusionary rather than inclusionary criteria.

5.2. CLASSIFICATION SYSTEMS FOR LD

"Classification criteria are the rules that are applied to determine if individuals are eligible for a particular diagnosis" (Reschly, Hosp, & Schmied, 2003, p. 2). Although the evaluation of LD in school-aged children is guided by the mandate of IDEA 2004 and its attendant regulations, diagnostic criteria for LD are also included in the Diagnostic and Statistical Manual of Mental Disorders, Fourth Edition, Text Revision (DSM-IV-TR; American Psychiatric Association, 2000), and the International Classification of Diseases (ICD-10; World Health Organization, 2006).

The classification criteria for learning disorders in each system are listed in Rapid Reference 1.4. The inclusion of relatively imprecise and vague words by all three systems is noteworthy and hinders practitioners' attempts to accurately and properly detect LD (Kavale & Forness, 2000, 2006). Despite the availability of numerous classification schemes, pupils between the ages of 3 and 21 who encounter academic difficulties are normally assessed in accordance with the requirements of IDEA 2004 (IDEA 2004, § 614) to ascertain whether they are in need of special education services.

The USDOE published the Federal Regulations (34 CFR, Part 300) with the goal of clarifying the statute and giving guidance to State Educational Agencies (SEA) as they worked to develop their own regulations because the classification category of SLD as described in the IDEA statute includes ambiguous terms. The 2006 Federal Regulations' guidelines included more specific instructions on how an SLD should be recognized.

5.3. METHODS OF SLD IDENTIFICATION AND THE 2006 FEDERAL REGULATIONS

Although the definition of SLD has remained virtually the same for the past 30 years, the methodology used to identify SLD changed recently.

According to the 2006 Federal Regulations (34 CFR § 300.307–309), a state must adopt criteria for determining that a child has SLD; the criteria (a) must not require the use of a severe discrepancy between intellectual ability and achievement; (b) must permit the use of a process based on a child's response to scientific, research-based interventions; and (c) may permit the use of other alternative research-based procedures for determining whether a child has SLD.

Since the publishing of the three alternatives for SLD identification, there have been numerous disputes. The debates surrounding the precise meaning of the guidelines, the requirements of a thorough evaluation, the implications of using response to intervention (RTI) as the only technique for identifying SLDs, and the lack of legal expertise among decision-makers have all been extensively written about and won't be repeated here.

Clarifying the three possibilities for SLD identification is the main goal of the next sections of this chapter because these alternatives are currently being used by all states.

5.3.1. Ability-Achievement Discrepancy

Because it helps operationally define unanticipated underachievement, a disparity between intellectual capacity and academic performance continues to be at the center of many SLD identification efforts.

The old ability-achievement (or IQ-achievement) discrepancy method, while a commendable attempt at an empirically based method of SLD detection, was riddled with issues.

The failure of the ability-achievement discrepancy method to identify SLD reliably and validly was summarized well by Ysseldyke (2005), who stated, Professional associations, advocacy groups, and government agencies have formed task forces and task forces on the task forces to study identification of students with LD.

Mega-analysis of meta-analysis and synthesizing of syntheses have both been done. There is not much scientific backing for test-based discrepancy models that identify students as having learning disabilities, according to nearly all groups.

Therefore, it was considered as a welcome reform in the law because governments could no longer demand the use of a significant gap between intellectual ability and success (IDEA 2004). The gap left by the repeal of the discrepancy mandate was addressed by a technique that permitted states to utilize a procedure based on a child's response to intervention to support SLD identification.

5.3.2. Response to Intervention (RTI)

Concerns regarding the method used to identify SLD gave rise to the idea of RTI. Examples include Bradley, Danielson, and Hallahan (2002), Learning Disabilities Roundtable (2005), and President's Commission on Excellence in Special Education (2002), which found that traditional methods of SLD identification, primarily ability-achievement discrepancy, were applied inconsistently across states and frequently resulted in student misidentification as well as over identification of minority students.

Due to these issues with conventional approaches, there was a "paradigm shift" (Reschly, 2004) based on the idea of treatment validity, "where it is conceivable to simultaneously inform, nurture, and record the necessity for and success of special therapy" (Fuchs & Fuchs, 1998).

RTI, at its most basic level, is a multilevel strategy for the early detection of pupils who are having academic or behavioral challenges. People only concentrate on RTI for academic difficulties in this chapter.

All students in the general education classroom receive quality instruction as the first step in the RTI process. Additionally, all students are screened to determine who is at risk of failing academically, particularly in the area of reading (Tier I).

Following a conventional treatment approach, students who are at risk for reading failure—those who have not benefited from the teaching offered to all students in the classroom—are subsequently given scientifically informed interventions (Tier II).

Students may be designated as non-responders and chosen to undergo extra, more intensive interventions in an effort to accelerate their pace of learning if they do not respond as expected to the Tier II intervention. One sort of intervention is followed by another until the desired response is attained when the first type of intervention does not seem to benefit the student.

Since IDEA was reauthorized in 2004, the inclusion of RTI as an acceptable alternative for SLD detection has generated the most debate. This is such that students who continually fail to demonstrate a sufficient response to increasingly rigorous interventions are automatically assumed to have SLD in districts that adopt an RTI-only approach.

Such an approach does not appear to be in compliance with the regulations. For example, according to the regulations, states must

- Use a variety of assessment tools and strategies to gather relevant functional, developmental, and academic information;
- Not use any single measure or assessment as the sole criterion for determining whether a child has a disability;
- Use technically sound instruments that may assess the relative contribution of cognitive and behavioral factors, in addition to physical or developmental factors;
- Assess the child in all areas related to the suspected disability;
- Ensure that the evaluation is sufficiently comprehensive to identify all of the child's special education and related service's needs; and
- Ensure that assessment tools and strategies provide relevant information that directly assists persons in determining the needs of the child.

RTI has been a significant factor in schools recently, especially in terms of influencing Tier I and Tier II assessments for intervention in the general education context, despite the fact that its use as a stand-alone approach for SLD identification is incompatible with the spirit of the law.

Screening and progress monitoring procedures have been elevated to new levels in an RTI model because of the emphasis on making sure students are receiving empirically based instruction and verifying their response to instruction through the systematic collection of data. This has led many to embrace this type of service delivery model for the purposes of both prevention and remediation.

RTI basically helps to increase accountability by providing data that shows whether or not learning has improved and enough progress has been made.

5.3.3. Alternative Research-Based Procedures for SLD Identification

The third option included in the 2006 regulations allows "the use of other alternative research-based procedures" for determining SLD. Although vague, this option has been interpreted by some as involving the evaluation of a "PSW" in the identification of SLD via tests of academic achievement, cognitive abilities, and neuropsychological processes.

5.4. HOW SLD MANIFESTS IN READING

5.4.1. Defining Reading Disability

Since the term learning disability (LD) was first used to describe a condition that interferes with education, it has been at the center of debate, study, and practice in school psychology.

It is obvious that this broad phrase has not been sufficiently defined, forcing academics, practitioners, educational institutions, and public policy makers to develop their own interpretations, and measuring methods to better capture the essence of this condition.

Figure 5.1. A student reading braille in class.

Source: Image by Flickr.

There is currently little debate over the fact that learning impairments are characterized by a wide range of heterogeneous ability deficiencies across a number of academic areas, including reading, math, written expression, and vocal language. However, the majority of education systems have embraced erratic justifications and very misguided ideas about how to operationally define, measure dependably, and intervene effectively with kids who show signs of a learning disability in the classroom.

Approximately 80% of students who have been recognized as having a learning disability, according to the United States Department of Education (2006), have reading skill deficiencies as their main problem. As a result, the majority of educational research has concentrated only on reading difficulties, sometimes known as developmental dyslexia, and has defined the illness by using rigorous cut-points to categorize pupils as having a problem or not.

As a result, there is a rather dichotomous perspective on pupils with reading problems, with only those students who manifest a condition being eligible for help and accommodations through an IEP.

There have been many theoretical attempts to effectively detect and assess underlying reading impairments in children, as well as, occasionally, incorrect conceptual assumptions. For instance, the discrepancy model has long been used by educational systems to help identify individuals with a particular learning problem (SLD).

With this approach, scholastic achievement in one or more core subjects—like reading, math, or written language—is evaluated, and it is determined whether or not the student's performance significantly differs from his or her general intelligence.

The discrepancy model focuses on more general aspects of cognition and achievement rather than on particular neurological processes that are exclusive to reading. The basic premise is that children with reading problems have the intellectual capacity to learn useful reading skills, but they underperform in school because they were born with a learning disability.

The discrepancy model has a number of drawbacks, such as an excessive reliance on a Full Scale IQ to capture the dynamic features of a person's reasoning abilities (Hale & Fiorello, 2004) and a lack of consensus regarding the degree of the disparity at different ages and grades (Feifer & DeFina, 2000).

According to Kavale and Forness (2000), nearly 50% of students classified as having a learning disability do not demonstrate a significant discrepancy between aptitude and achievement, due in part to the statistical imprecision of this method. Perhaps the most notable shortcoming of the discrepancy model was that it resulted in a wait-to-fail scenario, whereby students were forced to display a certain level of reading failure in order to qualify for special education services.

This was especially at odds with the National Reading Panel's (2000) conclusion highlighting the importance of early intervention services for children with reading difficulties. Simply put, the discrepancy model propagates an age-old educational myth that views reading disabilities along a one-dimensional continuum between those students with the disability and those without. According to Reynolds (2007), numerous neuropsychological studies of brain functioning have clearly shown the biological underpinnings of learning difficulties, with multiple subtypes and precise diagnostic markers clearly emerging.

Therefore, using ability-achievement discrepancy models to establish false cut-points as the only criteria for diagnosing learning disabilities simply disentitles students—most notably, students with lower IQs—from getting special education support and services. Human cognition is a multidimensional phenomenon that is distributed continuously and gradient ally throughout the brain, rather than linearly and modularly, as highlighted by Goldberg (2001).

Therefore, rather than merely creating artificial cut-points in a distribution of accomplishment test scores, there are degrees of variances in learning and cognition that must be studied through a multidimensional survey of brain activities.

Even though the neuropsychological literature offers a considerably more complex and supported perspective of the cognitive processes involved in learning, LD has still not been precisely measured, leading Kavale and Forness to conclude in 2000 that an operational definition of LD is still elusive.

Nevertheless, there has been significant progress in developing a more practical definition of LD, which is outlined in the book's later chapters.

States are no longer permitted to demand that school districts use a gap between IQ and accomplishment as being an essential criterion to designate pupils as having a reading disability after the 2004 reauthorization of IDEA.

Among the various features in this bill, states were finally given the option to forgo utilizing the discrepancy model in favor of the response-to-intervention (RTI) model to detect reading problems.

In other words, school districts were given the freedom to design a policy whereby, as part of a comprehensive evaluation, students who do not respond to evidence-based early reading programs may be regarded as eligible for special education services.

This is in contrast to the previous law, which required school districts to compare a student's overall intelligence with a nationally normed test of reading achievement to determine the presence of an educational disability.

RTI is nothing new. It has been utilized for many years in many districts primarily as a school-wide preventative program. What is novel, however, is that the federal special education statute specifically endorses RTI as a strong substitute for less efficient conventional approaches of establishing a student's eligibility for special education services (Canter, 2006).

RTI has received a lot of support, particularly from groups like the National Association of School Psychologists (NASP), because it gets around a lot of the problems with the conventional discrepancy paradigm. Additionally, RTI stresses the use of evidence-based teaching strategies in an effort to eradicate academic issues that are typically caused by inadequate curriculum or subpar instructional techniques.

In other words, the focus of RTI is more curriculum-centered than child-centered, with student underachievement in a core academic subject presumably due to poor instructional practices and implementation of inappropriate interventions.

In summary, RTI refers to an expansive array of procedures that can be used in conjunction with a comprehensive evaluation to determine eligibility and need for special education services within a problem-solving model (Feifer & Della Toffalo, 2007).

Regarding the identification of a specific reading disability, there is still a great deal of uncertainty regarding how far RTI's entangling web of influence can reach. Reynolds (2007) asserts that whereas RTI models place a greater emphasis on extrinsic elements that highlight child-school interactions, a disability is seen to be a specific condition that exists fundamentally within the child.

RTI is essentially more of a service delivery paradigm than it is a means of diagnosing a specific reading issue. Although curriculum-based measuring (CBM) techniques are emphasized in most RTI models and can be very helpful in aiding educators to track progress efficiently, CBM as a solitary measure is insufficient to identify the presence of a handicap.

The National Joint Committee on Learning Disabilities (NJCLD; 2005) came to the conclusion that employing CBM within a core RTI framework in the absence of other data is an inadequate technique of diagnosing a reading handicap.

5.5. HOW SLD MANIFESTS IN MATHEMATICS

Since mathematics is a difficult subject for most individuals to learn and is sophisticated and subtle, many children find it challenging. This is not because they have a learning handicap.

Nevertheless, about 7% of kids and teens have specific learning disabilities in math (MLD) as a result of underlying deficits or developmental delays in the cognitive systems that support math learning (Barbaresi, Katusic, Colligan, Weaver, & Jacobsen, 2005), and another 5% to 10% of kids and teens have persistent low achievement in math (LA) despite having average cognitive ability and reading achievement.

Compared to children with reading disabilities (RD), children with MLD and their LA classmates are the subject of far less research, yet significant improvement has been made over the past 15 years (Gersten, Clarke, & Mazzocco, 2007).

5.5.1. Definition, Etiology, and Incidence of Mathematics Learning Disability and Low Achievement in Mathematics

5.5.1.1. Definition

Currently, there is no agreed-upon test or achievement cutoff score used to diagnose MLD or LA (Gersten et al., 2007; Mazzocco, 2007). A consensus is beginning to emerge among researchers, however, at least with respect to the importance of distinguishing between MLD and LA (Geary, Hoard, ByrdCraven, Nugent, & Numtee, 2007; Murphy, Mazzocco, Hanich, & Early, 2007).

Children are classified as MLD when they perform below the 10th percentile on standardized mathematics achievement tests for at least two consecutive academic years, and LA when they perform below the 25th or 30th percentile but above the 10th percentile for the same period of time.

The "Cognitive Correlates" and "Diagnostic Markers" sections below show how these two groups differ in terms of the depth and severity of their mathematical difficulties as well as the underlying causes of those difficulties. Children with LA often have ordinary IQs, whereas children with MLD typically have IQs that are below normal.

Although some parts of their mathematics learning are influenced by the IQ gap between these two groups, this gap does not seem to be the main cause of MLD. Because of this, the value of a difference between math ability and IQ as a diagnostic criterion for MLD has not been proven (Mazzocco, 2007).

5.5.1.2. Etiology

Studies on twins and families imply that MLD may be caused by both genetic and environmental factors, as with other types of specific learning disabilities (SLD) (Kovas, Haworth, Dale, & Plomin, 2007; Light & DeFries, 1995; Shalev et al., 2001). Shalev and her coworkers discovered that people in the same immediate family as a child who has MLD are 10 times more likely to also be diagnosed with MLD than people in the general community are.

Kovas et al. discovered genetic, shared (between the pair of twins), and particular environmental influences to individual differences in mathematics achievement and MLD in a significant twin study of academic learning in primary school.

From one half to two thirds of the individual variance in mathematical achievement was related to genetic variation, and the remaining percentage to a combination of shared and individual experiences, depending on the grade and mathematics exam employed.

Individual variations in mathematics performance are influenced by the same genetic factors. In other words, individual disparities at all performance levels were caused by the same genetic variables that caused the MLD-related low performance (Kovas et al., 2007; Oliver et al., 2004).

These findings imply that MLD is not caused by specific genes, but rather by the same genetic factors that affect mathematics skill at the average to high levels of performance. One third of the genetic impacts were common to general cognitive ability, one third was unrelated to general cognitive ability but related to reading accomplishment, and one third was specific to mathematics.

As a result, around two thirds of the genetic influences on mathematical accomplishment and MLD are similar to those that have an impact on learning in other academic subjects, whereas the remaining one third solely have an impact on mathematical learning. Numerous children with MLD may experience RD or other issues that hinder their ability to learn in school, such as attention deficit hyperactivity disorder (ADHD), due to common genetic implications on academic achievement (ADHD; Barbaresi et al., 2005; Shalev et al., 2001).

Barbaresi et al. found that between 57% and 64% of individuals with MLD also had RD, depending on the diagnostic criteria used for MLD. These genetic influences, however, do not necessarily tell us about how effective future interventions may be, because changes in the individuals' environment may alter the relative extent of genetic and environmental influences on MLD status and/or related outcomes.

In any case, the research to date suggests significant environmental implications on MLD and math learning. For instance, schooling affects math achievement generally, and MLD therapies, even if they may not completely eradicate individual inequalities, increase math achievement of these children above and beyond the impact of general education.

5.5.1.3. Incidence

On the basis of several populations based, long-term studies and many smaller-scale studies, about 7% of children and adolescents will be diagnosable as MLD in at least one area of mathematics before graduating from high school (Barbaresi et al., 2005; Lewis, Hitch, & Walker, 1994; Shalev, Manor, & Gross-Tsur, 2005). An additional 5% to 10% of children and adolescents will be identified as LA (Berch & Mazzocco, 2007; Geary et al., 2007; Murphy et al., 2007).

5.6. HOW SLD MANIFESTS IN WRITING

5.6.1. Definition, Etiology, and Incidence of Writing Disabilities

Writing difficulties are intricate and varied, much like writing itself. Linking language, thinking, and physical abilities is necessary for writing. To write clearly, spell correctly, and translate thoughts into writing, a writer must use and integrate a wide range of skills.

A writing challenge in one area can exacerbate a writing challenge in another. For instance, a lack of fine motor control will immediately affect handwriting, which will subsequently affect the quantity and quality of written output. Writing is therefore a very difficult undertaking that has been compared to "an incredible juggling act" (Berninger & Richards, 2002).

5.6.1.1. Definition

The Diagnostic and Statistical Manual of Mental Disorders, Fourth Edition, Text Revision (DSM-IV-TR; American Psychiatric Association, 2000) describes a disorder of written expression as writing abilities that are significantly below what would be expected given the person's age, intelligence, and age-appropriate education.

In addition, the problem must seriously hinder the ability to do writing-intensive everyday tasks or attain academic success. Written expression is one of the eight criteria for inclusion under the category of particular learning disability in the Individuals with Disabilities Education Improvement Act (IDEA, 2004). (SLD).

Poor handwriting or incorrect spelling by itself is inadequate, according to the DSM-IV-TR and IDEA guidelines, to diagnose a written expression disorder. The inability to express oneself in writing must be hampered by writing difficulties. But frequently, lower-level abilities like handwriting and spelling are to blame for a person's problems with written expression.

Given that handwriting and spelling are the major basic abilities for writing in the primary grades, it is essential to focus on children who are having difficulty developing these abilities in order to identify writing issues early.

5.6.1.2. Etiology

A diverse variety of people with writing impairments exists. Numerous reasons, including medical, neurobiological, neuropsychological, and/or environmental ones, might contribute to bad writing. Writing difficulties have been connected to medical illnesses such fetal alcohol syndrome (FAS) and carbon monoxide poisoning (Bernstein, 2008), as well as brain injuries to the parietal lobe (National Institute for Neurological Disorders and Stroke [NINDS], 2009).

Studies on families and twins have revealed genetic factors that may be at play (e.g., Bernstein; Raskind, 2001). People who have certain language delays and disabilities are undoubtedly more likely to have writing issues. Having trouble with fine motor skills, language, visual-spatial abilities, attention, memory, or sequencing skills may have neuropsychological issues.

The causes of writing issues will also change depending on the kind of writing difficulty. For instance, whereas a problem with written expression is more likely to result from inadequate oral language development, a spelling issue may arise from a restricted capacity to retain the orthography (written symbols) of a language.

Writing issues may not become apparent until well into the second grade in some situations since reading skills may receive greater attention in the classroom. In fact, a student's writing issues could not become apparent until the student moves from the third to the fourth grade, when the writing requirements drastically increase and state tests are frequently given.

5.6.1.3. Incidence

The prevalence of students with some type of learning disability is typically estimated to be between 5% and 6% of the total U.S. school-age population (National Center for Education Statistics, 2009). For writing disability, the prevalence appears similar to that of reading disability; problems with written expression are estimated to occur in 2% to 8% of school-aged children, with a higher prevalence of boys than girls (Katusic, Colligan, Weaver, & Barbaresi, 2009; Wiznitzer & Scheffel, 2009).

The number of people with simply a particular writing handicap is difficult to estimate since people with writing disabilities frequently have comorbid conditions, such as disorders in reading, math, attention, or conduct.

In research on the prevalence of written language disorders, Katusic et al. discovered that 75% of the sample of students with written language issues (N 14 806) in a significant birth cohort had difficulties reading as well.

As a result, only around 25% of kids with writing impairments also have reading disabilities. However, teachers have reported a far greater incidence of handwriting issues, estimating that roughly 10% of their female pupils and close to one-third of their male students have handwriting difficulty (Rosenblum, Weiss, & Parush, 2004).

These results imply that writing disabilities have not received adequate attention. This is partly because of comorbidity problems, but it's also because researchers and teachers both don't place enough value on written language.

Evidence of the lack of instructional focus on writing in the U.S. schools can be found in reviewing the National Assessment of Educational Progress (NAEP) findings. According to the Nation's Report Card: Writing 2007 (Salahu-Din, Persky, & Miller, 2008), less than one-third of 4th and 8th graders and less than one-fourth of 12th graders were found to be proficient in writing.

5.7. HOW SLD MANIFESTS IN ORAL EXPRESSION AND LISTENING COMPREHENSION

Language-impaired children and adolescents exhibit a range of symptoms and require various levels of assessment and intervention. The educational diagnostician is in charge of selecting the exams and evaluations to utilize in order to pinpoint pupils' language strengths and shortcomings.

This involves consideration and should be based on choices of the factors that may need to be investigated in order to influence oral expression and listening comprehension. The contributions a child or adolescent makes to the process of using language for social interaction and learning are referred to as intrapersonal factors.

They comprise linguistic abilities, brain-behavior connections, and cognitive and affective factors. This chapter examines the growth and effects of these factors on vocal expressiveness and listening comprehension. Numerous standardized, norm-referenced assessments address the intrapersonal language and cognitive factors connected to oral expression and listening comprehension.

This chapter also covers the characteristics of tests and evaluations that gauge the contributions of various variables. The environment and culture in which the child or teenager is reared and expected to operate affect interpersonal variables. The educational environment of the school, the school's culture, the curriculum's aims and anticipated educational results, as well as the neighborhood and society at large, are among them.

It will be addressed how language impairments and the need for language use in social circumstances interact. Educational and academic evaluations concentrate on how well students interact with the curriculum, and these topics are covered in more depth in other chapters of this volume. Assessment of academic accomplishment will only be briefly discussed in this chapter.

5.7.1. Definition, Etiology, and Incidence of Language Disabilities

5.7.1.1. Definition

In order to learn and use the linguistic system for academic purposes and social interactions, one or more psychological processes must function normally. Language-based learning disabilities (LBLD) indicate problems in one or more of these psychological processes. They are frequently characterized as largely oral expression-based (oral language) or as a combination of oral expression and auditory comprehension challenges.

Language impairments are included in the broader category of particular learning disabilities under the Individuals with Disabilities Education

Improvement Act (IDEA) (U.S. Department of Education, 2004). If a pupil does not perform age-appropriately or does not reach grade-level expectations for oral expression or listening comprehension, a language handicap is assumed to exist.

The Diagnostic and Statistical Manual of Mental Disorders, Fourth Edition, Text Revision (DSM-IV-TR) (American Psychiatric Association, 2000) defines language disabilities from a clinical perspective as being either of the "Expressive" (code 315.31) or "Mixed Receptive-Expressive" (code 315.32) type. Expressive language disabilities are identified by the following criteria:

- Development of oral expression is significantly below the development of listening comprehension and nonverbal intellectual ability,
- Language disabilities interfere with academic, vocational, and professional achievement and/or social communication,
- The language difficulties are in excess of those usually observed in cases with cognitive, sensory, or motor deficits or environmental deprivation, and
- Symptoms do not meet criteria for a combined disability in oral expression and listening comprehension or pervasive developmental disorders (DSM-IV- TR, pp. 58–61).

"Mixed Receptive-Expressive" language disabilities are defined by the following criteria:

- Oral expression and listening comprehension are significantly below nonverbal intellectual ability,
- Language disabilities interfere with academic, vocational, and professional achievement and social communication and
- Symptoms do not meet criteria for pervasive developmental disorders (DSM-IV-TR, pp. 62–64).

The International Statistical Classification of Diseases and Related Health Problems, Tenth Revision (ICD-10) (World Health Organization, 2005) categorizes language disabilities as either "Expressive" or "Receptive" (codes F80.1 and F80.2).

In both definitions (DMS-IV-TR and ICD-10), oral expression disabilities are considered to constitute a separate clinical, diagnostic category, a concept that is challenged by Leonard (2009).

5.7.1.2. Etiology

The development of language is a complex process, and genetic, neuroanatomical, neurological, medical, and environmental factors can all have an impact on the functioning systems involved (Brown & Hagoort, 1999).

It's possible for language impairments to be secondary in nature. For instance, genetic syndromes including Down, Fragile X, and Tourette spectrum include language and communication difficulties (Dornbush & Pruitt, 1995; Prestia, 2003).

In addition, language disabilities are a core part of ASDs, and co-occur with attention deficit/hyperactivity disorder (ADHD), executive function disorders (EFD) such as obsessive-compulsive disorder (OCD), and psychiatric disorders such as bipolar and anxiety disorders and psychosis (Barkley, 1997; Brown, 2000; Culatta & Wiig, 2002; Pinborough-Zimmerman et al., 2007; Ottinger, 2003; Wetherby, 2002).

Traumatic brain damage can cause language problems at any stage of development. Language difficulties can also be brought on by prenatal and environmental causes, such as exposure to psychosocial stress during pregnancy and very low birth weight (Breslau, Chilcoat, DelDotto, Andreski, & Brown, 1996; Entringer et al., 2009).

It is widely acknowledged that children and teenagers with language problems include a diverse population whose impairments are brought on by a range of causes. Age-related cognitive demands and language requirements for academic pursuits and social engagement cause the group to grow increasingly diverse. As a result, linguistic impairments manifest themselves differently as people age (Larson & McKinley, 2003; Paul, 2000).

5.7.1.3. Incidence

Language impairment prevalence reports vary based on the type, severity, and age of the disability, as well as the inclusion and definition criteria. A study of kindergarten-aged children found that the incidence rate was 7.4% overall, with boys experiencing the condition more frequently (8%) than girls (6%).

According to other research (Gilger & Wise, 2004), children with early language problems are more likely to develop reading difficulties later in life (prevalence estimates range from 6% to 8% of school-age children).

According to a recent study of 8-year-olds, 6.3% of children have language difficulties, and boys outnumber girls by nearly two to one (1.8 to 1). (Pinborough-Zimmerman et al., 2007).

The percentage of language disabilities associated with ASDs has been estimated at 3.7%, with intellectual disability (i.e., IQ < 70) at 4%. The prevalence rates for mental health disorders that co-occur with language disabilities are reported at 6.1% for ADHD, 2.2% for anxiety disorders, and 1.7% for conduct disorders (Pinborough-Zimmerman et al.).

5.8. A RESPONSE TO INTERVENTION (RTI) APPROACH TO SLD IDENTIFICATION

5.8.1. Classification

An understanding of categorization, a field of study that has spanned many branches of science for many centuries, is essential to comprehending any approach to the identification of SLD. In accordance with a set of characteristics that describe how the observations are similar and dissimilar, classifications allow the division of a larger set of data into smaller subgroups.

Identification is the assignment of the observations to the more specific subgroups and is an operationalization of the definitions that result from the categorization. Biology makes clear the connection between categorization and identification by classifying plants into different species.

A hypothetical classification of mental and behavioral disorders that, like in other areas of medicine, is largely categorical and uses signs and symptoms for identification is the Diagnostic and Statistical Manual of Mental Disorders (DSM-IV-TR), published by the American Psychiatric Association (1994). (Also called diagnosis).

When a child's academic challenges are determined to be due to SLD rather than an intellectual disability or spoken language issue, classifications apply. The various identification models discussed in this book differ in the operationalization of the criteria for SLD identification, but they don't really differ in the major disorders' underlying classification or the crucial aspect of SLD that serves to set it apart from other academic issues—unexpected underachievement. The operationalization of the classification as a set of standards for classifying children into subgroups varies.

Therefore, every method of identification starts with a classification that describes the characteristics unique to the subgroups that need to be recognized. Specific subgroups of the greater population of people who encounter learning, achievement, and behavioral issues may be distinguished by these characteristics from the numerous other groupings (Morris & Fletcher, 1988).

The classification is based on postulated constructs that describe the characteristics of the many subgroups, including SLD, intellectual disability, ADHD, and other subgroups that may have behavioral, academic, and learning challenges (e.g., children with depression or motivational difficulties).

As a result, various disorders are classified, leading to identification (or diagnostic) criteria that are operationalized into a measuring system (definition), allowing determination of subgroup membership. The classification, as well as the operational definitions and criteria that come from it, are hypotheses that need to be continually assessed.

The measurement model operationalizes subgroups that are by definition unobservable and is observable. As a result, SLD cannot be observed directly, but it can be operationalized by describing the categorization and measurement methods that were used to do so.

Classifications tend to describe subgroups and, sometimes, individuals that represent ideal types, or prototypes. They are usually hierarchical and arranged in terms of larger to smaller classes that all share at least one common attribute, but differ on other attributes.

However, especially for subgroups like SLD in which the primary attributes are dimensional—that is, exist on a continuum with no natural demarcations (see Fletcher et al., 2007)—deciding about subgroup membership involves the placement of individuals along a set of multiple, correlated dimensions.

There are no natural boundaries, thus any conclusions resulting from the measurement model are necessarily arbitrary and heavily impacted by the measurement error present in the operationalization processes. If strict cut-points are used and the correlations between the dimensions are not taken into account, measurement error is a particularly serious issue (Francis et al., 2005).

Good classifications can be duplicated despite changes in the measurement model since they are trustworthy and independent of the particular measurement model. Additionally, they identify the majority of the key figures (i.e., have adequate coverage).

The ability to distinguish between the subgroups comprising a valid classification based on characteristics other than those used to define the subgroups is what makes excellent classifications legitimate, not just because subgroups can be recognized (Skinner, 1981).

For instance, if SLD is defined as a gap between IQ and achievement, there should be systematic disparities on cognitive, behavioral, and other factors not used to define the subgroups between poor achievers who match the IQ-discrepancy criteria and low achievers who do not (e.g., intervention response). Good classifications that satisfy these requirements enhance tasks such as communication and prediction.

5.8.2. RTI and SLD Identification

The benefit of recognizing SLD using an RTI service delivery system is that the instructional response components are already integrated into the identification process, speeding eligibility determinations and directly connecting special education services with general education services.

Frameworks for RTI service delivery also allow for a more flexible approach to evaluation, in which tools are chosen in accordance with theories regarding the causes of insufficient instructional response. The thorough evaluation serves as the foundation for each student's unique educational plans. Identification involves data from numerous sources in accordance with IDEA 2004.

5.8.2.1. What Is an RTI Framework?

The most important consideration in understanding RTI models is that they are not primarily for the identification of SLD.

Rather, the primary goal is the prevention and remediation of academic and behavioral difficulties through effective classroom and supplemental instruction, including those provided by all entitlement programs.

As such, RTI is a framework for effectively delivering and coordinating services in schools. RTI frameworks provide data that are relevant to identification of SLD and that lead to different approaches to referral and placement decisions related to SLD (Fletcher & Vaughn, 2009a).

In an RTI framework, a two- to three-times-per-year universal screening of pupils for academic and behavioral challenges takes place. Children who are at risk have access to multilayer interventions that start in general education classes and get stronger based on how well the pupils respond to the lessons. Intensity is raised by giving students more time, teaching in smaller classes, and changing the curriculum and interventions to suit each student's needs.

Brief assessments of progress, frequently based on a curriculum-based measurement (CBM) framework, are used to determine the need for more intensive interventions (Fuchs & Fuchs, 1998; VanDerHeyden & Burns, 2010).

The evidence that the general education curriculum's instruction has not been sufficient to meet the student's instructional needs may lead to the consideration of special education for a child who advances through multiple layers of intervention but fails to demonstrate adequate instructional response in relation to a benchmark set by the school, district, or state.

At this point, a thorough assessment would take place. The topic of suitable benchmarks is controversial.

Links to some form of national reference and state criteria for annual improvement, both of which are obviously conceivable from a CBM framework, however, make it easier to grasp these standards (Fuchs & Fuchs, 2004).

Tying metrics to the curriculum where progress is matched to regional benchmarks is suitable for instructional decision-making. However, unless there is a clear connection with national standards and proof of reliability and validity, caution should be exercised when adopting local standards for a legal eligibility condition.

One misconception regarding RTI models is that they demand that a child complete numerous levels of intervention before considering special education. In fact, during any stage of the RTI process, a kid may be recommended for a special education review (VanDerHeyden & Burns, 2010).

Referral raises the issue of what services special education can offer, though. Sometimes, a kid may require the civil rights protections provided by IDEA 2004 or may experience issues that the RTI framework is unable to handle (e.g., a speech and language disorder, or concerns about a pervasive developmental disorder). Even with techniques to SLD identification used before to IDEA 2004, the issue of what services and protections identification for special education would offer when a child was referred for special education arose. The main objective of RTI is to identify treatment requirements, and eligibility determination is not separated from intervention activities.

5.8.3. Reliability Issues

It is challenging to improve the coverage of classifications based on an RTI approach since there is no gold standard for identifying an inadequate response (or a child with SLD). This issue also pertains to any identification method for SLD, as identification will always be based on the operationalization of the model.

In general, strategies for recognizing insufficient student response to teaching are more consistent when identifying students who respond properly than badly (Barth et al., 2008).

In certain ways, people would argue that false negative errors (missing an inadequate responder) should be minimized, even while the false positive rate (identifying an adequate responder as inadequate) will rise, as the goal is to prevent missing kids who require more intervention.

Any psychometric technique based on cut-points is a discrepancy model and will not identify the same pupils as insufficient responders, whether identification is based on the assessment of instructional response, low accomplishment, or any sort of cognitive discrepancy (Francis et al., 2005).

For the evaluation of intervention response, this is unquestionably true (Barth et al., 2008; Burns & Senesac, 2005; Speece, Case, & Molloy, 2003). Uneven cut-points and the application of various assessments across procedures account for some of the variation between approaches.

The distinctions are dimensional, presumably exist on a continuum, and reflect the measurement error of the assessment, making it impossible to consistently identify individuals above and below a fixed cut-point on a dimension. Even if these factors are controlled, the lack of overlap should not be surprising (Cohen, 1983). In fact, kids that group together near the cut-point tend to be similar to one another.

For instance, Barth et al. (2008) analyzed the intervention response in 399 Grade 1 pupils in respect to cut-points, measurements, and methodologies widely mentioned for the identification of underachievers in a Grade 1, Tier 2 intervention (Mathes et al., 2005). In order to address the agreement of the various operationalizations of instructional response, measures of association (n ¼ 808) were computed.

Although agreement for identifying adequate responders was stronger, overall agreement between techniques remained modest, especially for identifying inadequate responders. Even when the latter accounted for the cutoff score, all at the 25th percentile, Speece et al. (2003) observed that dual-discrepancy models identified children as inadequate responders who were not recognized by straightforward poor achievement or level of performance assessments.

Although Speece et al. (2003) argued in favor of a dual-discrepancy model because of its focus on growth, a recent study questioned whether assessments of growth add to the information provided by level of performance at the end of the year on the same progress monitoring assessment (Schatschneider, Wagner, & Crawford, 2008).

Altogether, these issues with overlap, which occur for any model for LD identification, suggest that multiple criteria should be used, which is why the use of norm-referenced assessments of achievement in a hybrid model is encouraged.

5.8.4. Validity Issues

Comparing the emerging subgroups on factors not utilized to identify the members allows us to assess hypothetical classifications as well. So, using an RTI framework for identification should result in distinct groupings. 23 research on reading interventions for elementary school students (preschool through Grade 3) were compiled by Al Otaiba and Fuchs in 2002.

They stated that the majority of studies identified phonological awareness issues as a key trait of poor responders. A poor reaction was however correlated with issues with quick naming, phonological working memory, linguistic ability, attention and behavior issues, orthographic processing, and demographic factors.

Rapid naming, problem behavior, phonological awareness, letter knowledge, memory, and IQ were among the areas where adequate and inadequate responders differed, according to Nelson, Benner, and Gonzalez's 2003 meta-analysis of 30 studies. These areas also showed moderate to small effect size differences in the following order (larger to smaller).

Stage, Abbott, Jenkins, and Berninger (2003) compared cognitive functions in children who responded "faster" or "slower" to a Grade 1 intervention. In a univariate context, faster responders had higher scores on verbal IQ, phonological and orthographic awareness, rapid naming, and verbal reasoning. The slower responders were rated as more inattentive. Verbal IQ and discrepancies of verbal IQ and reading achievement did not contribute uniquely to responder differentiation. Al Otaiba and Fuchs (2006) compared groups of children who met adequate response criteria across kindergarten and Grade 1. Students consistently identified as inadequate responders performed more poorly on measures of morphonology, vocabulary, rapid naming, sentence repetition, and word discrimination, with more behavioral difficulties. Phonological segmentation was a weak discriminator of responder status.

5.9. CONCLUSION

The key components of identifying a particular learning disorder are outlined in this chapter. The concept of learning impairment and the categories of learning disabilities are covered in this chapter along with a brief history of the condition.

The methods of SLD identification highlighted in this chapter include ability-achievement discrepancy, response to intervention, and alternative research-based SLD identification processes.

This chapter also discusses the definition, etiology, and prevalence of each SLD manifestation, as well as how SLD appears in the areas of reading, mathematics, writing, oral expression, and listening comprehension.

REFERENCES

1. Dynega, M. S., Flanagan, D. P., & Alfonso, V. C., (n.d.). Overview of specific learning disabilities. In: *Essentials of Specific Learning Disability Identification*. Wiley. Available at: https://www.pdfdrive.com/essentials-of-specific-learning-disability-identification-essentials-of-psychological-assessment-d156836674.html (accessed on 14 October 2023).
2. Feifer, S., (n.d.). How SLD manifests in reading. In: *Essentials of Specific Learning Disability Identification*. Wiley. Available at: https://cloudflare-ipfs.com/ipfs/bafykbzaceb6wcisthyezk27 dvo3zekboqdh smmmtkqfhj6x5fltqknibthwni?filename=%28Essentials%20of%20psychological%20assessment%20series%29%20Dawn%20P. %20Flanagan%2C%20Vincent%20C.%20Alfonso%20-%20Essentials%20of%20Specific%20Learning%20Disability%20Identification %20%28Essentials%20of%20Psychological%20Assessment%29%20%20-Wiley%20%282010%29.pdf (accessed on 14 October 2023).
3. *IDEA Regulations: Identification of Specific Learning Disabilities*, (n.d.). sites.ed.gov. U.S. Department of Education. Available at: https://sites.ed.gov/idea/files/Identification_of_SLD_10-4-06.pdf (accessed on 14 October 2023).
4. Muktamath, V. U., Hegde, P. R., & Chand, S., (2022). Types of specific learning disability. *Learning Disabilities – Neurobiology, Assessment, Clinical Features and Treatments* [Preprint]. Available at: https://doi.org/10.5772/intechopen.100809.
5. Reschly, D. J., (2014). *Response to Intervention and the Identification of Specific Learning Disabilities*. alliedhealth.ceconnection.com. Wolters Kluwer Health. Available at: https:// alliedhealth.ceconnection.com/files/ResponsetoInterventionandtheIdentificationofSpecificLearningDisabilities-1390487901231.pdf (accessed on 14 October 2023).
6. Reschly, D. J., (2014). Response to intervention and the identification of specific learning disabilities. *Topics in Language Disorders*, *34*(1), 39–58. Available at: https://doi.org/10.1097/tld.0000000000000003.
7. *Unit 2 Specific Learning Disabilities (SLD)* (n.d.). egyankosh.ac.in. egyankosh. Available at: https://egyankosh.ac.in/bitstream/123456789/40001/1/Unit-2.pdf (accessed on 14 October 2023).

CHAPTER 6

Learning Disabilities Comorbid with Behavioral Developmental Disorders and Autism

Contents

This chapter talks about learning disabilities comorbid with behavioral developmental disorders and autism. This chapter explains about ADHD as a specific cause for learning disability. This chapter also provide highlights on developmental dyscalculia, nosological status and cognitive underpinnings. This chapter also helps to understand concept of autism spectrum disorder (ASD). This chapter also addresses learning disabilities in children with autism. At the end of this chapter, this chapter explains the important considerations for clinical intervention in SLP.

6.1. INTRODUCTION

Children under 19 years of age constitute a little less than half of world population and information about their mental health needs is a national imperative. Children with specific learning disorders (SLDs) exhibit academic difficulties disproportionate to their intellectual capacities. Prevalence of SLD ranges from 2% to 10%. Dyslexia (developmental reading disorder) is the most common type, affecting 80% of all SLD.

About 30% of learning-disabled children has behavioral and emotional problems, which range from attention deficit hyperactivity disorder (ADHD) (most common) to depression, anxiety, suicide etc., to substance abuse (least common).

The co-occurrence of these issues with SLD makes academic challenges much more challenging. Diagnoses in these situations are challenging and tricky, and academic improvement calls for an all-encompassing, holistic approach to care.

Because of the underdiagnosis and inadequate treatment of SLD, there should be more effort made to comprehend the co-morbidities, particularly in the Indian community. Because there is little research on co-morbid disorders and learning disabilities.

The classification of learning by certain academic skills is still used in the present conception of learning disorders (LDs), formerly known as academic skill disorders. Reading, mathematics, and written expression are among these abilities.

In each case, the skills are assessed using standardized tests whose results must be significantly below the level predicted given a person's age, intelligence, and degree of schooling for that age.

These deficiencies hinder academic performance, which results in failing or receiving poor grades. Low self-esteem, discouragement, social skill deficiencies, dropping out of school, difficulty finding work, and difficulty adjusting to social situations are additional characteristics that are related.

In the areas of a child's cognitive, verbal, emotional, social, and moral development, schools are essential and formative. Academic abilities like reading, writing, and math lay the groundwork for evaluating a student's success in the classroom.

Because of this, children of school age who experience learning difficulties may experience feelings of worry, inadequacy, and shame, which can result in behavioral problems. Any unfavorable input from a child's school is likely to affect how well they perform emotionally, socially, and in their families.

Children with LD display scholastic challenges that are out of proportion to their intelligence. They struggle to pick up scholastic abilities including reading, writing, math, and spelling.

Reading disorder (RD), mathematics disorder, disorder of written expression, and learning disorder not otherwise defined are the four categories under which learning disorders fall under the Diagnostic and Statistical Manual of Mental Disorders, Fourth Edition (DSM-IV). Depending on how the prevalence is measured and the definitions used in different countries, estimates of the prevalence of learning problems range from 2% to 10%.

6.2. ADHD AS A SPECIFIC CAUSE FOR LEARNING DISABILITY

Children with ADHD provide a significant challenge in the educational process due to their inability to pay attention, be patient, and comply with instructor directions throughout class. They also struggle with a range of learning issues.

ADHD is a clinically diverse neurobehavioral condition that is linked to high financial costs, family stress, and poor academic and employment outcomes. In adulthood, this syndrome is still present and poses a significant risk for addiction, risky conduct, unsatisfactory employment, a high divorce rate, etc.

This condition's diagnostics are subject to change throughout time. The condition was referred to as "minimal brain injury" or "minimal brain dysfunction" up until 1994, when it was termed for the first time as Hyperkinetic Disorder. Both manuals, the fourth edition of the Diagnostic and Statistical Manual of Mental Disorders (DSM-IV) and the International

Classification of Diseases (ICD-10) under the names "Hyperkinetic Disorder" (HKD) and "Attention Deficit Hyperactivity Disorder," list the three main symptoms of inattention, impulsivity, and hyperactivity (ADHD).

In DSM-IV, the diagnostic includes three different groups of children: the predominantly Hyperactive-Impulsive Type, the predominantly Inattentive Type, and the Combined Type of ADHD. It was approved that this disorder is more frequently found in boys with the ratio of boys to girls being approximately 4:1 for all three subgroups.

In May 2012, American Psychological Association was revising the Fourth Edition of the Diagnostic and Statistical Manual of Mental Disorders, which included some changes in the section on specific learning disabilities. Consequently, DSM-5 considers Specific Learning Disability (SLD) as a type of Neurodevelopmental Disorder that delays the ability to learn or use specific academic skills (e.g., reading, writing, or arithmetic).

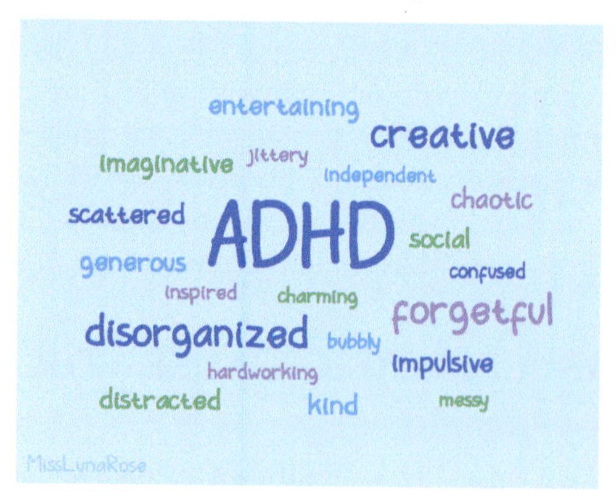

Figure 6.1. A word cloud of ADHD.

Source: Image by Wikimedia commons.

In this context, SLD is a clinical diagnostic that isn't often associated with the term "learning disabilities," which is typically used in the context of the educational system. SLD refers to the specific learning challenges that are present at the time of assessment in the three primary academic subjects of reading, writing, and mathematics.

The group of entities named as "Other Neurodevelopmental Disorders" includes Intellectual Disability, ASD, Attention-Deficit/Hyperactivity Disorder, and Communication Disorders and Motor Disorders. Consequently, whatever criteria for diagnostics are followed, ADHD stays as a huge cause for learning problems.

The differences in diagnostic criteria following different manuals have influenced to the different prevalence rates. As a result, HKD is estimated to be present in approximately 0.5% of children, whereas ADHD has been reported in between 5 and 11.4% of the population.

The differences in diagnostics have significant effects on both diagnosis and treatment because, depending on the criteria used, a child may or may not be considered to have a clinical disorder. This will have an impact on the choice of whether or not to include the child in the educational process and whether or not treatment is required.

Numerous experts have noted that there is a continuum between normal and aberrant behavior and ADHD. Particularly, behavioral studies of kids who tend to be the inattentive kind have discovered that these kids have some particular issues.

For instance, children who are inattentive are less impulsive and show less behavior issues than children who are hyperactive. In contrast, they exhibit more internalizing symptoms and are more socially distant, shy, and worried.

Additionally, they exhibit academic underachievement and learning issues more commonly. Youngsters who are not paying attention are easily confused, stare constantly, regularly daydream, and are drowsy, hypoactive, and docile, traits that are uncommon in children who are overly active.

More specifically, it was determined that inattentive children had deficiencies in the speed at which information was processed and in focused or selective attention, but the mixed form of ADHD is more characterized by a problem with sustained attention (persistence) and distractibility.

These results suggested that perhaps inattentive youngsters should not only be treated as a kind of ADHD but also as a separate set of disorders.

It has been established that dopamine-related genes (such as D1, D2, and D4) are implicated in the etiology of ADHD, despite the fact that genetic markers for the diagnosis of ADHD in children have not yet been discovered.

The possibility that this illness could affect members of the same family, particularly in twins, further supports some type of hereditary inheritance. Recent research has shown that autism and obsessive-compulsive disorder share genetic underpinnings and brain structures with ADHD (OCD).

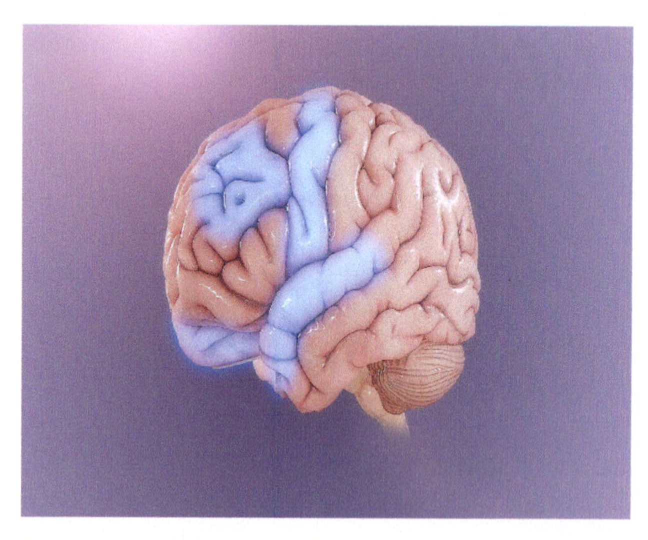

Figure 6.2. Some areas of the brain of an OCD patient which shows abnormal activity.

Source: Image by Wikimedia commons.

In all three situations, impulsivity is a common habit. Additionally, aberrant findings in the brain architecture, particularly in the corpus callosum structure, as well as extensive abnormalities in the white matter are found in these diseases.

However, children with OCD present fewer structural alterations in comparison with those with autism or ADHD. It is the possible reason that children with autism as well as ADHD manifest earlier specific symptoms in comparison with OCD, which could have a start even in adolescence.

Some rare genetic variants associated with autism and schizophrenia also increase a person's chance of having ADHD.

Eight copy number variants (CNVs) that are more prevalent in people with ADHD than in those without this issue have been discovered through genetic analysis. Autism and schizophrenia are also linked to these CNVs. This raises the novel theory that the biochemical bases for autism, schizophrenia, and ADHD may be the same.

However, while they can discover genes with a modest impact, findings do not support susceptibility genes for ADHD that have a higher impact. For chromosomal regions that need more research, whole genome linkage studies have shown some intriguing results.

Finding the endophenotype may be a helpful tactic for precise diagnosis, given the complexity of the ADHD phenotype and some genetic discoveries. A quantitative biological property that is heritable, trustworthy in reflecting the function of a distinct biological system, and assumed to be more directly related to the genetic basis of the disease than the clinical phenotype is known as an endophenotype, also known as an intermediate phenotype.

Figure 6.3. A researcher performing genetic analysis.

Source: Image by Flickr.

The combination of these two methods (endophenotype and genetic variations) may produce more conclusive findings. Increased theta power in an EEG recording is thought to be a potential biological indication of hereditary risk for ADHD in this situation.

In order to find possible neurologic basis for ADHD, many imaging techniques are used. Positron Emission Tomography confirmed that brain metabolism in children with ADHD is lower in the areas responsible for the attention, social judgment, and movement. It is confirmed also with fMRI, SPECT, or Blood Oxygen Level Dependent (BOLD) techniques. However, Quantitative Electroencephalography (Q-EEG) recording appeared to be more available, inexpensive, and useful indicator of brain metabolic activity.

It is confirmed that low metabolic activity is characterized by an increase in the slow activities (delta and theta waves) and a decrease in the fast beta activities in the region that provides the associated EEG signals. A study conducted by Monastra and his team provides compelling evidence for the value of the Q-EEG in the diagnostic assessment of ADHD.

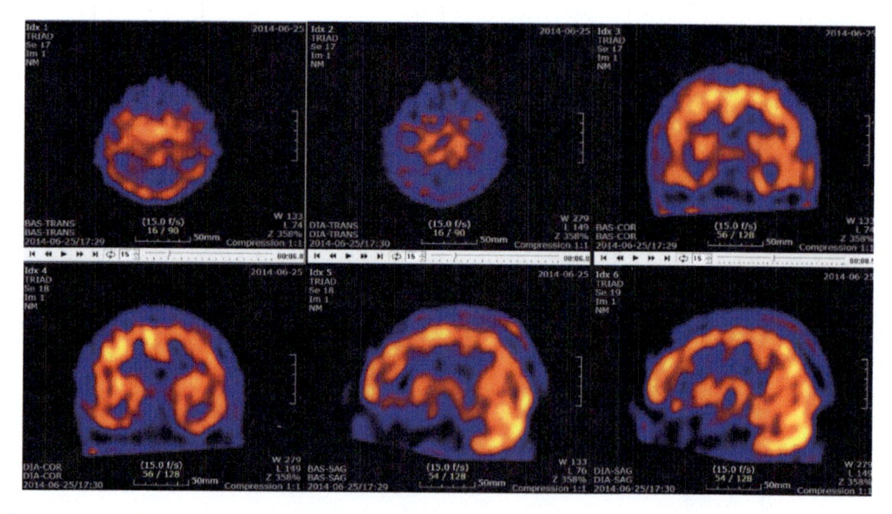

Figure 6.4. Brain SPECT with acetazolamide slices.

Source: Image by Wikimedia commons.

Many studies confirmed that the main brain system, which is impaired in ADHD, is the executive system. Two parameters are specific for the executive system:

- Arousal, as a generalized activation of the system; and
- Attention/focused activation of the system, associated with working memory, action selection, action inhibition, and action monitoring.

As was mentioned before, endophenotype is becoming an important concept in the study of ADHD. The endophenotype in psychiatry can be categorized as anatomical, developmental, electrophysiological, metabolic, sensory, or psychological/cognitive.

In contrast to the obvious behavioral symptoms, endophenotype serves as a simpler indicator for genetic process. In genetic analyzes of probands and families, it can be utilized as a quantitative variable and aids in defining subtypes of a specific condition.

This has led to the development of the Q-EEG spectrum classification of the ADHD population, which identifies four main endophenotypes: I subtype, which is characterized by an abnormal increase of delta-theta frequency range centrally or centrally frontally; II subtype, which is characterized by an abnormal increase of frontal midline theta rhythm; III subtype, which is characterized by an abnormal increase of beta activity frontally; and IV subtype, which is characterized by an excess of alpha activities at central, posterior, or frontal lobes.

Even so, a lot of school children's ADHD is misdiagnosed or underdiagnosed due to the complexity of the disorder. On the other hand, some hyper diagnoses are also feasible. For instance, many brilliant students in my research who had uninteresting regular school programs and had hyperactive behavior were diagnosed with ADHD.

The misdiagnosis may also be the result of other comorbid conditions such conduct issues, high general anxiety, depression, speech issues, ASD, or seizures that coexist with ADHD.

In this case, additional illnesses that are similar to ADHD may overlap with the actual disorder. According to neuropsychological theory, the same brain and cognitive processes that control attention and behavior are thought to be responsible for comorbidity.

6.3. DEVELOPMENTAL DYSCALCULIA: NOSOLOGICAL STATUS AND COGNITIVE UNDERPINNINGS

Today's civilization demands highly developed mathematics abilities. As cliche as it may sound, there is a substantial body of scientific data showing that higher mathematical competencies are linked to improved health outcomes, higher employability and incomes, and beneficial financial decisions.

Despite this substantial amount of research, many adults, and kids, especially in affluent nations, have difficulty doing basic math operations.

Numerous factors, such as financial, educational, and emotional ones, might cause math failure. Math is a difficult and abstract subject that mainly depends on formal school instruction. Additionally, as mathematical knowledge is typically cumulative, newer, more advanced, and abstract ideas are dependent on earlier understandings. This prior understanding can be picked up informally at school or intuitively by reciting a list of numbers in order.

Therefore, further conclusion will be a significant portion of the challenges kids have while learning or engaging in math-related activities stem from the complexity of mathematics itself. It is well known that, in contrast to other academic subjects, arithmetic learning difficulties can already be seen in young students during their first years of school.

The chronic and significant challenges some children have learning math, however, cannot be attributed to socioeconomic, educational, emotional, psychiatric, or intellectual issues. In these cases, the label developmental dyscalculia (DD) is often applied, and difficulties encompass a broad range of mathematical tasks, like reading and writing numbers in different formats, comparing numbers and quantities, and performing the basic arithmetical operations.

Some authors also indicate deficits in abilities concerning magnitude representation and the comprehension and use of symbolic codes to represent numerical information. The estimates for prevalence of DD vary from 3 to 6% of school-aged children.

There is still some disagreement over the diagnostic standards, neuropsychological foundations, and treatment plans despite the relative agreement on the challenges that define DD. Each of these three subjects will be covered in depth in the sections that follow.

6.4. NOSOLOGICAL STATUS

6.4.1. Diagnosis

Concerning the DD diagnosis, there are two key inquiries. The first query relates to the diagnostic standards, and three methods are frequently mentioned in the literature on the epidemiology of learning impairments.

The discrepancy criteria, which identify arithmetic learning disability from the difference between an average of above-average performance on general cognitive capacity (typically the IQ) and the low performance on standardized math exams, are perhaps the most widely used in research investigations.

Similar to the discrepancy criteria, the absolute threshold criteria define a disability merely by a low score on a standardized math exam. After examining the child's reactions to a variety of psycho-pedagogical therapies, the response to intervention criteria is used to establish the diagnosis.

In this method, the fundamental criterion for diagnosis is the persistence of the difficulty rather than the disparity between capacity and performance.

The definition of how poor a performance on an accomplishment test must be in order to diagnose DD is the subject of the second major query. The 30th, 25th, 10th, and 5th percentiles are the most often used cut off scores. Higher cut off scores (25th and 30th percentiles) are less cautious and inevitably more likely to provide false positive results. A lower cut off score is less likely to result in a false positive when classifying children and is more conservative.

According to some academics, the sample of people who are given labels based on higher cut off scores is less stable over time since their math challenges are more likely to be caused by social, educational, and motivational variables.

However, the group of people whose performance falls below the more cautious cut off values is more homogeneous, and their impairments are more likely to be due to cognitive issues.

According to Mazzocco, people who perform below the fifth percentile should be classified as DD, while people who perform below the thirty percentiles should be classified as having "mathematical difficulties."

6.4.2. Comorbidity and Cognitive Heterogeneity

The investigation of DD nosology also involves studying its comorbidities with other syndromes and how the cognitive profile varies among individuals. It is estimated that only 30% of the DD children are free of comorbidities.

The main comorbidities of DD are with developmental dyslexia and ADHD, with comorbidity rates of 40% for the first and between 25 and 42% for the second.

Math learning challenges can result from a variety of cognitive deficiencies, with comorbidities primarily caused by a combination of abnormalities, according to Rubinsten and Henik. For instance, the pure examples (for which the name DD is assigned) result from deficits in the intraparietal sulcus's ability to operate properly on the neurological level as well as the cognitive level's abstract representation of numbers.

The co-occurrence of impairments in number processing and attentional systems might explain the comorbidity of dyscalculia and ADHD. As a result, comorbidity with dyslexia is caused by a single impairment in the angular gyrus, which would impair the ability to connect symbols (such as Arabic words and numerals) to their intended meaning. Comorbidity instances would be referred to as MLDs (math learning problems).

6.5. COGNITIVE MECHANISMS

Following the diversity of activities involved in math and the heterogeneity of manifestations observed in mathematics difficulties, the cognitive mechanisms are also diverse and related to basic numerical representations, working memory, visuospatial reasoning, and language. In the following, the literature on each of these mechanisms will be reviewed in more detail.

6.5.1. Non-symbolic Representations

Like all other animals, humans are born with only a simple, language-free system that is used to understand amounts in the environment. Naturally, this system is incapable of processing numerical symbols, which are, from a phylogenetic standpoint, a fairly recent cultural innovation that needs to be adopted by the human brain through enculturation.

The object-tracking system (OTS) and the approximation number system are two versions of this inherited preverbal number knowledge that are each regarded distinct subsystems (ANS). Early in infancy, the OTS achieves its developmental plateau and accurately depicts small numericities up to four.

The representation of bigger numerosity's analogically and consequently with increasing imprecision is carried out by the ANS. According to a widely accepted hypothesis, the ANS approximates and logarithmically compresses numbers in accordance with the traditional psychophysical rules of Weber and Fechner.

Numerous research teams have focused their attention on the connection between success in mathematics and fundamental number representations over the past ten years. A small body of research has found that math performance and ANS accuracy are positively correlated.

It has also been demonstrated that kids with DD have difficulties performing even basic tasks that use ANS representations, like predicting the size of a group of dots numerically and contrasting two sets of dots.

A very well-known idea holds that DD results from a deficiency in the fundamental representations of numbers. According to some experts, the ANS is responsible for this deficient representation of numbers.

According to some studies, the numerosity coding—which is in charge of processing exact but discrete numerical numbers and is the foundation of all mathematical thought—is the dedicated numerical system in the DD. See Butterworth for a comprehensive examination of these theories.

6.5.2. Symbolic Representations

Non-symbolic representations are not the only type of fundamental numerical representation. In fact, understanding symbolic representations of numbers marks a turning point in the growth of mathematical thinking. Children pick up a series of numerical words, but they still have no concept of quantity.

Gradually, these number words are associated with non-symbolic numerical representation. The mapping between a list of words and their respective numerical representations (meanings) will be established gradually as children become able to perform a range of new tasks.

For example, they can use these numeric words to label a set of objects (say "six" when looking to six dolls at a glance). These activities only develop completely around the age of five, when children master the principle of cardinality.

In a meta-analysis research, Schneider and colleagues discovered that symbolic comparison activities have a larger correlation with performance on arithmetic examinations than non-symbolic ones. Additionally, research has found that children with DD perform less well than controls on activities requiring comparison of symbolic numbers, such as Arabic numbers and number phrases.

Rousselle and Noël's approach suggests that DD may also result from a problem obtaining non-symbolic representations from numerical symbols (access deficit hypothesis).

6.5.3. Language

Mathematics is influenced by language in a variety of ways. Memorizing the multiplication table, writing and reading numbers, and learning the Arabic code are only a few of the verbal processing-intensive mathematical tasks.

According to Simmons et al. there is a genuine verbal-numerical relationship because rhyme detection or phoneme elision activities, which are frequently used to test phonological awareness, are not related to math learning.

Another critical stage in the growth of mathematical abilities is the development of language skills. A specific situation is the capacity to translate between numerical notations, which is frequently evaluated via activities involving the writing and reading of numbers and is referred to as number transcoding.

Number transcoding is especially important early in school life, since it demands the understanding of basic lexical and syntactic components of Arabic and verbal numerals. As suggested by previous studies, understanding the place-value syntax of Arabic numbers and matching it with number words constitutes a significant landmark that young children must reach in order to succeed in mathematical education.

According to some scientific data, youngsters become proficient in the numerical codes after three or four years of formal education. Children still have difficulty writing and reading Arabic numerals in the first year of elementary school (about 7 years old). After a short while, by the time students are in third and fourth grade (8 and 9 years old), the majority of these challenges with Arabic numbers have already been resolved.

In a study that looked at kids with and without MLD and used more difficult number transcoding tasks, Moura et al. looked at this topic further. Children with MLD had considerable number transcoding issues, according to the results.

The extent of this discrepancy diminished with age, demonstrating that children with MLD tend to function on par with their peers who are average achievers. These challenges were more pronounced in Arabic number writing.

Importantly, independent of students' arithmetic abilities, most errors in the first through fourth grades are easily explained by the syntactic complexity of numerals, since most mistakes were found in numbers with more digits and more syntactically complicated numbers (like 1002, 4015).

Children with MLD struggle with the syntactic structure of Arabic numerals, particularly with 3- and 4-digit numbers, until the fourth grade, according to a rigorous analysis of transcoding errors, whereas typical achievers appear to get over similar challenges around the third grade.

Additionally, within the first year of primary school, typical achievers appear to have a well-developed understanding of lexical primitives, whereas children with MLD exhibit a small but significant proportion of lexical errors (e.g., writing twelve as 20).

The frequent comorbidity between DD and dyslexia provides additional significant support for this connection between verbal and numerical skills. According to epidemiological research, over 40% of dyslexic kids also struggle in math.

Some studies suggest comorbidity rates up to 70%, which may be overestimated because of diagnostic criteria and constructs evaluated by standardized arithmetic and reading tests. Importantly, the comorbidity between DD and dyslexia is greater than would be expected by chance if the two entities were fully segregated independently.

An influential hypothesis states that children with developmental dyslexia struggle with numerical activities that rely on verbal codes, such as number transcoding and learning arithmetic facts.

6.5.4. Working Memory and Attention

The literature has extensively discussed the relationship between working memory and attention, as well as mathematical ability. In actuality, working memory resources and planning are needed for a wide range of numerical operations, including number transcoding, intricate calculations, and problem solving.

A significant portion of children with DD also have comorbid attention deficit hyperactivity disorder, according to Rubinsten and Henik (ADHD). It's interesting to note that the intraparietal sulcus, a part of the brain important for numerical development, is also engaged in a number of non-numerical processes, such as reasoning and attentional control.

Recent research suggests that attentional control is a key cognitive indicator of DD. According to Gilmore et al. frequently used dot comparison tasks need inhibitory control mechanisms because of tactics designed to adjust for nonnumerical visual characteristics.

Surprisingly, the executive function component of magnitude comparison tasks has a stronger relationship with math ability than the numerical component does. Similar to this, Szucs et al. hypothesized that children with DD struggle more than their usually developing peers to suppress irrelevant nonnumerical information.

6.5.4.1. Visuospatial Abilities

Visuospatial abilities are one of the most important skills related to arithmetic achievement, along with working memory. They are mostly related to performance in multidigit calculations, particularly those requiring borrowing and carry-over techniques.

Although there is evidence that visuospatial skills play a role in calculation, there is no well-defined visuospatial subgroup of DD, making a pure visuospatial deficiency in children with DD less obvious than the other cognitive skills mentioned above. The so-called nonverbal learning handicap has generated much discussion regarding the co-occurrence of math and visuospatial difficulties. The visuospatial component of working memory is observed to be impaired in children with DD, despite the fact that there is disagreement over whether or not there is a visuospatial impairment in DD. Importantly, it is usually noted that under these situations, the linguistic portion of working memory is intact.

Despite the fact that the cognitive underpinnings of numerical representations and mathematical performance have only recently been studied, a substantial body of scientific evidence has already been gathered, enabling significant advancements in our understanding of how mathematical abilities develop as well as in the detection and treatment of mathematical difficulties.

Even so, there are still a number of unanswered questions in this extensive field of study. Longitudinal and replication studies are particularly important at the moment.

6.6. AUTISM SPECTRUM DISORDER

Developmental impairment known as ASD is brought on by variations in the brain. Some ASD sufferers have a recognized distinction, like a genetic disorder. Other factors are still unknown. ASD is thought to have a number of underlying reasons that interact to alter how people typically develop. There is still a lot people don't know about these factors and how they affect people with ASD.

People with ASD may behave, interact, communicate, and learn differently than most other people. Frequently, their appearance does not distinguish them from others. People with ASD may have a wide range of skills.

For example, some people with ASD may have advanced conversation skills whereas others may be nonverbal. Some people with ASD need a lot of help in their daily lives; others can work and live with little to no support.

ASD begins before the age of 3 years and can last throughout a person's life, although symptoms may improve over time. Some children show ASD symptoms within the first 12 months of life. In others, symptoms may not show up until 24 months of age or later.

Some ASD children develop new skills and reach developmental milestones up until the age of 18 to 24 months, at which point they cease doing so or lose the abilities they previously possessed.

Figure 6.5. A word cloud of autism spectrum disorder.

Source: Image by Flickr.

Adolescents and young adults with ASD may struggle to make and keep friends, communicate with peers and adults, or comprehend what is appropriate behavior in the workplace or at school.

Because they also have illnesses like anxiety, depression, or attention-deficit/hyperactivity disorder, which affect persons with ASD more frequently than those without ASD, they may be noticed by medical professionals.

6.7. LEARNING DISABILITIES IN CHILDREN WITH AUTISM

Many times, cognitive strategies used by children with ASDs do not fit the typical developmental profile. As a result, it should come as no surprise that numerous studies on education and literacy will center on how children with this illness learn. Unfortunately, the reality is far different.

Despite the fact that many creatures have the ability to learn, only humans purposefully impart knowledge, according to Fonseca.

According to the literature, problems learning conditional links between concepts and stimuli might affect a person's life and their ability to communicate with others.

Integration of auditory and visual stimuli depends heavily on communication. In this approach, human engagement with the environment leads to environmental cognition, and the relationship between sensory stimuli and learning is the result.

Figure 6.6. Four images depicting autistic children: A girl covering her ears due to auditory sensitivity, a boy passionately talking about his favorite subject (cats), a girl lining up objects and finger flicking (stimming).

Source: Image by Wikimedia commons.

6.7.1. Learning by Children with ASD: Language, Social, and Cognitive Factors

Language is known to develop mostly as a result of significant events and circumstances. Although it depends on linguistic skills, physical health, and cognitive development, the environment's expectations and support are crucial to a child's learning process.

Interaction with other significant individuals is necessary for the development of a socially shared code that results in the attribution of meaning to the world's many elements and experiences. Meaningful events and experiences are also necessary for language and memory.

Even though skills acquired through systematic training typically yield quick benefits, they are quickly lost if they are not put to use or connected to important contexts.

Based on these concepts, it would seem plausible to assume that children with ASDs have certain learning disadvantages since they have a social incapacity that is a characteristic of ASDs, with varying degrees of social interaction impairment.

In this way, it is acknowledged that language impairment in children with autism is not always linked to linguistic structures, even though some children do have issues with them.

Language challenges in children with ASD are mostly pragmatic abilities-related and involve varying degrees of inabilities, from lack of touch to subtle difficulties with interaction and conversation skills.

It is crucial to comprehend the child's context and environment, evaluate the impact of each child's limitations, and create intervention plans that address the most effective and timely intervention for this reason, among others.

Several recent studies show that including families in the therapeutic process of children with ASD increases better outcomes and prognosis than traditional one-on-one therapeutic approaches.

Authors like Winnicot consider emotional health as the development's "back bone," allowing cognitive and linguistic development and therefore enabling successful learning processes. Regardless of the causal relation and of the hierarchy among these areas of development, the importance of emotional health to learning is unquestionable.

Perceiving and processing sensorial information and positively assimilating and interpreting information in order to build and learn healthily and creatively—that is, so that cognitive processing really occurs—depend on emotional health.

The number and impact of studies emphasizing the value of involving parents and carers is growing, and the results are becoming more and more consistent in showing that these processes' success is positively influenced by both the quality of life of parents and carers and their participation in intervention processes for children with ASD.

Research on the learning abilities of people with ASD and ADHD has been prompted by the symptoms that frequently show up in people with ASD who also fit the ADHD diagnosis.

It is crucial to think about both diagnoses from a neurocognitive perspective, posing queries and conducting studies involving tasks that call for abilities like executive function (EF), theory of mind (ToM), language, and even correlations between them in order to look for potential causal connections.

A goal-setting and goal-accomplishing cognitive process, including the skills required for it, is how executive function is now defined. They include cognitive flexibility, inhibitory control, and working memory. Working memory is the capacity to retrieve previously stored information to complete a task. The ability to suppress any behaviors or knowledge that might obstruct or complicate the completion of a task or goal is known as inhibitory control.

The EF of the person with ASD affects their learning, autonomy, and social life. EF is intimately related to communicative abilities. Because of this, it might be challenging to comprehend how EF impairment directly affects kids with ASD. Even the studies cannot agree on EF deficits in this cohort at this time.

ASD individuals do not exhibit greater impairment than other groups with typical development (TD), ADHD, and developmental language disorder (DLD) indicating that this may not be the primary impairment of the disorder. However, some studies show deficit and risk indicating the causal relationship between EF and other abilities.

Even when matched for IQ and school age, some researchers, like Kado and collaborators, indicate in their publication that children with ASD and ADHD perform similarly in terms of working memory, but that these children do worse than TD children.

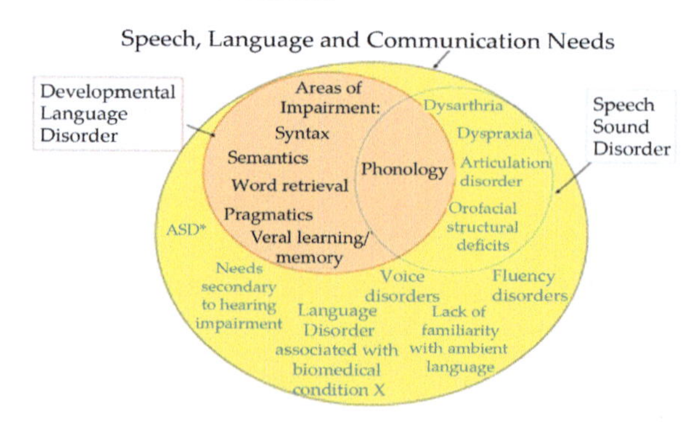

Figure 6.7. A Venn diagram comparing the impairment in common speech, language, and communication needs.

Source: Image by Wikimedia commons.

When compared to those without ASD matched for IQ, other studies like Roleofs and collaborators did not discover any appreciable variations in working memory between adolescents and adults with ASD and intellectual handicap. Some studies divide the evaluation of this cognitive function into verbal working memory and visual or spatial working memory in an effort to better understand the relationship between working memory and language. Hill's paper from 2015 is a really intriguing study that aims to explain how working memory and language proficiency are related.

Children with ASD and DLD aged 5 to 8 had their working memory assessed and compared. Children with and without language impediment made up the two groups of ASD kids in the study.

Children who spoke properly performed better than those who had language difficulties. Furthermore, in the majority of verbal working memory activities, children with DLD and reduced language performance were comparable to that of children with ASD, indicating their interdependence. Additionally, inhibitory control results in this.

The findings of inhibitory control studies in children with ASD are diverse. Some indicate significant losses, while others find no differences compared to ADHD and DT. A widely used test to verify this ability is Stroop, which requires a refined language skill. Corbett and his collaborators performed several inhibitory control tests, with and without the need for verbal expressive language.

In the test, requiring verbal ability, children with ASD and ADHD had worse performances than TD children. In the test where the verbal expressive ability was not required—children should hear or saw a certain number to answer or not—children with ASD performed worse than children with DT and ADHD.

It's crucial to remember that the job requires language skills even in the visual working memory exam, which is meant to not require them.

The similar tendency also appears in studies that aim to measure cognitive flexibility through tasks using some degree of expressive or comprehensive language.

The lack of sensitivity to these skills in neuropsychological examinations, which are meant to evaluate language abilities, has been a common issue in most suggested assessments. In most cases, these evaluations are conducted by psychologists who lack the expertise necessary to identify language deficiencies, let alone to distinguish or specify the language structures necessary for such purposes.

Many people mistakenly view language merely as an expressive or verbal act, which is fundamentally incorrect. They also fail to examine language's cultural component or even to assess language competence alone, frequently taking the child's cognitive processes into account.

And as was already mentioned, this information is crucial to elucidate a potential causative connection or to throw light on a potential connection between cognitive and language domains, not just in children with ASD.

6.7.2. Learning to Read

For kids with regular development, learning to talk can come effortlessly from taking part in and observing conversations with their parents and other members of their community.

In contrast, learning to read and write is a difficult process that involves several interconnected steps, such as realizing how the visual symbols relate to the spoken language.

Since writing is regarded as a representation of language, several papers discuss the significance and interdependence of strong oral language development for the achievement of written code acquisition.

According to the clinical neuropsychology literature, children with any developmental or learning issue benefit from having their cognitive strengths and limitations assessed. Given the diversity of therapeutic settings for children with ASD, determining a child's unique strengths and weaknesses aids in better focusing educational plans and medical care as well as identifying any potential problem areas.

Westerveld et al. argue that learning to read is just another challenge for children with ASD. In their study, they found that approximately 30–60% of these children present some difficulty to develop literacy. It is important to highlight that even higher functioning children are also part of the statistics.

Jones et al. described that the cognitive heterogeneity of children with ASD is an element that makes it difficult to characterize the academic difficulties of this population. In addition, they report that cognitive abilities may not be congruent with their writing operations.

According to Fletcher and Miciak's article, a child's cognitive test deficiencies may not always point in the same direction as their learning challenges. A child's learning difficulty is not "why" they have a cognitive deficiency.

Individual disparities in language skills in the areas of phonology, semantics, and syntax have been discovered in the literature as a potential explanation for this diversity in the development of reading and writing in children with ASD.

According to Davidson and Weismer, reading difficulties can be divided into those that affect comprehension or decoding skills. To take into account what is known about reading ability in people with ASD, it is crucial to understand the history of reading instruction for kids with extraordinary educational needs.

Gabig found that children with ASD performed less well in vocabulary tests, which may have an adverse effect on phonological processing abilities. She also discovered that several decoding-related skills seem to be mostly unaltered.

The relationship between phonological awareness and reading abilities is not strong due to the fact that the causes of the phonological deficiency in autism are still unclear. However, it does interfere with the quality of lexical and mental representations.

Others have questioned whether specific linguistic material flaws or issues with perception, timing, or long-term memory are to blame for poor reading performance.

Overall, studies show that while reading comprehension may be comparable to that of typically developing learners, children with ASD typically struggle to integrate information.

In other words, individuals struggle to recall and integrate the meanings required for reading comprehension, including the capacity to draw connections between the information read and their existing knowledge and the capacity to draw conclusions.

According to the research, the majority of autistic children have average reading comprehension skills and can correctly spell words according to their age and grade level. The literature, however, is still unable to explain why phonological awareness follows the successful phonetic decoding demonstrated by autistic children.

There have been a number of studies that question whether children with ASD would perform worse while decoding pseudowords than when reading sight words due to rote memorizing of the visual shape of words. Most of their findings suggested that autistic kids do not exhibit a preference for visual recognition of sight words over decoding of pseudowords.

It implies that kids with ASD are able to recognize written words utilizing their visual and phonological systems. Accordingly, findings incline us to think that kids with autism can gain from additional access points to produce strong reading and writing skills.

Hyperlexia is frequently one condition presented by children with ASD. It is characterized by a child's precocious ability to read (far above what would be expected at their age). As with all individuals, children with hyperlexia have a wide range of skills and deficits.

The high abilities to decode do not exclude the possibility that children may have a cognitive, language learning and/or social disorder.

What experts argue is that content that can be "formally" taught can be more easily learned by children with ASD. Already "intuitive" content such as phonological awareness skills would be less understood by this population.

Corso et al. investigated the relationship between several neuropsychological processes and reading tasks. They came to the conclusion that executive function tasks showed the strongest significant connections.

Pellicano said that there are only studies with the fractionation of these functions, that is, as if only one of these components can be especially disturbed in autism, and that there are no studies that precisely study the nature of executive functions in autism.

Studies that contrast how well kids with ASD do in terms of their theory of mind abilities are also frequently available (ToM). According to certain studies, it is uncommon to find kids with impaired executive function but normal theory of mind skills.

Understanding the nature of these skills cannot be disregarded during the evaluation of reading and writing skills because their application is crucial to mental and behavioral functioning.

One explanation for why people with ASD may struggle to portray situations involving theory of mind is that they struggle to integrate information that is pertinent to both the context and their own self-representation.

This would provide an explanation for the text comprehension issues that are frequently noted in this demographic, particularly the issues with understanding pragmatic and nonliteral language features.

Between disruptions, there may be differences in EF and literacy functional deficiencies. It is possible to learn which systems may be compromised and, more significantly, how to activate them by evaluating them and determining their deficiencies.

6.8. IMPORTANT CONSIDERATIONS FOR CLINICAL INTERVENTION IN SLP

All of the children's deficiencies in oral or written language may be taken into account in the intervention strategy. It's crucial to link details about the student's facilitating pathways, whether they are auditory, visual, or motor. The therapist should then look at whether different processing modalities have an impact to get a fuller picture of the child's future perceptual abilities.

Technology is reportedly employed in educational settings as a powerful tool for engaging students, according to Bosseler and Massaro.

Some writers contend that if people ensure the use of materials that cover the various paths, learning can happen only as a result of repeated exposures without needing feedback and official intervention from the therapist. Bosseler and Massaro noted that children benefited from both hearing and seeing, however that spoken language can better direct language development than modalities alone.

What people should anticipate is that in order to apply functionality and employ stimulating content in a meaningful way, it must be learned operatively, processed, stored, and associated to a set of experiences.

Currently, there are already some available therapeutic methods that can be developed by parents at home. However, there are not yet numerous clinical articles that allow a more accurate interpretation of the results. Thus, there are limitations in measuring the effectiveness of these approaches in treating autistic children, especially in the long-term.

There are authors who emphasize how important it is to encourage these types of family-based therapeutic approaches as key interveners; however, understand that caregiver training should be done very carefully so that such interventions are not inadequately developed and reinforce difficulties and changes in child development.

As can be seen, environmental support is crucial to a child's ability to learn. The results imply that children with ASDs may experience certain learning disabilities as a result of their social impairment caused by ASD characteristics.

According to the literature, parental involvement, and support in intervention processes with children with ASD have a favorable impact on the procedures' results. Since the carers have provided the knowledge and resources, the intervention approach should include all of these opportunities and resources for oral and written language stimulation.

Our ultimate objective for these children is to establish a link between learning and functionality because there are learning problems among children with autism.

6.9. CONCLUSION

This chapter provides a summary of the relationship between autism, behavioral development disorder, and learning difficulties. This chapter's introduction describes ADHD as a particular cause of learning impairments and developmental dyscalculia. Highlights from this chapter are also included for ASD and learning difficulties in autistic children. A discussion of the crucial factors for clinical intervention in SLP is provided toward the end of this chapter.

REFERENCES

1. Moura, R., Garcia, S., & Lopes-Silva, J. B., (2020). Developmental dyscalculia: Nosological status and cognitive underpinnings. *Learning Disabilities – Neurological Bases, Clinical Features and Strategies of Intervention* [Preprint]. Available at: https://doi.org/10.5772/intechopen.91003.
2. Padhy, S. K., Sahoo, M. K., & Biswas, H., (2015). Psychological co-morbidity in children with specific learning disorders. *Journal of Family Medicine and Primary Care*, *4*(1), 21. Available at: https://doi.org/10.4103/2249-4863.152243.
3. Pop-Jordanova, N., (2020). ADHD as a specific cause for learning disability. *Learning Disabilities – Neurological Bases, Clinical Features and Strategies of Intervention* [Preprint]. Available at: https://doi.org/10.5772/intechopen.91272.
4. Sun, I. Y. I., Cortez, A. C. M., & Fernandes, F. D. M., (2019). *Learning Disabilities in Children with Autism*. IntechOpen. Available at: https://www.intechopen.com/chapters/69030 (Accessed: December 19, 2022).
5. *What is Autism Spectrum Disorder?* (2022). Centers for Disease Control and Prevention. Centers for Disease Control and Prevention. Available at: https://www.cdc.gov/ncbddd/autism/facts.html (accessed on 14 October 2023).

CHAPTER 7

Assessment of Speech and Language-Based Learning Disabilities

Contents

This chapter talks about the contradictions around inter-collegial collaboration regarding differentiated assessment for pupils with dyslexia in Greek state secondary schools. This chapter explains the child with learning difficulties and their writing. This chapter provides highlights on the transition possibilities for adolescents with intellectual disabilities into adulthood. This chapter also explains the speech therapy work with children having specific language impairment (SLI). At the end of this chapter, this chapter also explains the speech therapy impact on SLI in Russia.

7.1. CONTRADICTIONS AROUND INTER-COLLEGIAL COLLABORATION REGARDING DIFFERENTIATED ASSESSMENT FOR PUPILS WITH DYSLEXIA IN GREEK STATE SECONDARY SCHOOLS

In two Greek state secondary schools, the topic of inter-collegial cooperation regarding differentiated testing and marking for students with dyslexia is covered in this chapter. Provision for dyslexia calls for interdepartmental cooperation. According to Mackay, all staff members should have access to portraits of all students who have particular learning issues, as well as their unique teaching and learning approaches.

In the Hunter-Carsch study, one successful step undertaken by SENCOs was the establishment of student profiles. In one school, SEN directories and student profiles were implemented to improve communication between SEN personnel and curriculum topic teachers.

The challenge for special needs instructors in reaching out to all subject teachers regarding specific kids is also mentioned by Pollock and Waller. They propose that a list of students in need of assistance be frequently circulated, stressing their individual need. They also advise teachers to provide information about students with dyslexia.

As far as the Greek context is concerned, Arapogianni reported lack of contact and collaboration of teachers with other professionals. Lappas also reported lack of communication and collaboration between learning support teachers and mainstream teachers in Greek primary schools because of the lack of responsibility of the head teachers for the provision for specific learning difficulties, which lay only with the learning support teachers.

Similar approaches (semi-structured interviews) were used to examine whether inter-collegial communication is successful from the perspectives of parents, students, teachers, and head teachers, but not from those of learning support teachers and policy agents, as Lappas did. Additionally, my research was done in Lappas senior schools rather than primary schools.

7.1.1. Theoretical Framework

It was necessary to develop a theoretical framework that examines collectively how people learn inside organizational systems. One such framework was offered by Engestrom's work and activity theory. When Vygotsky attempted to explain the learning process, he proposed that learning allows people to think or do things that are beyond their capacity and that this is done in a historical, cultural, and social context, with one or more people. This was the beginning of the sociocultural activity theory.

Vygotsky believed that human activity happens when the subjects, those whose actions are analyzed, resolve a shared problem, an 'object,' by using 'tools' to achieve a goal. Engeström describes how the current understanding of activity theory has evolved through three generations of research.

The first generation contributed to activity theory the idea of 'mediation,' which was represented in Vygotsky's triangular model linking the subject and the object through mediating artefacts.

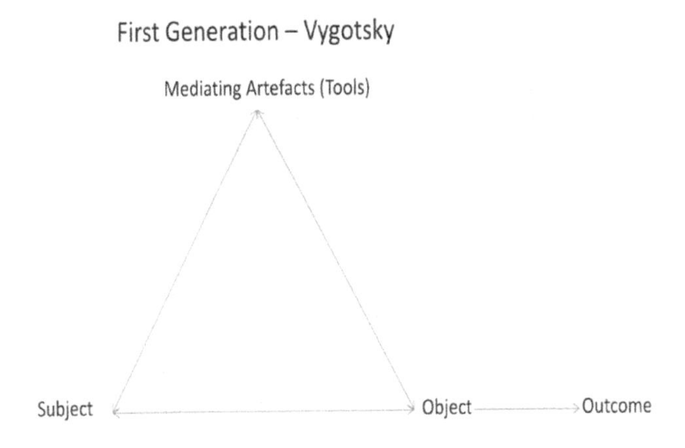

Figure 7.1. Vygotsky's mediated action triangle.

Source: Image by Wikimedia commons.

Engeström expanded the triangular depiction of an activity system in the second generation, which was based on Leont'ev's work. This allowed for the investigation of activity systems at an organizational level rather than a focus on the individual actors using tools. The addition of the components of community, regulations, and labor division to the Vygotskian triangle indicates the social or organizational factors in an activity system. The choice of activity theory as the theoretical framework for the data collection and analysis was made since it permitted the inclusion of various participant groups and the examination of their relationships.

The second activity theory principle, multi-voicedness, was helpful because it enabled the examination of several perspectives on the same topic, including those of EFL teachers, students, parents, and the Ministry of Education.

Therefore, the English as a Foreign Language (EFL) instructor 1 and one dyslexic student, George, are the topics of learning for the activity system in School 1, the institution where the study was conducted. Differentiated assessment could be an object of learning, or what the students are working on.

An activity system's goal is the product of the "creative endeavor" that can be made if the issues are fixed. Inclusion of students with dyslexia may be a goal.

The community representing the wider sociocultural influences includes the context of the activity, that is, the people who are concerned with the same object: the headteacher of the school, the other students and teachers, the Local Education Authority (LEA) and the Ministry of Education. Therefore, the activity is a collective one and not an individual action of the teacher only or the students only.

The division of labor refers to the division of tasks between the EFL teacher, the headteacher and student. The rules are the principles regulating the actions of the participants and they can be both written and unwritten, for example, the national policies on dyslexia and their interpretations by the headteacher of the school as well as the routines and professional practices of the teachers.

Activity theory is frequently associated with the use of case studies that take context and its specifics into account because it is extremely contextual and investigates specific local practices. A case study was an acceptable design that made use of activity theory as a theoretical foundation.

A case study was appropriate since it aimed to explore the complexity of dyslexia provision in sufficient detail and required the use of multiple sources for data collecting.

7.2. THE CHILD WITH LEARNING DIFFICULTIES AND HIS WRITING: A STUDY OF CASE

One goal of the Mexican educational system is for children to learn traditional writing in the early grades of elementary school. For this reason, it is important for students to comprehend the alphabetic code's purpose and significance. They can join a discursive community in this way.

The students in the elementary school are a diverse mix. Some students exhibit varying degrees of writing proficiency. This is because of the supportive social and familial environments for literacy. As a result, some kids have had more opportunity than others to engage in reading and writing activities.

As a result, by the end of the academic year, some students still do not understand the alphabetical basis of writing. They exhibit initial or intermediate writing acquisition level characteristics. Children find it challenging to learn writing simultaneously, at the time that the educational system or teachers recommend.

Additionally, there can be students in the classroom that have learning challenges. Some kids are taught by the Department of Special Education. Students with exceptional educational needs demonstrate more learning challenges than their peers.

To complete the educational goals, they need more resources. These scholars emphasize that special education needs vary from person to person. These requirements result from the interaction between a student's surroundings and personal traits.

Therefore, any child may have special educational needs, even if he/ she does not have any physical disability. However, some students with learning difficulties do not have a complete assessment about their special educational needs.

On the one hand, their school is far from urban areas; on the other hand, there are not enough teachers of special education for every school. In consequence, school teachers do not know their students' educational needs and teach in the same way. Thereby, students with learning difficulties do not have the necessary support in the classroom.

Writing-related learning impairments can be quickly identified. Special education students struggle to connect phoneme and grapheme, which makes it difficult for them to acquire the alphabetical principle of writing. Children thus exhibit their conceptualizations of writing in various ways.

Teachers may edit the writing that their students produce because they don't write in a traditional manner. Stigmatization of special education students occurs in the classroom. They are viewed as less desirable. Children don't pass the school year when it's over.

As a result, the goal of this essay is to describe a youngster with special needs who attends a multi-grade rural school in Mexico. The child is shown writing a list of words both with and without the aid of a picture in this text. Analysis includes figuring out how the youngster approaches writing, his conceptualizations of the process, and any challenges or errors he encounters. These errors are signs that you're learning.

This young man resides in the country. He exhibits unique educational needs in terms of learning. Because he lives in a rural outpost, he has never received specialized attention. He had some learning challenges despite being integrated into the regular school system.

He had a reputation for not being a good student. In light of this, this work explains Alejandro's writing and his activities following two years of preschool and one year of primary school.

7.2.1. Children with Learning Difficulties and Their Diagnosis

According to the National Institute for the Evaluation of Education, Mexican education system provides basic education (preschool, elementary, and secondary school) for students with special educational needs. There are two types of special attention: Centre of Multiple Attention (CAM, in Spanish) and Units of Service and Support to Regular Education (USAER, in Spanish).

Children with particular educational needs visit this Centre in the first one. These kids receive care in accordance with their basic educational needs. In the second, special education teachers visit classrooms and offer assistance to pupils.

Teachers in the schools are also given information by these teachers. This promotes inclusiveness and educational equity in Mexican schools.

The psycho-pedagogical assessment is a suggestion made by the Mexican educational system to find students that need special education. Student with greater difficulty is identified by teacher. An expert teacher administers various tests that have been predetermined separately.

This Assessment is Organized as Follows:

Physical Appearance: The teacher gives a description of the child's appearance. These characteristics reveal, among other things, the kind of food the student consumes, the care given to him or her, and the level of parental involvement.

Conduct seen during the assessment: The teacher should note the following in this section: the circumstances under which the assessment was conducted attitude, conduct, and interests of the youngster.

Child's Development History: This section presents conditions in which pregnancy developed, physical development (ages in which child held his/her head, sat, crawled, walked, etc.), language development (verbal response to sounds and voices, age in which said his/her first words and phrases, etc.), family (characteristics of their family and social environment, frequent activities, etc.), hetero-family history (vision, hearing, etc.), medical history (health conditions, diseases, etc.), and scholar history (age at which he/she started school, type of school, difficulties, etc.).

Present Condition: In this, there are four aspects:

- It refers to a student's general characteristics, such as their intellectual (information processing, attention, memory, understanding), motor (functional skills to move, take objects, position of his or her body, etc.), communicative (phonological, semantic, syntactic, and pragmatic levels), adaptational, social-interactional, and emotional development (the way of perceiving the world and people). Although there is not enough information about them, each one states the instruments he offers.
- The second consideration is the degree of curricular competency. The teacher determines what the student is capable of performing in respect to the objectives and subject matter of the prescribed curriculum.
- The third factor has to do with learning preferences and want to learn. It describes the actual surroundings in which the child works, their interests, their degree of attention, their approaches to problem-solving, and the rewards he receives.
- Information regarding the student's environment, including aspects of the home, family, and societal context that affect the child's learning, makes up the fourth aspect.

The ability to detect children's general educational needs is provided by psycho-pedagogical assessment. The schoolteacher could learn about the kids' challenges in this way. It is, nonetheless, a generic evaluation. It covers a number of topics but doesn't delve deeper into any of them.

As a result, it doesn't suggest a new evaluation. It comprises of showcasing one child's writing challenges, his conceptualization of writing, and some errors he makes.

7.2.2. Students With Learning Difficulties and Their Scholar Integration

The Mexican educational system has been attempting to provide special education programs to pupils in basic education since 1993. Promoting the inclusion of these kids in normal education classes was the first step.

But all that was accomplished was the student's inclusion in the school. As a result, the educational system looked for ways to give teachers recommendations. Students that struggle with learning can be assisted in the classroom at the same time in this way.

The attention given to kids with learning challenges, whether they have physical limitations or not, has been directly correlated with educational inclusion. However, this procedure suggests that the school will change. For this, it is vital to enlighten the educational community, raise awareness among educators, keep teachers current, and collaborate with family members and specialist teachers.

Currently, the Mexican educational system views educational integration as a process in which each student who has learning challenges is treated individually. The goal of educational integration is to modify the curriculum to fit the needs of the kid. Curricula adequacy is one of the strategies used to assist pupils with learning challenges. This is a suggestion for an individual curriculum. To meet the kids' specialized educational demands is its main goal. The current Mexican educational system suggests that curricula should be flexible to support learning processes. However, it's crucial to take into account what the child already understands about a certain topic.

It's important to understand how youngsters acquire written language in order to better understand how to teach them. If teachers do not have enough knowledge about their students, it is impossible to create a curriculum that is adequate. Children are, nonetheless, seen as knowledge creators. As a result, the procedure has learning challenges.

7.3. ALEJANDRO'S CASE: AN EXAMPLE

Information about Alejandro's private life is provided here. He introduced himself to the people when they went to his school for additional investigation. The boy remained silent in class, so they concentrated on him. He did not participate in the activities and sat in a corner of the work table constantly. To learn more about him, this has been discussed with his teacher and mother.

Alejandro is a student of an elementary multigrade rural school. He was 7 years old at the time of the study. He was in the second grade of the elementary school. His school is located in the region of the "Great Mountains" of the state of Veracruz, Mexico.

It is a rural area, marginalized. To get to this town from the municipal head, it is necessary to take a rural taxi for half an hour. Then, you have to walk on a dirt road for approximately 50 min.

Alejandro's family is integrated by six people. He is the third of the four sons. He lives with his parents. His house is made of wood. His father works in the field: farming of corn, beans, and rising of sheep. His mother is a housewife and also works in the field. They have a low economic income.

They consequently get a scholarship. He also has an elder sibling who struggled with learning in school. His mother claims that both of her children struggle with learning. However, they lack the funds to support their boys' learning challenges. Additionally, their home is far from any special institutions.

The youngster has struggled with learning his entire life. He spent two years at preschool. At this level, he did not, however, acquire the required abilities. This child was mute and nonverbal during class. Teachers at the preschool thought he was deaf. However, he engaged in conversation with his classmates at scholar recess. In the classroom, Alejandro took his time using words to express himself.

Alejandro continued to struggle with learning as he started kindergarten. He also kept to himself during class. He merely observed what his peers did. He was inactive during class. He simply drew some lines in his notebook after removing it from his rucksack.

He occasionally exchanged words with his peers. Alejandro was asked a question, but he remained silent. He did not respond and lowered his gaze. He simply ducked his head and remained for some time.

Alejandro participated in activities apart than those of his peers while he was in the second grade. He painted some drawings that his teacher had drawn for him. On other occasions, the instructor gave him some letters to paint. Over several hours, the toddler completed every activity. He took his time doing his workout. On occasion, he spent two hours painting some drawings.

Although Alejandro requires specialized attention, he has not received it. He has not had a full psycho-pedagogical assessment at school by specialized teachers. His school does not have these teachers. Also, the child was not submitted to neurological structural examination or neurophysiological studies to exclude an organic origin of his learning difficulties.

His parents do not have enough financial resources to do this type of study for him. In addition, one specialized institution that can do this type of study for free is in Mexico City. It is so far from child's house. It would be expensive for the child's parents. Therefore, he is only attended as a regular school student.

7.4. ALEJANDRO'S WRITING

In this part, Alejandro explains how he writes. Alejandro, who is seven years old and in the second grade of the elementary school, is already mentioned. Because the youngster has already completed one year of primary school, according to his instructor, he should be writing in a normal manner. However, this is not the case. While the majority of his peers write in a formal style, he does not.

There are three parts to this section. Writing words is discussed in the second section, writing for pictures is discussed in the third section, and the first section shows how Alejandro wrote his name and how he recognizes letters and numbers.

7.4.1. Alejandro Writes His Name and Some Letters and Numbers

Alejandro had to write his name, as well as a few letters and numbers he is familiar with, in the first section of the assignment. Two circumstances led to the request for his name. The interviewer also spoke with other students at the same school; thus, the first reason is to identify the sheet.

Additionally, each student's group's written products needed to be identified. The second reason was to watch how he wrote and recognized letters and numerals in his name. The boy was instructed to sign his name at the top of the sheet by the interviewer. Alejandro took a moment to consider the directions when the interviewer gave them. He wasn't pressured or cut off. He remained still for some seconds. The kid looked all about before turning to the sheet. Once again picking up the pencil, he penned the following on the paper.

In the interview, Alejandro's writing was examined. Was there anything missing, he questioned. Alejandro knew his name, the interviewer was certain, and his writing was incomplete. But Alejandro was serious, and he took his time studying the material.

The interviewer inquired as to whether his name was finished. "No," the child replied. The child was questioned about his memory of his name. Alejandro shook his head in denial. They then moved on to their next duty.

Alejandro created the idea behind his name. He may have had some chances to sign his name, in our opinion. He may have been instructed by his teacher to sign his notebooks as part of the classwork. Alejandro chose letters with traditional sound values, as can be seen.

This is due to the fact that he used his name's first three letters: ALJ (Alejandro). His name's initial two letters are represented by the first two letters. He then puts "J" in place of "E" (ALE-) (ALJ). Alejandro says he doesn't recall the others, though. This may indicate that while he has his name memorized, at that particular time he was unable to recall the remaining letters, or these letters are all that he can recall.

Subsequently, the interviewer asked Alejandro to write some letters and numbers he knew. The sequence was: a letter, a number, a letter, another letter, and number. In every Alejandro' writing, the interviewer asked the child what he wrote.

For this task, Alejandro wrote for a long time. He did not hurry to write. He looked at sheet and wrote. The child looked at the interviewer, looked at the sheet again and after a few seconds he wrote. The interviewer asked about every letter or number.

Alejandro distinguishes between letters and numbers, as can be seen. Every signal was correctly written by him. That example, he responded appropriately when asked to write a letter or a number by the interviewer. Alejandro is able to distinguish between what is appropriate for reading and what is not by using this method.

People must also note that the child only uses a small number of letters. His writing lacked consonants. He exclusively made use of the vowels A (capital and lowercase) and E. (lower). It demonstrates to us how he distinguishes between capital and lowercase letters. Additionally, he knows what vowels and letters are because to the child's response to the interviewer's question about them.

7.4.2. Writing Words from the Same Semantic Field

To find out what the child already understands or has developed regarding the writing system, ask the youngster to write words on the board at random. Although it is known that Alejandro has learning disabilities and has not developed a normal writing style, nevertheless it is required to ask him to write a few words.

This is for tracking and evaluating his writing abilities, the body of knowledge he has amassed, and the challenges he faces. Each term has the standard form in Spanish printed next to it. Additionally, these words are written in English in the parenthesis.

At the beginning of the interview, Alejandro did not want to do the task. He was silent for several seconds. He did not write anything. He looked at the sheet and the window. The interviewer insisted several times and suspended the recording to encourage the child to write.

Alejandro mentioned he could not write, because he did not know the letters and so he would not do it. However, the interviewer insisted him. After several minutes, Alejandro took the pencil and started to write.

Alejandro spent a minute or two writing each word. He occasionally needed more seconds or minutes. He turned around and took a glance at the sheet. At other moments, he was silent and turning the sheet over. Additionally, it has been established that he requires space to compose. This demonstrates his insecurity and lack of writing knowledge.

He was terrified of being wrong and that the interviewer would penalize him for it, which made him feel insecure. He can receive a grade when he makes a mistake in class. He is ignorant since he is unfamiliar with several letters and has a limited understanding of the writing system. Alejandro must therefore consider writing and find for ways to portray it. The kid needs more time to write because of this.

The lack of a phoneme-grapheme link established by the youngster has been noted. When reading every word, he merely moves his finger from left to right. He doesn't create a connection between the letters he utilized. There is no correlation between the number of letters in each word and its length. Additionally, because there can occasionally be variations in the quantity and type of letters, the kid does not create a constant. Alejandro used letters unrelated to the conventional writing of the words. For example, when he wrote GATO (cat), Alejandro used the following letters: inpnAS. It is possible to identify that no letter corresponds to the word. Perhaps, Alejandro wrote those letters because they are recognized or remembered by him.

Alejandro only uses a small number of standard letters. He does this by using the vowels A, E, I, and O. These vowels were less commonly utilized by the child. Every word contains at least one vowel. Alejandro used two vowels when writing PEZ (fish). It is further noticed that he either writes these vowels at the start of the word or at the end. It is not known why he arranges them that way, though. Perhaps he uses this as a differentiating concept.

In Alejandro's writing, there is distinction between the qualitative and the quantitative. In other words, he did not consistently write every word. His writing is unique in every way. Every word contains a unique mix of letters in a different number. Two words have different letters when they have the same number of letters.

When Alejandro wrote MARIPOSA (butterfly), he used five letters. The number of letters is less than what he used for GATO (cat). Maybe he wrote that because the interviewer said "butterfly is a small animal." This is because the cat is bigger than the butterfly. Therefore, it may be possible that he used lesser letters for butterfly.

Figure 7.2. MARIPOSA (butterfly).

Source: Image by Wikimedia commons.

The word "dog" (PERRO) has five letters in Spanish. 5 letters were written by Alejandro. In this instance, Alejandro's writing contains all the required letters. But it appears that he is exempt from any writing regulations.

This is due to two factors. The first is that the size of the animal does not correspond. Since the horse is bigger than the dog, Alejandro needed less letters for the horse.

Second, PERRO (dog) has two syllables and CABALLO (horse) has three. Alejandro represented two syllables by using additional letters. Additionally, a pseudo-letter is seen to exist. Horizontally, it resembles an inverted F as well as a D and a B.

When Alejandro wrote the word PEZ (fish), the interviewer first enquired as to how many letters it required. The youngster remained silent. When the interviewer repeated the question, the student responded that he was unsure.

The interviewer then instructed to write PEZ (fish). Alejandro did nothing but stare at the sheet for a while before speaking. He was repeatedly questioned by the interviewer, but he never responded. Alejandro penned: E. after a while. The child was asked by the interviewer if he was done. He made a head-nod denial. He began writing after one minute. Six letters were found in his writing, as it is noticed. The majority of the letters are capital.

In three words, Alejandro utilized letters backwards. They could be regarded as fictitious letters. But if looked closely, it can be seen that they resemble regular letters. They are written differently by the child—inverted.

Perhaps Alejandro has a writing guideline. His sentences are made up of a minimum of four letters and a maximum of six. He has created this regulation. The length of orality or the thing it refers to have no bearing.

Further, it can be told that Alejandro writes in a crude manner. He is still learning the writing system. The process of phoneticization is not yet in place. This level has not yet been reached by the youngster. He merely employs letters devoid of their usual sound value. He occasionally employs pseudo-letters, and there is no correspondence to phoneme-grapheme.

Alejandro's writing process was discussed. This description results in the following conclusions:

Alejandro is a student of an elementary regular school. He presents learning difficulties. He could not write "correctly." However, he did not have a full assessment by specialized teachers. His school is so far from urban areas and his parents could not take him to a special institution.Therefore, he has not received special support. Also, there is not a favorable literacy environment in his home. His teacher teaches him like his classmates. Usually, he has been marginalized and stigmatized because "he does not know or work in class."

Because Alejandro was a youngster who was constantly fidgeting in class, attention has been paid to him. It must depict his writing errors as a necessary element of his learning process rather than as a negative.

Errors serve as process indicators. They help to define the person's abilities. They make it possible to pinpoint the knowledge being applied. Errors can be viewed as elements that have a didactic value in this sense.

Alejandro demonstrated some writing skills as well as some knowledge. The child recognizes and can tell between letters from numerals. If he conceptualizes their usage in each instance is unknown. Because he didn't include any numbers in the words when he wrote, he demonstrated his understanding that letters are for reading.

For Alejandro, the writing directionality is a challenge. Both from right to left and from left to right, he writes. People did not understand why he did that. The causes are unknown. However, it's critical to identify any variables that may have influenced the youngster to write in this manner.

The student hasn't yet established a phoneme-grapheme connection. He has not yet mastered the basics of writing. He writes in both regular letters and fictitious letters. The quantity and diversity of letters used in writing are not set in stone. However, it is not examined that how the students felt about writing. When he reads his own compositions, he defends them and makes up letters to stand in for certain words.

There is still a small number of letters available. He made use of a few alphabet letters. Alejandro must therefore interact with many texts rather than being taught each letter individually. despite the fact that "he does not know those letters." He will take various components and resources of the writing system in this way.

The amount of time he spends writing is crucial to us. He initially balked at writing for a few minutes. After that, he penned each word for one or two minutes. As was already noted, Alejandro might not have felt confident performing the assignment.

He may have believed that the interviewer would criticize him for writing "incorrectly." He couldn't seem to write. Therefore, it's critical that mistakes made by kids in class are not suppressed. People can learn about a child's knowledge and learning requirements by looking at their mistakes.

It has been said that Alejandro did not benefit from his classwork. Among other things, he painted sketches and letters. This was to keep him occupied. As a result, it is crucial that the youngster engage in reading and writing exercises. He will be able to participate in scholar activities and won't be isolated from his classmates in this way.

It is crucial that students with learning disabilities express their opinions through their writing. Please don't edit their writing. They are not regarded as beings who are incompetent. It is important to keep in mind that learning takes time. More time will be needed for those kids than for their classmates.

In Mexico, special education is significant. However, it is essential that the teacher be given knowledge and have access to expert teachers in the classroom rather than treating the student with learning issues in isolation. The student who struggles with learning can then be included in class, academic activities, and reading and writing exercises.

Although Alejandro was thought to have learning disabilities, his writing process is shown. It is clear that he has certain difficulty, but he also understands several writing system components.

7.5. TRANSITION POSSIBILITIES FOR ADOLESCENTS WITH INTELLECTUAL DISABILITIES INTO ADULTHOOD

The prospects for transitioning young people with intellectual disabilities into adulthood remain a complex topic that the healthcare and non-healthcare systems frequently overlook. The absence of information, skills, and resources has a detrimental effect on the potential of transition given the duties and functions that the healthcare system, non-healthcare system, and families must fulfill to address the transition possibility issue.

The development and provision of working skills must be prioritized in order to position adolescents with intellectual disabilities into adulthood. Consideration should be given to transition options for all adolescents with intellectual disability.

Adolescence is a time of transition, involving multidimensional changes, namely biological, psychological and social. These changes occur simultaneously and at different paces for each adolescent. Extant literature reports that the world is home to 1.2 billion adolescents aged between 10 and 19 years. Transition for adolescents is not only biological, but it also includes emotional transition.

The United Nations statistics has reported that there are more than 600 million people with disability and that 80 million live in Africa. There is also estimation that more than 300,000 adolescents have intellectual disabilities.

Majority of adolescents with intellectual disabilities (IDs) adolescents would be excluded from acquiring some education and employment opportunities, as well as to suffer discrimination Nyangweso. In addition, Meleis, Sawyer, Im, Messias, Schumacher transition is perceived to be complicated.

Due to advancements in healthcare and allied technologies, adolescents who have IDs will live to maturity. Transitioning from adolescence to adulthood is very difficult for adolescents, especially for those with intellectual disabilities who may continue to be completely dependent on their parents for emotional wellbeing, according to Pandey and Agarwal. Despite the fact that transitions are almost normal given how frequently they occur.

7.5.1. Transition as a Concept

The concept of 'transition' has been in existence for more than three decades. It is among the concepts that are debated on its meaning and uses in literature.

Transitions occur throughout life and are the processes faced by all humans, from birth, to adolescence and to adulthood, from being immature to mature and from being dependent to independent. Transition is often associated with movement from a more shielded environment to a more self-directed environment.

It is characterized by the capacity for decision-making and self-care. Numerous life alterations are also a part of transition. These include leaving home after parental death to go to an orphanage, leaving parents to go to boarding school, and any other life events that can need moving from one place to another.

The definition of transition given by Chick and Meleis is "a passage or movement from one state, condition, or place to another." According to Ally et al. transitions are intended to raise a person's quality of life. It is a transition from one area of dependency to another where one can carry out everyday tasks with little assistance. The authors went on to say that it is about a person's cognitive and adaptive functioning. The majority of teenagers find the transitioning process to be quite challenging, and adolescents with intellectual disabilities may find it to be even more challenging.

Transition is described by Shaw and DeLaet as a procedure, a moment in time, and a perception. In order for the transition process to be successful, persons with ID, their families, carers, and the healthcare system must cooperate.

According to the authors, the period from when a transition is anticipated until the new status and change are realized constitutes the transition. Last but not least, the authors believe that rather than being an event, transition depends on how each individual interprets it. Additionally, the environment in which the transition process occurs affects this.

Since 18 is generally seen as the age of maturity, teenagers are expected to have attained some level of independence and be able to make important life decisions like choosing a job and a career by the time they turn 18.

According to Patterson and Pegg, historical evidence shows that teenagers with IDs were treated poorly and were not let to live alone. Those with intellectual disabilities have difficulties because of these presumptions and attitudes.

7.5.2. Transition of Adolescents with Intellectual Disabilities

Multiple restrictions in mental, emotional, cognitive, and physical functioning are traits of intellectual impairment. People with intellectual disabilities exhibit extremely problematic behaviors that demand constant monitoring.

The term "intellectual disability" is also a source of much debate. There isn't a single definition that works for everyone yet.

For instance, it is believed that people with intellectual disability's social and practical skills differ significantly from what is accepted as normal by his or her society (American Association of Intellectual and Developmental Disabilities (2011 cited in Aldersey).

On the contrary, Werner and Lancaster et al. define ID as characterized by significant limitations in intellectual functioning with an IQ below 75 which originates before the age of 18 years. To this end, intellectual disability has been defined by limitations in intellectual functioning and adaptive behaviors. They need more attention and assistance to cope with activities of daily living Shogren and Plotner. The transition of adolescents with ID into adulthood is challenging in that they are expected to go through psychological and social maturation just like their able counterparts. There is a range of issues associated with transition of adolescents with ID into adulthood.

Rehabilitation and special education concerns are among them. The majority of nations, particularly those that are emerging, do not, however, have the necessary infrastructure in place to help them reach this milestone. Most of the time, there aren't any programs or regulations that can meet their needs.

In Africa, where it is deeply ingrained in the culture, the concept of disability is still evolving. Disability in the African setting is connected to supernatural reasons, which has an impact on how family members would approach the person with ID.

According to Aldersey, a person's disability in Africa is a product of their culture. Etiyiebo and Omiegbe concur with this assertion that society views people with intellectual disabilities as less than human.

Examples of additional studies in Africa that define intellectual disability in accordance with societal norms include those from Botswana, Zimbabwe, and Cameroon. In the majority of African nations, these unfavorable preconceptions have resulted in the exclusion of people with ID from society at large.

This has even prompted some families to conceal their adolescent children, allowing them to mature alone without a smooth transition. Therefore, it is not surprising that the majority of Africa lacks legislation that are pertinent to those with ID, which presents numerous difficulties for them and their families. The majority of these difficulties are related to social, professional, and parenting issues.

7.6. SPEECH THERAPY WORK WITH CHILDREN HAVING SPECIFIC LANGUAGE IMPAIRMENT

The challenges of differential evaluation and in-depth research of SLIs in children are rapidly evolving in world science, and in Russian speech therapy in particular. The authors' descriptions of the signs and symptoms help grasp the underlying causes of a condition known as "SLI."

This enables a thorough examination of the mechanisms underlying impeded development, as well as the formulation of speech therapy's tactics and directions.

Figure 7.3. Speech therapy camp.

Source: Image by Flickr.

Thus, in Russian science, the quest for further approaches to a transdisciplinary examination of the issue of aiding children with SLI in special education in general and speech therapy in particular remains highly relevant. It might be said that current speech therapy as a science has a lot of paradoxes in its definition.

On the one hand, there is a need to find new and improving existing approaches to the speech therapy work with children with SLI. On the other hand, methodological, substantive, organizational, and other aspects of new and modernized approaches to solving the designated problem are insufficiently developed.

The resolution of the existing contradictions, of course, occurs, and will continue to take place in scientific research of several generations. However, today, people can say that a personalized approach in speech therapy work with SLI children meets the abovementioned social challenges and contributes to effectively overcoming pressing contradictions in general, inclusive, and special education.

Scientists began writing on the emergence of a tailored approach in Russian teaching at the turn of the 20th century. Personalization in education has been interpreted in several ways, allowing for multiple interpretations of the phenomena. It is possible to define personalization as the process of acquiring by the subject universal human, socially significant, individually distinctive properties and qualities that enable him to fulfill a particular social role in a unique way, creatively build communication with others, and actively influence their perception and assessment of their own personality and activities.

At the same time, the term "personalization in education" is often used in Russian scientific research, interpreted extremely variably as: a special form of organization of the educational process, taking into account the peculiarities of personal differences of students; one of the directions of modernization of the system of continuous education; a process aimed at the development of students' abilities and interests; a factor of development of cognitive activity of trainees; and a means of building a personal educational route.

The personalization of education is also regarded as a didactic principle, which states that all other aspects of the educational process, including their content, ought to be developed in accordance with the interests, requirements, and goals of those taking part in educational activities.

The diversity of interpretations, however, is a reflection of the fact that educational processes in Russia generally place a high priority on the dynamic development of pedagogical paradigms that place the student's personality and his multifaceted interests and needs at the center of pedagogical processes.

Additionally, it makes sense that a tailored approach is important in the diagnostic and development work done by a speech therapist with children who have SLI.

7.7. SPEECH THERAPY IMPACT ON SLI IN RUSSIA: ALGORITHMS OR PERSONALIZATION?

Russian speech therapists have established reliable methods for dealing with kids who have particular language difficulties over a long period of time. These algorithms base their evaluation of the linguistic and speech development of such children on the traditional Russian level approach.

Russian speech therapy has long understood the essence of SLI as a developmental speech-language disorder that manifests systemic underdevelopment of all language components and encompasses all speech processes (from the 1960s of the previous century).

In this context, national evaluation methods for kids with SLI have been identified and are currently being used successfully in Russia.

These models assemble an interdisciplinary team of experts who examine children thoroughly, assess the state of various functions, and come to a conclusion and make suggestions for working with a specific child (psychologist, pediatrician, neurologist, speech therapist, teacher-representative of the school, and if necessary, other specialists).

As a member of this team, the speech therapist does his evaluation. Technology and didactic materials may vary, but it must always include the following: gathering information on the child's language and speech development and the speech environment in his family; understanding speech and language structures; and the condition of vocabulary, grammar, phonetics, dialogical and monolog utterances (in relation to the age indicators of normative development).

The diagnostic program also includes an examination of the state of language analysis and synthesis operations (beginning at 3 to 4 years of age), the state of literacy fundamentals (beginning at 6 years of age), and later (between 7 and 8 years of age), an examination is added to the aforementioned writing, counting operations, reading, and other academic skills.

For many decades, scientific research data, covering various regions of Russia, confirmed the idea of professor R.E. Levina, and, later, professor T.B. Filicheva that the speech-language status of children with SLI can be understood as very different, varying within different levels: from the first level (lowest) to the fourth level (somewhat close to the lower limits of the age norm).

The national practice of speech therapy allows detecting a delay in the development of speech/language in children from 2 to 3 years of age with a normative state of intelligence and hearing, in order to subsequently consider these children as a risk group for detecting SLI in them, starting from 3 years.

As a result, from this age on, it is normal in Russia to refer to a condition found in a child as a disordered development of language and speech rather than a condition that is delayed. The national psycho-pedagogical classification of speech-language disorders reflects the background of this approach.

Beginning at age three, a hierarchy of short level features used in Russian speech therapy attests to the underdevelopment of language and speech processes in children with SLI:

Children in the first level are essentially non – speakers who can only understand a very small number of words. Instead of stringing together these words into a phrase, they use single basic words, amorphous root words, sound complexes, and word fragments.

There are no word endings, understanding and use of prepositions is not observed. Word formation is not available. A child cannot compose a story on his own. Monological speech is practically absent.

A dialog with such a child shows his active use of nonverbal means of communication. The phonetic side of speech is significantly disturbed; sounds from different phonetic groups are not formed. Children do not understand the tasks aimed at distinguishing the verbal sounds.

The second level—the beginning of the sentence development: children begin to combine two or three words into a simple sentence. However, these sentences are characterized by violations of structure and content. Understanding of speech lags significantly behind these normotypic children.

Prepositions, which allow for differentiating the number, size, gender, activities, and signals of things, as well as morphemic components of words, are skipped or altered by children.

Initial attempts to form words may contain serious substantive and structural flaws. Children engage in conversation, but they don't start it; instead, they just say one or two words in return. Still, there remains a propensity for nonverbal communication.

Children cannot recount the story, discuss the incidents, etc. It is unable to carry out tasks involving linguistic sound distinction. Multiple isolations are features of how various sound groups are pronounced.

The third level is defined by the use of a straightforward sentence that contains numerous lexical and grammatical faults. It becomes possible for third-grade students to construct simple and even some types of complex sentences.

However, there are glaring flaws in these sentences, including lexical modifications, omissions, rearrangements of the sentence sections, replacement of word ends, and replacement of prepositions (e.g., according to the genus-specific characteristics of words).

Although they can actively participate in conversation, kids tend to play a more passive role. The story can now be self-compiled, and the text can be retold. Additionally, stated faults in the text's transmission, composition, cause-and-effect, logical, and chronological links are permitted.

Persistent, ongoing errors are a feature of word creation and changes in word forms based on grammatical categories (choice of morpheme, choice of grammatical model, word design, etc.). There is an improvement in the capacity to recognize some native language sounds.

However, sounding phonemes do not differentiate as they ought to be based on children's ages. They discovered improper pronunciation of sounds belonging to various phonetic categories.

The fourth level characterizes residual manifestations of mildly expressed underdevelopment of vocabulary, grammar, phonetics, and storytelling. Single, but persistent manifestations of impaired development of language and speech are noted in almost all areas, but as minimal manifestations.

Such micro-manifestations in the underdevelopment of speech and language, however, are systemic. They show the need for further continuation of the work of the speech therapist.

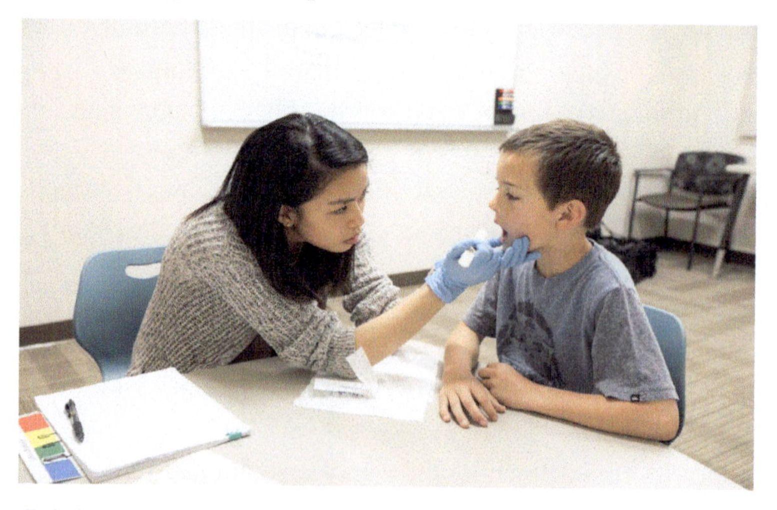

Figure 7.4. Speech pathology students help patients at the Maryjane Reese language, speech, and hearing center.

Source: Image by Flickr.

On the one hand, these characteristics of the level assessment of the status of speech and language in children indicate an algorithmized knowledge of the fact that SLI can be characterized by underdevelopment of the examined processes of various severity.

On the other hand, while evaluating a child with SLI's language and speech, this method already indicates personalization (if there are common characteristics of underdevelopment inherent in one or another level).

A comparison is made between each child's speech-language data and markers of the age norm. Indicators of inadequate language and speech development in each individual child are also made apparent at this time.

Speech therapists in Russia successfully develop efficient algorithms for the best treatment for kids with SLI in accordance with this multi-layered approach, which has been supported by hundreds of scientific studies and many decades of scientific and practical practice.

These algorithms are based on figuring out the child's current level of language and speech development, as well as the level that is promising and doable for him during development work, while also taking into account the child's social demands.

Currently, training programs for kids with SLI take into account these speech therapist work algorithms (e.g., programs for overcoming SLI in preschool children).

These child training packages provide speech therapists with a clear and straightforward work flow. It includes a strategy for working with a child (with a first, second, third, or fourth level of speech-language underdevelopment), the work's content, the key principles for forming children's lexical, grammatical, phonetic, and syntactic possibilities, as well as the potential outcomes that the speech therapist hopes to achieve in his work.

So, in working with children whose level of speech and language capabilities is assessed as the minimum (first level), the speech therapy is aimed at:

Development of Understanding of Speech: to teach according to the instructions of a speech therapist to recognize and show objects, actions, signs, understand the generalizing meaning of a word, differentially perceive who and where, and understand appeal to one or more persons, grammatical categories of the number of nouns, verbs, guess objects according to their description, determine elementary cause-effect relationships;

The Development of Active Speech Activity: in any phonetic design, to name parents, close relatives, imitate the cries of animals and birds, sounds of the world, musical instruments; give orders—go, sit, give; make up the first sentences from amorphous root words (mama pi—mama, go to sleep), convert imperative verbs into singular verbs of the present tense, make sentences according to the model:

- Who? What does?

- Who? What does? What? (e.g., Katia (mom, dad) is sleeping; Anna drinks milk).

Simultaneously, exercises are conducted to develop memory, attention, logical thinking (remembering 2–4 objects, guessing the removed or added object, remembering and selecting pictures of 2–4 parts).

The concept of combining a personalized approach with algorithmic and individual techniques is currently highly well-liked and rapidly evolving in Russia with regard to enhancing speech treatment. Aspects of individualized care for kids with SLI are being developed in particular.

Given the wide range of comorbidity of the state of disturbed verbal and nonverbal processes in these children, the speech therapist's personalization of the content, means, and technologies will vary significantly when working with such children, depending on the scientific, technological, informational, and social resources of society.

When there are genuine opportunities for logical integration with other approaches that are supported by science and experience, the adoption of a tailored approach in speech therapy seems to be the best option.

It is based on the skillful application of both traditional and contemporary scientific data from the fields of speech therapy and related sciences, accounting for variable and combinatorial components in the structure of a systemic speech and language impairment understanding of the unique needs and opportunities of children (social, activity, educational, etc.), the relationship in the work interdisciplinary team of specialists, attracting justified technological solutions, etc.

7.8. CONCLUSION

The evaluation of speech- and language-based learning difficulties is summarized in this chapter. This chapter illustrates the inconsistencies in inter-collegial coordination surrounding differentiated assessment for dyslexic students. In public secondary schools in Greece. The writing of the learning-disabled child is also explored (a case study).

Highlights on Alejandro's case and the options for transitioning young people with intellectual disabilities into adulthood are given in this chapter's middle section. The speech therapy work done with kids who have specific language difficulties is described in this chapter's final section. The effect of speech treatment on Russia's specific language handicap is also discussed in this chapter.

REFERENCES

1. Domitilo, G. M. E., (2020). The child with learning difficulties and his writing: A study of case. *Learning Disabilities – Neurological Bases, Clinical Features and Strategies of Intervention* [Preprint]. Available at: https://doi.org/10.5772/intechopen.89194.
2. Grace, M. R., & Thupayagale-Tshweneagae, G., (2020). Transition possibilities for adolescents with intellectual disabilities into adulthood. *Learning Disabilities – Neurological Bases, Clinical Features and Strategies of Intervention* [Preprint]. Available at: https://doi.org/10.5772/intechopen.89174.
3. Law, J., Dennis, J. A., & Charlton, J. J. V., (2017). Speech and language therapy interventions for children with primary speech and/or language disorders. *Cochrane Database of Systematic Reviews* [Preprint]. Available at: https://doi.org/10.1002/14651858.cd012490.
4. Rontou, M., (2020). Contradictions around inter-collegial collaboration regarding differentiated assessment for pupils with dyslexia in Greek state secondary schools. *Learning Disabilities – Neurological Bases, Clinical Features and Strategies of Intervention* [Preprint]. Available at: https://doi.org/10.5772/intechopen.91922.
5. Volodarovna, T. T., & Borisovna, F. T., (2020). Speech therapy work with children having specific language impairment: Algorithms and personalization. *Learning Disabilities – Neurological Bases, Clinical Features and Strategies of Intervention* [Preprint]. Available at: https://doi.org/10.5772/intechopen.91185.

CHAPTER 8

Issues and Challenges in Assessing Learning Disabilities in Children

Contents

This chapter will discuss various issues and challenges in assessing learning disabilities in children. At the beginning of this chapter, this chapter explains different types of learning disabilities. This chapter also provides highlights on the challenges in the assessment of students with special learning needs. This chapter also helps to understand the issues that remain unanswered in specific learning disabilities. At the end of this chapter, this chapter explains the issues in identification and assessment of students with learning disabilities.

8.1. INTRODUCTION

A neurological disorder known as a learning disability affects the brain's capacity to send, receive, and absorb information. A youngster with a learning disability could struggle with comprehension in general as well as with reading, writing, speaking, listening, and mathematical ideas.

A set of conditions known as learning impairments includes dyslexia, dyspraxia, dyscalculia, and dysgraphia. Disorders of different types can coexist.

"Specific learning disability means a disorder in one or more of the basic psychological processes involved in understanding or in using language, spoken or written, which may manifest itself in an imperfect ability to listen, speak, read, spell or to do mathematical calculations.

The term includes such conditions as perceptual handicaps, brain injury, minimal brain dysfunction, dyslexia and developmental aphasia.

The term does not include children who have learning problems which are primarily the result of visual, hearing or motor handicaps, or mental retardation, emotional disturbance or environmental, cultural or economic disadvantages."

Make sure the child receives a thorough checkup from his or her family doctor or pediatrician before moving further with a psycho-educational assessment. This will provide the doctor the opportunity to rule out any underlying medical issues that might be impairing the child's ability to learn. To rule out or correct any impairments, make sure the child has undergone a vision and hearing screening.

Keep the child's primary care physician or pediatrician up to date on the child's learning difficulties. The child's doctor might take an active part in the healing process. If the child's needs seem to be more complex, he or she will be able to recommend the parent to experts.

Psycho-educational evaluations for learning difficulties are often carried out by suitably qualified psychologists and psychological associates. Psychologists who conduct psycho-educational evaluations ought to ideally have training in either clinical child psychology or educational psychology, as well as previous experience dealing with kids. The Psychological Association of the jurisdiction should also have granted him or her a license to practice psychology.

Look for a psychologist who can do the examination in the child's native tongue if the child is not quite fluent in English or French. Both the local children's mental health agency and the child's school board (accessible through the school's principal) offer publicly sponsored assessments for learning disabilities.

However, there are typically very large waiting lists for these services. It would be a good idea to add the child's name to these waiting lists and find out whether any services are provided for kids with learning difficulties.

Private evaluation costs might range from $1,500 to $2,500 depending on how much time is needed for the evaluation (4–8 hours, 1–3 visits). These evaluations can be initially costly, but they can pay off in the early detection of the handicap and the management techniques needed to manage it.

The majority of the time, provincial health plans do not cover psychological therapies. However, you might wish to inquire about the coverage of psychiatric therapies with the additional health insurance.

After the evaluation, the assessing psychologist should offer a written report. This should include an explanation of the tests that were used, a statement of the test results, a breakdown of the interviews that were performed, and conclusions and suggestions. The evaluation ought to highlight both the child's areas of need and their strengths.

A copy of the report should be given to the child's school and school board so that they can make specific academic accommodations for the child. To ensure that the kid receives the assistance and support they need, this information is essential.

Figure 8.1. Approximately 30% of children have emotional problems.

Source: Image by PickPik.

8.2. ISSUES IN LEARNING DISABILITIES: ASSESSMENT AND DIAGNOSIS

According to the National Joint Committee on Learning Disabilities (NJCLD), improper diagnostic techniques and methods have led to incorrect classifications of people and dubious incidence rates of learning disabilities.

Such approaches and processes lead to the incorrect inclusion of persons who's behavioral and learning issues are not related to learning disorders and the incorrect exclusion of individuals whose deficits are signs of particular learning disabilities.

The NJCLD views the following issues as important to an understanding of current concerns:

- Lack of adherence to a consistent definition of learning disabilities that emphasizes the intrinsic and life-long nature of the condition;
- Lack of understanding, acceptance, and willingness to accommodate normal variations in learning and behavior;
- Lack of sufficient competent personnel and appropriate programs to support the efforts of teachers to accommodate the needs of children who do not have learning disabilities but who require alternative instructional methods;

- Insufficient supply of competently prepared professionals to diagnose and manage exceptional individuals;
- The false belief that underachievement is synonymous with specific learning disability;
- The incorrect assumption that quantitative formulas alone can be used to diagnose learning disabilities;
- Failure of multidisciplinary teams to consider and integrate findings related to the presenting problem(s);
- Lack of comprehensive assessment practices, procedures, and instruments necessary to differentiate learning disabilities from other types of learning problems; and
- General preference for the label "learning disability" over "mental retardation" or "emotional disturbance," which leads to the misclassification of some individuals.

In this statement, the NJCLD tackles these issues and stresses the significance of combining the processes that result in a diagnosis of learning disability and eligibility for services.

It should be pertinent to policymakers, educational administrators, normal and special educators, staff involved in related services, parents, activists, and those who identify, assess, diagnose, and assist those with learning difficulties.

1. Learning Disabilities Show Up Differently Over Time, in Different Situations, and in Different Levels of Severity.

- Like other disabling conditions, learning difficulties can manifest in mild, moderate, or severe ways.
- From early infancy through maturity, appropriate processes must be employed to test and identify people who may have learning difficulties. Various age groups have different procedures.
- Both academic and non-academic contexts may see issues related to learning difficulties. As a result, methods used to diagnose people should incorporate information gathered from all pertinent locations.
- Professionals should follow people who exhibit particular signs of learning difficulties or who are thought to be at risk for them to see if an evaluation or other special services are required. In particular, young toddlers under the age of 9.

2. Differential diagnosis is required to distinguish between and within other disorders, syndromes, and factors that may hinder the development and use of abilities in the areas of listening, speaking, reading, writing, reasoning, and mathematics.

- Differential diagnosis is a process that calls for the creation of hypotheses about the cause and characteristics of the presenting issue. All potential etiological options must be taken into account when learning difficulties, low accomplishment, underachievement, or maladaptive behavior may be caused by one of multiple variables.
- Low accomplishment may be primarily caused by intellectual limits, sensory impairments, and unfavorable emotional, social, and environmental circumstances, which should not be mistaken with learning disorders.
- A required but insufficient criterion for the diagnosis of learning disorders is the documentation of underachievement in one or more areas.
- Evaluation of a person's strengths and shortcomings is necessary for the diagnosis of learning difficulties.
- The possibility that a person also has a learning disability is not eliminated by linguistic and cultural differences, poor instruction, and/or social and emotional neglect. The same is true for those who also have other disabilities such mental retardation, sensory impairments, autism, or significant emotional or behavioral disorders. These people may also have concurrent learning challenges.
- Diagnostic decisions must not be made only on the basis of test results. Such a technique can led to an excessive dependence on test results, a failure to adequately take into account unique behavioral and social qualities, and a failure to adequately integrate other evaluation data.
- It is not acceptable to diagnose learning problems solely on the basis of discrepancy formulas.
- IQ test results (IQs) are not the only indicator of intellectual capacity. Intra-individual variations in abilities and performance are disregarded by diagnostic criteria that only take IQ into account.

- Learning difficulties can show up as language impairment or other symptoms that affect performance on IQ tests. The impact of particular limitations on measures of intellect must therefore be taken into account when choosing tests and interpreting the results.

3. To make a diagnosis and plan an effective intervention program, a thorough assessment is required.

- A number of activities and procedures are included in assessment in order to ensure a complete collection of data that can be used to determine a person's status and needs.
- The methods used to evaluate learning difficulties should take into account the current issues.
- A thorough evaluation must include techniques for figuring out how well a person performs in the following areas: motor, sensory, cognitive, communication, and behavior. The following areas should be evaluated when a learning disability is suspected: speaking, reading, writing, reasoning, math, and social skills. But the evaluation must concentrate on the presenting problem(s) and potential related (s).
- Information from case histories, interviews, and firsthand observations is crucial, especially when it comes from parents, teachers, and the person who may have a learning problem. The knowledge aids in assessing symptoms, behaviors, and signs historically.
- Valid, trustworthy, and up-to-date normative data are requirements for standardized exams. Test administration, scoring, and interpretation policies must be strictly followed. Performance should be stated using standard scores rather than grade or age equivalents since they have the maximum degree of comparability across measurements. If a formula is employed to determine the gap between aptitude and achievement, regression must be corrected for.
- Curriculum-based assessment, task and error pattern analysis, diagnostic instruction, and other non-standard procedures are effective sources of extra information, particularly when data are not available through standardized testing.
- The assessment's information and data must be used to create the intervention plan. This strategy must cover the full spectrum and

all levels of seriousness of the identified issue.

- Determining the individual's current level of performance and functional needs should serve as the foundation for any interventions and services. Planning for the program should take independent living, social, personal, and employment demands into consideration.

4. To assess, diagnose, and decide on service provision, a multidisciplinary team is required.

- To diagnose learning disorders, a multidisciplinary team is required. The team's members must be equipped with the variety of skills required to evaluate and make diagnostic judgments.
- Information for assessments that determine a person's status and needs is gathered from a variety of sources. The multidisciplinary team analyzes, combines, and analyzes the data from different sources while also developing service choices.
- Those who performed the assessments must be in the room when the diagnostic choices are made. Parents and those professionals interested in delivering direct services should be part of the team when detailed program and service plans are prepared. When appropriate, the person with a learning disability should also be included.

5. A Clear Distinction Must Be Made Between "Diagnosis of Learning Disability" and "Eligibility for Specific Services."

- Diagnosis of learning disabilities should never be denied to an individual because the specific eligibility criteria for a given program have not been met.
- When a diagnosis of learning disabilities is made, appropriate services must be provided.
- Programs for individuals with learning disabilities should not be used as placement alternatives for those with other learning and behavioral problems.
- The availability of funding must not influence the determination of eligibility for services.
- It is improper to deliberately diagnose an individual as teach disabled to generate funds.

8.3. CHALLENGES IN THE ASSESSMENT OF STUDENTS WITH SPECIAL LEARNING NEEDS

The necessity for educators to reevaluate the techniques of assessment utilized is brought on by the fact that learners with special needs in education demand teaching and learning approaches that may differ from the traditional approaches.

Teacher-training programs in Zimbabwe and other poor nations in Africa usually do not give teachers the tools they need to cope with students who have unique learning needs. The purpose of this lecture is to critically examine the challenges associated with evaluating kids that have specific learning needs.

Assessment is typically thought of as a process that allows for the evaluation, recording, and reporting of the level of a learner's accomplishments. Continuous observation or summative assessment are used to make judgments.

Teachers and outside examiners serve as the assessors. Zimbabwe has ratified the Salamanca (1994) international convention, which supports inclusive education and is dedicated to the creation and delivery of high-quality education that is defined by equity and access.

Learners with special needs are individuals whose teaching and learning requirements cannot be fully satisfied by conventional teaching approaches, according to the Zimbabwe education sector policy. According to Clark et al. there should be curriculum differentiation and a variety of instructional approaches.

When they advise that education should be made relevant, adaptable, and responsive in order to promote effective achievement and the development of students as self-regulated learners, Johnstone and Chapman add to this idea. This implies that assessments of students with special needs must necessarily take these variances into account.

Due to the technical nature of inclusion, the numerous specialized abilities, competencies, resources, and staff experience needed, a number of issues must be resolved in educational settings while assessing students with special needs. Every learner is different, and each one deserves to be evaluated on their own merits while taking into account any particular circumstances.

Among many other needs, hearing loss and deafness, vision loss and blindness, dyslexia, mental retardation, and brilliant students are among the specific learning needs that teachers find difficult to recognize and assess in classroom settings.

According to Bahr and colleagues, the tenet that the right to education is a fundamental right and the cornerstone of a just society informs the practice of inclusive education. This idea condemns the exclusion, segregation, or discrimination of students for whatever reason from admittance to public mainstream schools.

Regardless of the intentions, the problems that result from the adoption of these noble positions in schools are numerous. The ultimate goal of educational assessment is providing an appropriate instructional program for the student in order to enable them to grow and realize their unique potential.

According to Goodwing, assessment and inclusion are naturally connected, and that equity in schooling relies on both. Since the government of Swaziland advocates for the practices of an inclusive educational system, they recognize that assessment is critical to the achievement of such inclusion.

It is acknowledged generally that assessment has a direct influence on teaching and learning, and that its power can be harnessed and directed towards positive outcomes. It is important that pupils with special needs derive maximum benefit from assessment to ensure maximum participation in school, and eventually society.

However, not all of the teachers in schools have the necessary training to recognize and evaluate students with special needs. The majority of special needs students in Swaziland, according to the writer, move through the educational system without receiving a fair assessment.

Missed assessments prevent students from participating in some educational programs, such as modified classroom instruction, curricula, tests, and exams. Only after being diagnosed with special needs may learners obtain these benefits.

Many Swaziland students with special needs fail to excel in specialized programs in schools because there are so few students who are assessed. Some students are left without assistance because there aren't enough school-level intervention teams with the necessary expertise to assess the learners' various special learning requirements right away.

Primary school teachers are more likely to come across a student with disabilities and special learning needs in their classroom now that the free primary education program appears to have increased the number of learners with special needs at the primary school level.

These teachers confront difficulties in providing greater classroom support due to the requirement to assess kids with special needs, and yet it is extremely difficult for teachers to obtain this information for a sizable portion of their pupils.

Currently, the institutionalized center for challenged persons serves as the sole evaluation facility for the entire nation. There may have been a sizable number of pupils with special needs who were not examined since the ability of the one primary center to provide countrywide coverage is constrained or limited. Zimbabwe's assessment of students with special needs lacks a clear set of policy criteria.

This stands in contrast to the circumstances in the majority of industrialized nations, where laws and regulations on assessment specify what should happen for pupils at various stages of learning. For instance, Greece's "Education of Individuals with Special Educational Needs" law (Law 2817/2000) mandates that pupils with special needs be identified within their first year of elementary school.

This law also specifies the use of a special screen-test system at the start of every school year by the local Diagnostic Assessment and Support Centers for the entire Greek student population. It is hoped, that, these measures will lead to an integrated Individualized Educational program for every student identified as having special needs.

In schools, the learners are still minors and the need for guardians to authorize their assessment is problematic because these are not always forthcoming. However, if there are laws and clear procedures to be followed, teachers and school administrators will be able to refer the learners to specialist centers and practitioners to get help at an early stage.

This is demonstrated by the Greek case, where pupils with special needs were identified and enrolled in conventional classrooms, which are thought by experts to be the most conducive to the education of all students.

Who should be evaluated and when should the evaluation occur are not entirely obvious. Most of the time, assessment occurs by accident or not at all. It is common knowledge that assessments are one of the key components of successfully integrating kids with special needs into regular classrooms. Despite the fact that many students with special needs are enrolled in school, formal assessments are not always conducted.

These students are consequently denied the opportunity to take use of the modifications that are available, such as specialized instruction and altered exams. These kids then frequently have difficulty with the standard curricula and exams. This frequently results in such students quitting school as a result of dissatisfaction, failure, and a lack of defined career prospects.

Deep-seated issues with the assessment of students with special learning needs arise from imprecise policies, the lack of effective teacher preparation programs, and the lack of teacher support systems for the various types of learning requirements that the kids present.

If the issues with assessment of these learners are to be effectively addressed and the learners are to be empowered to reach their unique maximum potentials in life, there is also a need for legal frameworks to be in place to safeguard the learners with special needs from neglect, social stigma, and prejudice.

8.4. ISSUES THAT REMAIN UNANSWERED IN SPECIFIC LEARNING DISABILITIES

Specific learning disabilities (SLDs) are defined as "heterogeneous group of conditions wherein there is a deficit in processing language, spoken or written, that may manifest itself as a difficulty to comprehend, speak, read, write, spell, or to do mathematical calculations and includes such conditions as perceptual disabilities, dyslexia, dysgraphia, dyscalculia, dyspraxia, and developmental aphasia.

8.4.1. Distinction between Terminologies – Disorder, Disability, Difficulty, and Slow Learner

Although they are frequently used interchangeably, learning disorders, learning disabilities, and learning difficulties are not the same thing. Significant academic challenges that youngsters have are referred to as disorders, but this is not enough to support a formal diagnosis.

The Diagnostic and Statistical Manual of Mental Disorders and the International Statistical Classification of Diseases and Related Health Problems, both of which are regarded as authoritative manuals for mental health practitioners, both use the term "disorder" as a medical term.

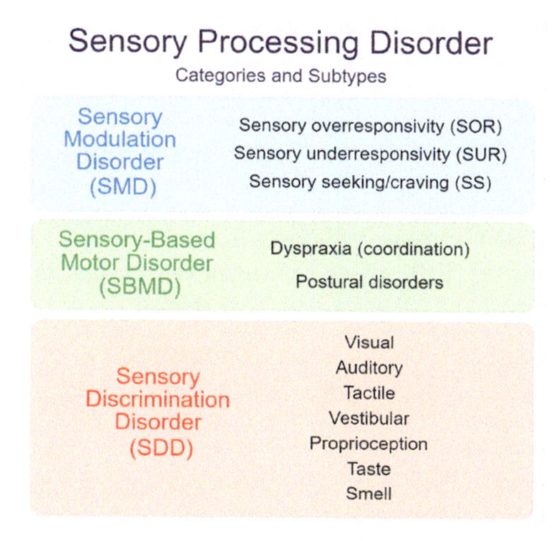

Figure 8.2. Sensory processing disorder (SPD) – categories and subtypes.

Source: Image by Wikimedia commons.

The Right of Persons with Disabilities Act (RPWD Act, 2016), notifications from the Ministry of Social Justice and Empowerment (Department of Empowerment of Persons with Disabilities), and the Individuals with Disabilities Education Act (IDEA) all use the term "disability" in relation to SLDs (United States federal law).

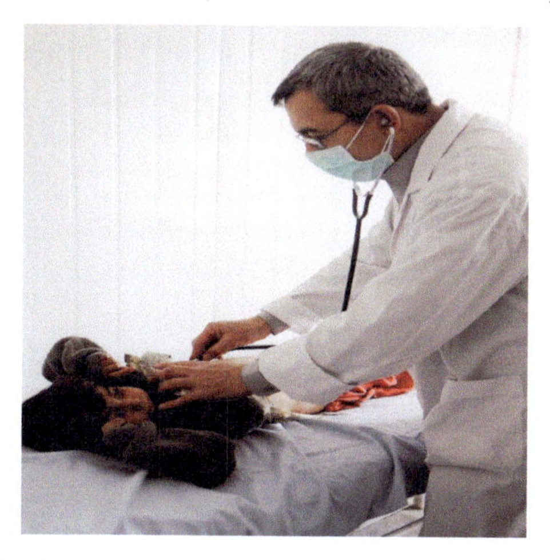

Figure 8.3. A pediatrician doing checkups of child.

Source: Image by Wikimedia commons.

The rights of students with disabilities are safeguarded by this federal legislation. A pupil must be a "kid with a handicap" in order to qualify for these statutes' special disability certificates and services. SLD is a recognized clinical diagnosis given when a person satisfies certain criteria as determined by a qualified individual (psychologist, pediatrician, etc.).

For a variety of reasons, including behavioral, psychological, and emotional problems, the fact that English is not their mother tongue, ineffective teaching methods, high absenteeism, and inadequate curricula, children with "learning difficulties" underperform academically. Once they receive support and instruction based on solid research, these kids have the capacity to perform at levels that are age-appropriate.

Those students are referred here who have below-average cognitive talents but who are not considered impaired as "slow learners." The youngster who learns slowly is not regarded as mentally retarded since, despite progressing more slowly than the ordinary child, he is nevertheless capable of obtaining a modest level of scholastic accomplishment.

8.4.2. Problems with Languages

The LDs were seen as a concern in English-speaking nations in the oriental globe. Not many attempts were made in this area because to a lack of awareness and allegedly lower incidence rates in Asian nations like China and India.

Researchers in the West blamed outdated teaching methods and overcrowded classrooms for this issue. On the other hand, eastern scholars link it to issues with linguistic adaption brought on by the phonetic complexity of the English language.

Hindi has direct spelling-sound connection; thus, one writes exactly how he/she speaks. However, English has some well-known characteristics that make it difficult to learn and require memorization of the random word spellings.

For example, there are a lot of words in English language with silent letters which makes the language much more difficult, because here the person needs to remember formations such as psychology, pseudo, pneumonia, and walk.

Those children having difficulty in process of learning find it difficult to comprehend. People reading and writing Hindi and other regional languages also do suffer from learning difficulties. It is seen equally in other languages as well. The child is unable to learn orthography, syntax, and phonetics of language because of which it becomes imperative for the teachers to adopt such teaching practices and for the school authorities to facilitate the learning process of these children.

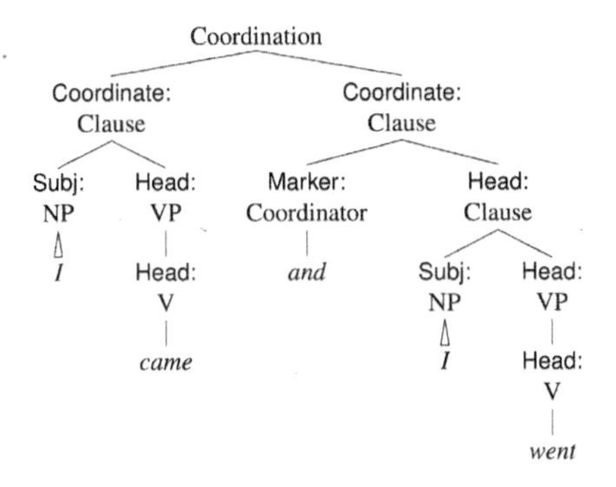

Figure 8.4. This is a syntax tree for the coordination of clauses, "I came and I went." The coordination is composed of two coordinate clauses. The first is "I came." The second clause has the coordinator "and" in marker function and a head clause. The head is "I went."

Source: Image by Wikimedia commons.

8.4.3. Lack of Standardized Assessment Tools

Since some nations have a multilingual population, it's critical to evaluate the SLD issue in a child's mother tongue. There are several different LD assessment batteries, each with advantages and disadvantages.

Some of the assessment batteries, such as the NIMHANS Index for Specific Learning Disabilities and the AIIMS SLD: Comprehensive Diagnostic Battery, are frequently utilized, although there are no criteria that have been thoroughly developed for all of the subtests.

Many batteries are written in regional languages, which limit their ability to be used across the country. About 100.4 million pupils attend schools with a Hindi medium, yet some tests, including the NIMHANS Index for Specific Learning Disabilities, can only be given to English-medium students.

The materials utilized to make the batteries are not uniform. Assessment is challenging since the age categories for the existing batteries have not been included, particularly when the student is to be tested in tenth- or twelfth-board classes for the production of a certificate to qualify for benefits.

8.4.4. Complexity of Gradation in Learning Difficulty and Disability

One class is equivalent to one standard deviation in the evaluation process used to diagnose learning problems. As a result, if a child performs two classes below his or her true standard, that child is diagnosed with learning disability, and if the performance is one class below, that child is diagnosed with learning difficulties that does not constitute a disability.

There is a lack of knowledge among policymakers about this point of divergence. No accommodations are made for struggling students.

The situation gets worse because parents and school administrators are unsupportive. Students are unable to take breaks and must endure their suffering in silence. Clinical psychologists help pediatricians, psychiatrists, and teachers discern between learning difficulties and disabilities in children.

The certification and intervention processes are hampered by this uncertainty. A special educator and a parent must work together to address the issues of students with learning difficulties that do not constitute disabilities as early as possible using specific approaches of intervention.

8.4.5. Provisions for Specific Learning-Disabled Students

After a series of consultation meetings and drafting process, the Rights of People with Disabilities Act, 2016 was passed by both the houses of the Parliament. It was notified on December 28, 2016 after receiving presidential assent.

The list was expanded and it included SLDs in it. A bill was introduced in Rajya Sabha on March 24, 2017, entitled "The Children with Specific Learning Disabilities (Identification and Support in Education)."

It highlighted the need for special facilities in educational institutions, setting up detection and remediation centers, guidelines for certification of children with SLDs, and so on.

The Ministry of Social Justice and Empowerment's (Department of Empowerment of Persons with Disabilities) notification on the process to be followed when certifying people with disabilities was published on January 15, 2018. The Gazette placed a strong emphasis on SLD diagnosis, certification, and screening.

The government should be commended for this endeavor, which aims to standardize certification while also highlighting its significance. Despite this action, there remain several problems that warrant caution. Psychiatrists are not eligible to participate in the certification process.

Child and Adolescent Psychiatry clinics are typically referred by schools for students experiencing academic challenges or academic decline.

Figure 8.5. Croydon child and adolescent mental health services, Croydon, London CR0.

Source: Image by Flickr.

The whole evaluation of the pupils referred by schools is done by a team of psychologists and psychiatrists. Along with pediatricians and psychologists, psychiatrists are strongly advised to be involved in the procedure as well because they have specific training in mental health and developmental issues of children and adolescents.

Second, the Gazette lists the tests to be used for IQ testing to ensure uniformity, but when it comes to SLD testing, it should be left to the judgment and expertise of the psychologists.

The tools that will be utilized should be the newest and have standards that can be applied to the target population as a whole. Due to the large range of sociodemographic and regional variations that can affect test results, the same tests cannot be applied across the entire nation.

The CBSE has made the initiative to offer LD kids a discount. These accommodations come in the form of a scribe and additional time, a third language exemption, subject flexibility, the ability to use calculators in math, and the ability to read out the question paper to a dyslexic student. Additionally, these pupils are excused from making spelling mistakes, providing thorough replies, and other requirements.

According to the recent circular issued by CBSE, no school can deny admission to students with disabilities in mainstream education. It has also recommended regular in-service training of teachers in inclusive education at elementary and secondary level, as per CBSE guidelines.

Many other boards and state boards are also offering concessions, but there is no uniformity in rules for demanding certificates. Some boards demand only a certificate of SLD and some require a detailed report along with the certificate; some need renewal while some accept one-time certification.

These provisions have advantages and disadvantages. Some parents insist on certifications even though their kids do not have LDs. They do not emphasize corrective action. This causes these clauses and certification to be abused. This is a delicate matter that has to be addressed with care. Others may not be aware of these accommodations, which causes the child's handicap to persist.

8.5. HOW TO ADDRESS THE CHALLENGES FACED BY CHILDREN WITH SPECIFIC LEARNING DIFFICULTIES

Every child develops his or her unique style of reading, speaking, writing, and expression. Some might perform really well, while others might struggle. Every person has the potential to learn effectively or not. They each have a different learning style.

Early detection of learning disabilities in children is essential. Professionals employ particular assessment methods to diagnose SLD. To differentiate between the other disabilities that include different severity levels, such as mild, moderate, severe, or profound, it is important to use a specific evaluation technique.

Children with Specific Learning Difficulties (CWSLD) have one or more talents that are impaired, which contributes to their poor comprehension of spoken or written language. This shows up as a limited capacity for speaking, listening, spelling, or even performing mathematical computations. Let's learn more about how distinctive SLD is.

8.5.1. Challenges Faced By CWSLDS

A correct first diagnosis of the issue is one of the biggest challenges CWSLDs encounter. As a result, their poor level of performance is mostly a result of inadequate formal teaching experience. Numerous of them experience a variety of challenges that go unnoticed; additionally, the negative effects of the environment, culture, and economy make these challenges even more severe.

A learning disability is not always simple to identify. Even though the indicators seem to indicate a slow learning issue, one should never presume that they know what their child's trouble is. Most parents simply don't want to acknowledge that their child actually has a problem.

As a result, the issue becomes more serious as valuable time is squandered making the child learn by heart and memorizing the course materials. As a result, it's critical to have the child evaluated and tested by a trained specialist as soon as parents can.

8.5.2. Signs and Symptoms

There are certain major symptoms which children with SLD show on a day-to-day basis and these have been mentioned below.

At an individual level:

- Confused
- Low self-esteem and self-confidence
- Difficulty in focusing on a specific task
- Distracted easily
- Unable to express oneself
- Recalling a proper instruction
- Difficulty in adapting to the environment

At school Level:

- Slow speed of writing
- Poor spelling
- Process of writing is effortful and tiring
- Handwriting is immature
- Difficulty choosing correct spelling alternatives
- Poor sentence and paragraph structure

- Difficulties in oral rhyming, blending and segmenting sounds in words
- Delayed speech and language development Limited spoken vocabulary
- Poor understanding of Phonetics
- Difficulty in the acquisition of letter knowledge

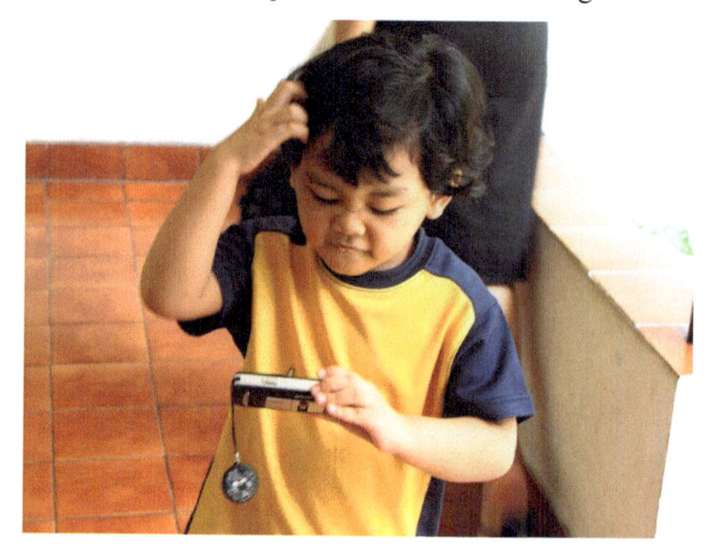

Figure 8.6. Confused symptoms of a child.

Source: Image by max pixel.

8.6. ASSESSMENT TOOLS TO IDENTIFY STRENGTHS IN STUDENTS WITH SPECIAL NEEDS

8.6.1. Behavioral and Emotional Rating Scale

Michael H. Epstein's Behavioral and Emotional Rating Scale, Second Edition (BERS-2). The BERS-2 is a questionnaire that can be completed by the child, the parent, or the teacher. It is intended to assess the personal qualities and competences of kids between the ages of 5 and 18. such as "asks for aid," "accepts a hug," and "is popular with classmates."

8.6.2. The VIA Inventory of Strengths (VIA-IS)

The VIA-IS, developed by Martin Seligman and Christopher Peterson. The

VIA inventory, which stands for "Values in Action," is one way the "positive psychology" movement is put into practice (Seligman, a former president of the American Psychological Association, is one of the founders of this movement).

This model contains twenty-four strengths, including humor, inventiveness, curiosity, zest, humility, and appreciation of beauty. Children (between the ages of 8 and 17) can take the VIA Strengths Survey for Children online (anonymous results are used in research at the University of Pennsylvania).

8.6.3. Dunn and Dunn Online Learning Style Assessments

These assessment tools are based upon the learning style model of Drs. Rita and Kenneth Dunn, which focuses on 25 factors important for understanding how a child learns (e.g., environmental, emotional, social, physiological, and psychological). There are separate assessments for different age groups (ELSA, grades 2–4; LSCY, grades 5–8, LIVES, grades 9012).

8.6.4. Search Institute's 40 Developmental Assets

These are resources that point to a collection of abilities, exposures, connections, and behaviors that help children grow into successful, resourceful individuals. There are distinct lists for various age groups (early childhood, grades K-3, middle childhood, and adolescents).

For adolescents, the list can include cultural competency, honesty, responsibility, caring, and leisure reading. The Developmental Assets Profile survey, which is available to kids between the ages of 11 and 18, will be mailed out by the Search Institute upon request. Results and next actions will then be delivered.

8.6.5. Clifton Youth Strengths Explorer®. (For Ages 10–14)

The StrengthsFinder for adults was likewise created by the Gallup Poll Group. evaluates 10 potential student talent themes, including (Discoverer, Achiever, Future Thinker, and Organizer). This online test takes roughly 15 minutes to finish and consists of 76 paired comparison items.

8.6.6. Torrance Tests of Creative Thinking (TTCT)

These tests, which have been in use for 60 years and were created by creativity specialist Dr. E. Paul Torrance, were initially intended to evaluate students in elementary schools. There are two basic types of writing: figurative (picture-oriented) and verbal (word-oriented), which assess fluency, creativity, adaptability, and imagery richness. Kindergarten through adult appropriate.

8.6.7. Multiple Intelligences Developmental Assessment Scales (MIDAS)

Dr. Branton Shearer's MIDAS. One of the few trustworthy and valid tools to assess multiple intelligences in kids or adults (linguistic, logical-mathematical, spatial, musical, interpersonal, naturalist, intrapersonal, and bodily-kinesthetic). The management of the scales is given with fundamental certification.

8.7. ISSUES IN IDENTIFICATION AND ASSESSMENT OF STUDENTS WITH LEARNING DISABILITIES

Learning Disabilities are manifested differently over time, both in severity and with varying settings and environment. The identification, comprehensive assessment for diagnosis, and service provision to the Learning Disabled needs to be effectively integrated, and differential diagnosis is necessary to distinguish between and among other disorders, syndromes, and factors that can interfere with the acquisition and use of listening, speaking, reading, writing, reasoning, or mathematical abilities and planning of an appropriate intervention program by a multidisciplinary team, with a clear distinction between 'Diagnosis of Learning Disability' and 'Eligibility for Specific Services' (NJCLD).

The development and validation of identification criteria, identification tools, identification of causes of a specific learning disability, identification of co-occurring deficits with learning disabilities in an individual, and the effects of learning disabilities on a person's intellectual functioning and educational, personal, and social functioning are thought to be the main issues in the identification and assessment of learning disabilities.

The following concerns must be resolved in order to identify and assess children with learning disabilities in a timely manner and to allow for timely treatment and remediation of the children:

8.7.1. Lack of Proper Research in the Area

Learning Disabilities is relatively a new and less explored area, with only selected centers and departments being interested and involved in researching this field. The educational system in the country lays particular emphasis on 'knowing' rather than 'learning,' and 'theory' in place of 'application,' and is therefore inappropriate for students with Learning Disabilities.

Since there is a dearth of indigenous research and a predilection for and domination of Western adaptations in the absence of an adequate need-based assessment, it is crucial to look into the issues surrounding assessment and repair.

The non-government and private sectors do the majority of the research and intervention in the field of learning disabilities, with little meaningful interaction and collaboration between them and the state educational authority.

Even though early identification and prevention programs and early intervention in basic reading skills in primary-grade general education classrooms can reduce the number of students with reading problems by up to 70%, a divide still exists between the personnel in the health and educational fields in both the private and public sectors, impeding the effectiveness of medical interventions (Lyon, et al., 2001).

In studies on dyscalculia, the deficits are discovered to point to two patterns of brain dysfunction: one where there are deficits in auditory perception, semantic memory, and phonemic discrimination, whereas no deficits are present in visual-spatial skills, indicating that such children are more lacking in reading and spelling than in arithmetic.

These deficiencies have been understood to be a sign of left hemisphere injury. The other type of dyscalculia is characterized by deficits in visuospatial perception, visuo-spatial analysis, tactual discrimination, and finger agnosia, but not in auditory function.

This group does mathematics more poorly than they do reading and writing, and they also exhibit deficiencies in right hemisphere-damaging neuropsychological tasks (Rao, 2003).

Studies done across several countries prove that the typologies have clinical significance from the view point of diagnosis, and warn against the improper clubbing of all children with Dyscalculia into one group, stressing on the rehabilitation programs for these children to be planned carefully keeping in mind the nature of dysfunction.

Within the multifactorial framework, the gene-gene and gene-environment interactions may be a reason for the different symptoms in the Dyslexia spectrum resulting in other conditions like Attention Deficit Hyperactivity Disorder (ADHD) and Central Auditory Processing Disorder (CAPD) which surface in future implying that 'Specific Learning Difficulty' is more than just a difficulty with learning involved, and one of the symptoms (McGrath et al., 2006).

8.7.2. Lack of Proper Diagnosis and Timely Intervention

The 15% prevalence percentage of learning disabilities that is widely accepted is thought to be overstated, while studies also indicate that learning disabilities are underreported.

While better research, a broader definition of reading disability, a focus on phonological awareness, and a greater identification of girls with learning disabilities can be credited with the increase in the rate, it also has some illogical causes, such as the general and unspecific definitions of learning disabilities lacking specificity, a lack of financial incentives to identify students for special education, and the insufficient preparation of teachers by educational institutions (Lyon, 1996: 55–76).

There is no clear agreement on the diagnosis of learning disabilities, whether they should be divided into different subtypes, or whether the methods used to teach dyslexic youngsters are equivalent to those used to teach other struggling readers.

According to whether the person has Dyslexia, Dyspraxia, Dyscalculia, Dysgraphia, or a combination of these, the many Specific Learning Difficulties that appear in them may be the result of an overlap of a variety of symptoms (Nicholson, 2002: 55–66).

The many external or environmental factors on the learning challenged child have a considerable impact on how Dyslexia affects their academic progress, especially in light of the overlapping symptoms that are expressed in the "Dyslexia ecosystem."

The causal variant within the multi-factorial framework is to involve gene-gene and gene-environment interactions leading to the various symptoms on the dyslexia spectrum, including other conditions like ADHD and Central Auditory Processing Disorder (CAPD), depicting the Specific Learning Difficulty as just another difficulty with the involved learning and only one of the symptoms (McGrath et al., 2006).

In order to prevent some learning disabilities, vulnerable families may benefit from education. Strong evidence linking developmental dyslexia to dyspraxia, dyscalculia, and dyslexia indicates the presence of genes influencing the condition at multiple chromosomal loci that are responsible for the condition's various manifestations (Williams and O'Donovan, 2006: 681–689). (McGlannan, 1968: 185–191).

Earlier, a substantial discrepancy between a child's aptitude, typically operationalized by IQ, and their reading performance were an indication suggesting children as having reading difficulties (Gunning, 1998; Francis et al., 1996a: 132–143).

And though the discrepancy-based method was widely used, there appeared to be several conceptual and measurement problems that warranted an alternative method of identification of dyslexics and other poor readers (Francis et al., 1996b: 3- 17; Shaywitz et al., 1992: 145–150).

The overall academic success in higher classes can be predicted with reasonable accuracy by using reading outcomes at early grades (Torgesen & Wagner, 2002) and early identification of children at risk for reading difficulties (Shaywitz et al., 1992; Juel, 1988).

Inadequate diagnosis processes lead to the incorrect inclusion of people with learning and behavioral issues that are not related to learning disabilities as well as the exclusion of people whose impairments are signs of Specific Learning Disabilities. Due to this, learning disabilities have unclear prevalence rates (NJCLD).

Studies confirm that children identified as having reading difficulties would not have required "learning disability status" if their difficulties had been recognized at an early age. Children at high risk who receive intervention during early schooling illustrate significant improvement in academic performance over the period of time (Schenck et al., 1980). (de Hirsh et al., 1966; Strag, 1972).

Therefore, effective training in phonological awareness, phonics, fluency development, and reading comprehension strategies should be included in prevention and early intervention programs to help children acquire effective reading skills (Lyon, 1996).

The attitude of regular teachers, who frequently consider children with disabilities to be the responsibility of the resource teachers and hold them to be a "disturbance" to the class causing distractions that delay course completion, is a major barrier that the children with disabilities experience at school (Agbenyega, 2007; Wall, 2002; Yu et al., 2011: 355–369). As a result, they ignore their presence and concentrate on carrying out their lesson plans (Das, & Kattumuri). While teachers' intentions are generally seen as good and accommodating, it is discovered that they lack the propensity to successfully engage kids with special needs in the classroom (Gerber, 1992: 213–231; Soni, 2004). Another obstacle is their insufficient comprehension of their students, despite the fact that there appears to be a want to learn (Sengupta & Biswas, 2003).

However, there is no evidence of acceptance of a total inclusion (Avranides & Norwitch, 2002: 129–147). The beliefs, attitudes, and perceptions of regular teachers about students with disabilities and inclusive education play a significant role in the acceptance of these students and also the commitment of regular teachers in implementing and promoting inclusion (Opdal & Wormnaes, 2001: 143- 161; Minke et al., 1996: 152-186; Villa et al., 1996: 29–45).

8.8. CONCLUSION

The problems and difficulties involved in evaluating learning deficits in children are discussed in this chapter. This chapter's introduction describes the different categories of learning disorders as well as the difficulties associated with diagnosing and treating them.

This chapter's highlights on the difficulties in assessing kids with unique learning needs are presented in the chapter's middle section. This chapter also discusses the problems with special needs that remain unresolved.

How to deal with the difficulties faced by kids with particular learning disabilities is covered toward the end of this chapter. Highlights on the evaluation methods used to find students with special needs who have strengths are also provided in this chapter.

REFERENCES

1. Armstrong, T., (1970). *7 Assessment Tools to Identify Strengths in Students with Special Needs (and all Kids)*. The American Institute for Learning and Human Development. institute4learning. Available at: https://www.institute4learning.com/2013/09/03/7-assessment-tools-to-identify-strengths-in-students-with-special-needs-and-all-kids/ (accessed on 14 October 2023).
2. Assessments for Learning Disabilities, (n.d.). Children's support by lifeworks. *Children Support Solutions*. Available at: https://childrensupportsolutions.com/five-signs-learning-disability/assessments-for-learning-disabilities/ (accessed on 14 October 2023).
3. *Exploring the Invisible: Issues in Identification and Assessment of ...* (n.d.). www2.hu-berlin.de. Available at: https://www2.hu-berlin.de/transcience/Vol6_No1_2015_91_107.pdf (accessed on 14 October 2023).
4. *Issues in Learning Disabilities: Assessment and Diagnosis*, (1994). American Speech-Language-Hearing Association. American Speech-Language-Hearing Association. Available at: https://www.asha.org/policy/tr1994-00140/ (accessed on 14 October 2023).
5. Kohli, A., Sharma, S., & Padhy, S. K., (2018). Specific learning disabilities: Issues that remain unanswered. *Indian Journal of Psychological Medicine, 40*(5), 399–405. Available at: https://doi.org/10.4103/ijpsym.ijpsym_86_18.
6. Mapolisa, T., & Khosa, M. T., (n.d.). *Challenges of Assessment of Students with Special Learning Needs*. ResearchGate. Available at: https://www.researchgate.net/publication/302029058_Challenges_of_Assessment_of_Students_with_Special_Learning_Needs (accessed on 14 October 2023).
7. Mathur, A., (2019). *How to Address the Challenges Faced by Children with Specific Learning Difficulties*. YourStory.com. Available at: https://yourstory.com/socialstory/2019/06/challenges-children-specific-learning-difficulties (accessed on 14 October 2023).

INDEX

C

D

E

F

G

H

I

L

M

N

O

P

U

V

W